THE POLITICS OF IRONY

THE POLITICS OF IRONY

Essays in Self-Betrayal

Edited by
Daniel W. Conway and John E. Seery

St. Martin's Press
New York

Excerpt from "On an Occasion of National Mourning" in *War Stories* (University of Chicago Press, 1980) reprinted by permission of Margaret Nemerov.

Excerpt from "East Coker" in *Four Quartets*, copyright 1943 by T. S. Eliot and renewed 1971 by Esme Valerie Eliot, reprinted by permission of Harcourt Brace Jovanovich, Inc. and Faber and Faber Ltd.

First published in the United States of America in 1992

Printed in the United States of America

ISBN 0-312-04801-7

Library of Congress Cataloging-in-Publication Data

The politics of irony : essays in self-betrayal / edited by Daniel W.
  Conway and John E. Seery
    p. cm.
   ISBN 0-312-04801-7
   1. Political science—History. 2. Irony—Political aspects.
I. Conway, Daniel W. II. Seery, John Evan
JA81.P642 1992
320.5'09—dc20   91-44679
                                      CIP

In memory of
Gregory Vlastos—
Ironist, Moral Philosopher, Friend

CONTENTS

Part II
Contemporary Contestations:
Feminism, Culture, Resistance, Play

Part III
The Ongoing Discourse of Irony: An Exchange

INTRODUCTION

But "ironic" politics? The word combination seems all too strange and especially all too frivolous for one ever to find it valid, much less to admit that politics is altogether and always of ironical character.

—Thomas Mann, *Reflections of a Nonpolitical Man*

Writing in 1917 as a self-proclaimed "nonpolitical" man, Thomas Mann insists on a deep antagonism between irony and politics. Mann defines irony as the "self-betrayal of the intellect," an unrelenting, self-referential skepticism that mercilessly questions, and thus threatens to undermine, all political commitment. Politics often makes for strange bedfellows, but even the most compromising politician ought never to trust an ironist, who will forever remain fickle and fiendish.

Mann's skeptical appraisal of the prospects for an "ironic politics" reflects a common understanding of irony as antipolitical, or political only by default. So understood, irony is relegated to the periphery of political life, where it sometimes provides consolation or escape for the downtrodden, disgruntled, and disempowered. Preserving a therapeutic and modest sense of freedom under desperate conditions, irony customarily attracts naysayers, snobs, slaves, pessimists, buffoons, scoundrels, and cowards. Ironists, Benjamin DeMott once declared, are "sickniks."

Although irony may equip the dispossessed with a much-needed critical perspective and even underwrite a minimal political agenda, it is generally regarded as irremediably parasitic and antisocial. The individual's ironic triumph is often achieved at the expense of others and is liable to vitiate the public ideals of the society as a whole. Echoing the judgment of Socrates' accusers, political theorists often warn that an unchecked irony can poison and potentially topple the body politic. Mann's skepticism would seem to suggest that he, too, accepts the either/or dilemma posed to the Athenian judges: Irony or Politics?

Or does he? What if Mann's "nonpolitical" separation of irony and politics were *itself* ironic? In that event, Mann's self-proclaimed aversion to politics might actually reveal an aspect of political life that is often overlooked. It may be the case that Mann both does and does not mean what he says about irony. He may *also* be claiming, via insinuation, that "politics is altogether and always of ironical character." We might think of Mann as simultaneously and paradoxically embracing parallel truths, namely that irony is both subversive in character *and* intimately linked to politics.

Mann himself suggests such a double reading. Despite his avowed reservations concerning "political irony," he nevertheless deploys this term in his "nonpolitical" manifesto. Irony's "self-betrayal of the intellect" becomes "political," he says, when performed in the service of "life." Yet Mann's uneasy experiment with "political irony" as a new third term does not suggest a resolution to the either/or antagonism between irony and politics. "Political irony" instead conjoins and negotiates between its component terms, preserving and even exaggerating the tensions between them. Mann's exercise in self-referential irony introduces the idea that irony can betray even its own antipolitical character, thus enabling an unexpected and unlikely turn toward politics. Under certain unique conditions, he seems to suggest, the self-betrayal of the intellect itself becomes political and yields a fleeting, fragile moment of affirmation and empowerment. If taken ironically, Mann's appraisal of irony would illuminate a political dimension of irony that is usually overlooked by irony's critics.

Having discerned this potentially political moment of irony, we must be careful not to overestimate or romanticize its capacity for affirmation. Hegel, for example, cautions us not to confuse irony with power, and Nietzsche exposes Socratic irony as expressing a secret death wish. Agents of irony frequently subvert public values and the ideals of others. Irony would never be chosen in the "original position" as the optimal political strategy and is usually embraced only reluctantly, in moments of desperation caused by crises in history, politics, and economics. For the most part, then, Mann is right to insist on a strict separation of irony and politics. Still, as Mann's own self-referential irony suggests, this separation is artificial and ultimately impossible to sustain—a point often elided by those political theorists who endorse a similar separation.

Mann may or may not be recommending this ironic take on politics. Whether he holds such a position is finally irrelevant, and any further appeal to authorial intention might prove inimical to his irony. So long as we defer to Mann and allow him (or anyone else) to set our agenda, we compromise our own prospects for a skeptical embrace of political irony. In order for Mann's irony to *exemplify* the self-betrayal that he *describes*, and thus complete its provisional turn to politics, we the readers must intervene and reconstitute the paradox that Mann bequeaths to us. As Gregory Vlastos argued on behalf of Socrates, irony shifts the burden of interpretation onto the reader and thus indirectly promotes moral autonomy. Having acknowledged this burden, along with the legacy of parasitism that attends it, we accept the overture that Mann and his text apparently extend to us and "autonomously" reopen the investigation of political irony. Mann does not have the last word on irony and politics; nor shall we in this volume.

Why political irony now? The issue has surfaced before in American intellectual life, from the wartime essays of Randolph Bourne (also in 1917) to the post-World War II writings of Reinhold Niebuhr. While irony still has its enemies, including those humorless commentators who categorically deny its political import, and while there may be some point to Jean Baudrillard's facile observation that "the irony of community is missing" in America, the recent resurgence of interest in the politics of irony, cutting across various academic disciplines, is impossible to ignore. Certainly the writings of Paul de Man, Jacques Derrida, Michel Foucault, Richard Rorty, Hayden White, Marshall Berman, Wayne Booth, Donna Haraway, Vlastos, and others have contributed to this growing fascination.

The proponents of irony have been overwhelmingly successful. Many contemporary "postmodern" scholars have touted irony as the master trope of our times, for irony, they say, lurks behind or within virtually every text and readerly strategy. They sometimes delight in what they see as the political consequences of their irony, as evidenced in its subversive effects on traditional hierarchies and artificially enforced relations of power. In fact, the timing of this volume may seem somewhat odd, especially in academic circles, for irony has apparently won the day.

Precisely because irony now rules, however, the politics of irony warrants further investigation. We worry that the triumph of irony within academic circles signals the domestication of irony, that this new vanguard of professional ironists might not be sufficiently ironic about its own enterprise. The seemingly expansive gesture of installing irony as a master trope can actually serve to contain and sanitize it. For example, some postmodern ironists are free to celebrate the corrosive power of irony only because they arbitrarily confine irony to tropology. They customarily beg the question of irony's wider, "extratextual" influence, pretending that their academic activity is inherently and necessarily political. Suddenly the academy finds itself guided by professional ironists who ingeniously collapse the binary distinctions between textuality and worldliness and yet who seem extremely vulnerable to the charge that they have only interpreted the world ironically, in various ways, but have not changed it. Having gentrified irony, these scholars apparently share few of Mann's reservations about its ambiguous relation to politics, and thus foreclose any possible access to his intimation of an ironic politics. They have made the world safe for irony, but only by proscribing those "self-betrayals of the intellect" that Mann associates with political irony.

Those of us who pursue with all earnestness the politics of irony must therefore remain ever vigilant of the ironies of irony. Unlike those scholars who turn to irony for redemption, we must remain steadfastly ironic about our own investment in political irony. We must abandon all hopes that irony can serve as a political panacea, and we must live in constant fear and trembling that we, too, are domesticating this trope and thus violating its spirit. We gratefully accept the insights that irony affords us into politics, yet we do not presume that irony necessarily liberates us in the process. With these provisos and disclaimers in mind, we offer to our readers the following essays, which aim to take seriously both the corrosive nature of irony and its episodically political manifestations.

The Politics of Irony: Essays in Self-Betrayal presents ten essays—all previously unpublished and written specifically for this volume—that explore the ironic dimensions of politics. Although most scholars hold the respective claims of irony and politics to be irreconcilable, these authors variously examine the wayward premise that politics is perhaps unavoidably ironic. The composition of the volume is uniquely cross-disciplinary, featuring authors from the fields of political theory, women's studies, literature, and philosophy, all of whom address issues that lie at the intersection of these disciplines.

The volume is divided into three parts. The first four essays attest to a history of political irony in the works of Plato, Swift, Goethe, and Nietzsche; the next four essays examine the contemporary significance of irony in the politics of feminism, interpretation, resistance, and postmodern play; and the volume ends with an exchange between Jean Bethke Elshtain and Richard Rorty on the possibility of an ironic commitment to liberal ideals.

Part I

HISTORICAL STUDIES:
PLATO, SWIFT, GOETHE, NIETZSCHE

1

Spelunkers of the World, Unite!

John E. Seery

I have a suspicion that some of the most conscious artists of earlier times are still carrying on ironically, hundreds of years after their deaths, with their most faithful followers and admirers.

—Friedrich Schlegel, "On Incomprehensibility"

Except in outlying areas and certain oddball pockets of (mainly Straussian) resistance, Plato's politics do not enjoy a happy reputation today. He is out of favor. Whitehead's remark that all of Western philosophy is but a series of footnotes to Plato now reads like a searing condemnation. It has become common genealogical practice to track down and triumphantly name Plato as the source of many of the philosophic ills that still afflict us. The list grows long: first metaphysician; rationalist; redeemer; logocentrist; ocularcentrist; eurocentrist; phallocrat. He split our selves, he divided our world, he privileged mind over body, speech over writing.[1] Applied to politics, his nasty little lies made us yearn for false unities and transcendent verities and One-Over-the-Many objectivities. Socrates' deathly vexations were bad enough; but then Plato, the crypto-necrophiliac, had to enshrine Socrates' negativity beyond the grave by erecting a monumental memorial to his teacher. Versed in deconstructive strategies, we now know better. His works imprisoned us for nearly three thousand years, but the nightmare—a Gothic horror story—is over. Plato is dead, Plato is dead. Let's read something else.

But what if, just what if, this elaborate story now in vogue about the history of Western philosophy, beginning with Plato as the founder of the Forms, turns out to be deeply mistaken about Plato? What if Plato never really was a *Platonist*? The scandal would be enormous. *How could we all have been so wrongheaded?*

Everything will depend on what we mean by Platonic irony (separate from Socrates' famous irony) and its implications for politics. Leo Strauss and Jacques Derrida are two moderns who have discussed irony in connection with Plato's writings, but both view Plato essentially as a Platonist, an absolutist, a metaphysician, a believer in his own Forms (although political practicability is a separate issue, especially for the Straussians). This essay is meant as a step in the direction of rehabilitating Plato, though the rehabilitation is liable to produce unexpected results that will hardly support the traditional readings of Plato—nor will it confirm the respective Straussian or Derridian understandings of irony. A correlate point (for concerned methodologists) is that irony may be the one case of writing that eludes contemporary deconstructive analysis.

Reading irony is tricky, and a newcomer to this trope should be apprised from the outset that she or he should never hope for a complete identification of the beast, at least not within the span of a normal lifetime. Characteristically, those who have claimed to have spotted irony in texts follow a procedure whereby a critical mass of interpretive hunches about a work accumulate to the point that one gathers enough confidence to go public with them, and then one blurts out the word "irony" in much the same register as one would shout "bingo" at a charity bake sale. The maddening aspect about irony is that, for most ironical texts in question, certain textual incongruities (he seems to be winking at me) appear deliberate and yet the poor reader can find no explicit authorial account for them. This is why deconstructive strategies consistently fail to arrest irony: For reading irony requires that we readers grant the author a benefit of the doubt, namely about the willingness to sustain a prolonged pretense, to carry on—in Goethe's words—these "very serious jests." The ironical author is one who attempts to strike a delicate balance between authorial implication and authorial inscrutability— and if we readers don't have a theory in hand of the *author*, to whom we can extend a benefit of doubt, then we can hardly begin to develop a sense of authorial inscrutability. (None of this commits us to a claim that all textual meanings flow, and only flow, from authorial intentionality; there is plenty of room for deconstructive cleverness as well.) All sorts of historical obstacles have probably worked to prevent us from granting Plato such a bene-fit—we like to patronize the ancients in general, insisting that they must have believed literally in their quaint mythologies and that they were somehow incapable of mock-serious reverence toward their own cultural pieties. We read the Greeks through Christian eyes, in which case Plato becomes a dualist and eschatologist. We read him through our rationalistic understandings of Descartes, and the Enlightenment, and Hegel, and Nietzsche, and Heidegger's Nietzsche, and Derrida's Heidegger; and eventually one must wonder a bit whether Plato has been lost in the shuffle. My point isn't that we should if we could try to recover some original intention, but we must at least be alert to the possibility that Plato, for one, attempted long ago to engage *us*, as readers, in oblique dialogue by way of his reportage of Socrates' dialogues, and that the text is, as it were, pretext. But enough about method (such dreary talk could go on forever).

In this essay I want to work toward a rehabilitation of Plato by focusing on the apparent irony of his longest dialogue, the *Republic*. The overall case about Plato will thus be incomplete in the pages that follow. Surely a more ambitious rereading of some of the other dialogues would support the present thesis; rereadings of other dialogues would probably detract. As for the latter, it may well be that Plato departed from or abandoned his own irony at some point in his later career; then again, maybe he just decided to camouflage it better. Such questions will need to be put on hold until another day.

Even to professional readers, it is not clear what the main subject of the *Republic* is supposed to be. Some say that the dialogue is about education, some say it is about individual psychology, others say it is about utopian politics. For purposes of economy, I want to suggest the following, interrelated themes: the *Republic* is about *reading*, the *Republic* is about *death*, the *Republic* is about the pursuit of political *justice*, and the *Republic* is about *us*, the readers of this book.

The *Republic*, curious text that it is and fascinating because of its complexities, has drawn generations of readers into its pages and has inspired thousands of pages of commentary in learned response and dutiful explication. Reverential philosophers and philologists have pored over its arguments line by line. After such excruciatingly erudite endeavors, some, even today, have issued the conclusion that the *Republic* represents a coherent argument over the whole of the work—about the nature of justice, or about the supraworldly presence of the Forms (*eidos*), or about the tripartite division of the soul, or about the need for philosopher-kings to rule, and so on. Others have credited themselves with the insight that *Republic* contains numerous fallacious, half-baked, and thoroughly unconvincing arguments. Only a rare few of these more rebellious readers have suggested that such claims may be deliberately specious or mock.

Another school of readers has looked up from the "arguments" of the *Republic* in order to attend to the drama of the dialogues. These commentators have suggested to us that the best way to read this strange book is to focus on the development of the characters in the dialogues (Thrasymachus, Adeimantus, and especially Glaucon). The explicit text may be concerned with the hypothetical education of some would-be philosophers, but the important subtext is that Socrates' interlocutors undergo a change in temper over the course of the conversation. Presumably we readers, privy to such down-to-earth spectacles, are somehow to draw certain conclusions on the basis of our witnessing these characterological metamorphoses.

But I want to suggest that even this second approach runs the risk of burying our noses too closely in the book. In reading the *Republic*, we need to look up from the elenchic arguments and up from the drama as well.[2] The real dialogue and the greater drama of the work involve a subliminal, extratextual exchange between Plato, as author, and us, as readers. Plato is trying to turn the dead letter of the written page into a living dialogue,[3] and he has a whole array of devices at his disposal to prompt us toward such an engagement. His tactics, I want to propose, are not meant to be manipulative or underhanded or self-concealing, but are the way they are, subtle and indirect, because he values our independent discovery of them and our considered participation in his project. He cannot simply tell us what he wants to tell us, we have to find out the point of it all by and for ourselves, and there is good reason for all of this circumlocution and subterfuge, as we shall see.

The *Republic* in various critical moments draws our attention to the activity of reading (and to the activity of writing).[4] Such sections should strike us as a little odd coming from the character Socrates, for nowhere are we told that Socrates writes anything, nor do we have a sense from the many Platonic dialogues that Socrates is as much a reader in life as he is a talker. In such passages, we might suspect that we are beginning to detect the self-conscious presence of Plato, who seems to drop clues that we are to read this text of his with a certain critical distance, for appearances can be deceiving.

One such clue seems to be dropped in the pivotal passage on the difference between reading the "letters of justice" in individuals or in polities (368d-e). Up to this point the characters in the dialogue have been grappling (for the most part unsuccessfully) with the question of the comparative rewards of justice versus injustice, and we readers, frankly, have been struggling along with them. When Socrates proposes that he and his auditors are rather "shortsighted fellows" who can't very well read the smaller letters of justice, and thus the group ought to pursue such letters writ large, we readers of this text begin or ought to begin to suspect that Plato, the author, seems to know that we have been squinting pretty intensely at this book of his, and the results thus far have been pretty hazy. The hint in effect doubles as a commentary upon the material to follow: We readers have been tipped off that the text is aware of itself as a text, and that we ought to be equally aware of ourselves as active readers. So what does this mean?

Cut to the most famous of all sections in the *Republic*, a section that is the climax of the "large-lettered" political section, a section that seems to hold the secret key to it all, namely the Allegory of the Cave in book seven. Socrates up to this point has deployed all sorts of ploys, arguments, images, illustrations, metaphors, and stratagems to try to convince Glaucon and company of the virtues of pursuing justice (*dikaiosyne*), and these pretty patterns have largely failed to convince. Now, as a last resort, Plato takes us deep into a cave, where we learn about some strange little stick figures who are chained in such a way that their heads cannot turn so that they must stare straight ahead at a wall in front of them, and some puppeteers behind them cast shadows on the wall, which constitute these stick figures' entire reality, or so they believe. At this point in the dialogue, someone (probably Glaucon) interrupts and remarks that this cave image depicts an "odd picture and an odd sort of prisoner." To make his point more directly, Plato might have substituted "shadow" for "picture" in this last remark. For surely this entire cave parable is an allegory about us, the earnest readers who are trying to make sense of this cave story. Socrates (or Plato, as it were) admits as much in the next line, when he says that these pictures are "like us."

Professional Platonic interpreters generally jump in at this point and explain that Plato's cave story reinforces the "divided line" analogy that immediately preceded it (509d-513e), the point of which is that we humans live in a world of mere appearances, that true reality lies in a world somehow beyond this one, that true philosophers in the know are aware of this great schism, and that ordinary people allow their immediate surroundings to pass for ultimate reality. Certain philosophers, unchained, can ascend to the world of knowledge, bask in the bright lights of *logos*; and then, if somehow they can compel themselves or allow themselves to be compelled to turn around and return to the land below full of chained stick figures, at least they, the philosophers, will know that the shadows are but shadows.

But I think Plato has perpetrated a little joke upon generations of all-too-earnest readers—though it was a joke that was probably intended to be an *inside* joke (we readers have let him down). Plato knows that the idea of a deep cave myth will sound mysterious and alluring to attentive readers. As they read, they will visually construct this odd picture, and their imaginations will run wild: What does it mean, what does it all mean, where is the answer? They will scour the details for deep hidden truths, and they will study these lines extremely carefully. A parallelism emerges: So enthralled as they read about about these stick-figure prisoners staring straight ahead at the wall in front of them, Plato's readers, he hopes, will eventually catch themselves staring ahead at the page in front of them. The spell will be broken, and maybe they will laugh a little at themselves. If these words in front of us are like shadows on the wall, then we must question even these words, these pages, this entire book, now in front of us. Interpretation will not be easy.

Plato has dropped enough hints that we are to read this grand myth with critical reserve, and the comic reflexivity of the prisoner image should at least suggest that Plato doesn't want his readers to stare at this myth with complete credulity. Still, subsequent generations of spellbound readers have mined this myth for only the most straightforward of interpretations. Plato, they say, is extending to us, in so many words, the saving vision of philosophic reason; he is revealing an otherworldly source of knowledge and goodness; he is explaining Socrates' death at the hands of the Athenians. Upon such a reading, the myth suggests answers to many of the big questions in life (i.e., truth with a capital "T" exists, go find it and bring it back).

Yet the myth is playful and admits itself as such, and I suspect that Plato expected his immediate readers to recognize it as such (and also to make the easy recognition that the myth is centrally preoccupied with the already-dead Socrates). Surely the Allegory of the Cave—whatever else it is—is Plato's play upon Aeschylus' play upon the Prometheus myth—though for some reason this not-so-cryptic allusion is seldom mentioned in Platonic commentary.[5] The imagery of chains, fire, caves, shadows, and a miserable humanity would immediately recall the Prometheus story to a Greek audience. Prometheus, it should be recalled, was the one who discovered mortals living "deep in sunless caves" (452). They were "confused and purposeless," passing like "shapes in dreams." And in those days, humans "had eyes, but sight was meaningless" (447). Out of goodwill to humans, Prometheus stole fire from the gods and taught humans skills for practical living. He was the one, well before Socrates or Plato, who gave humans mind and reason (444). He was the one who invented number for humans and set words down in writing. He taught them many useful skills which helped them to attain wealth and greatness (463), and he showed them all the treasures of the earth—bronze, iron, silver, and gold hidden deep down. In addition to cunning and ability, Prometheus gave us "blind hopefulness" (252) by turning our eyes away from death (249).

That the Allegory of the Cave is an obvious play upon the Promethean myth should lead us in certain interpretive directions and foreclose others. Prometheus helped to found cities, but Plato apparently still finds humanity wanting. Such purely practical skills are insufficient. We are, the allegory seems to suggest, still residing in caves, we still can't really see though we have eyes, Prometheus' fire didn't really liberate us, we are all chained as he.

But the point of this satiric commentary cannot be, as the traditional Platonic reading would have it, that Plato is making a pitch for greater reason, greater enlightenment, as the solution to our woes. Prometheus already gave us reason (*nous*). The shadows are still shadows, we have eyes but still do not really see, but the implication need not be that there is literally a greater reality behind the shadows. This allegory is not fundamentally about epistemology, it is not about the intellectual bankruptcy of the Athenians who tried Socrates, it is not just a dramatized justification for philosophers to rule.

The *Protagoras* dialogue gives us a clue as to Plato's ulterior point (not every Platonic dialogue need be consistent with every other, but these two, the *Protagoras* and the *Republic*, were probably written about the same time, most Platonic scholars have agreed). In Socrates' version of the Prometheus story, Prometheus gave humans *techne* and fire, but he failed to grant them political wisdom (319d). Thanks to Prometheus, humans could fight off beasts for they knew the art of warfare, and such warlike tendencies eventually drew them together to form fortified cities. But because humans did not know how to conduct themselves politically, Socrates says, they would injure each other and scatter again, and thus their cities would self-destruct, and the human race itself would be put again in jeopardy. Zeus then sent them, by way of Hermes, the qualities of respect for others and a sense of justice, "so as to bring order into our cities and create a bond of friendship and union" (322c).

The allegory then, as an update to the Prometheus story, presents a roundabout claim about the need for political justice—which surely is a main theme of the *Republic* as a whole—but the pursuit of justice here cannot simply be a matter of beholding some new transcendental source of light (the usual reading): Plato cannot simply be calling for a second theft of fire from the gods! Rather, the play upon the Prometheus myth connects the allegory with another prominent theme, also recurrent throughout the *Republic*, of the relation between *sight* and the *consequences of justice*: What are the visible benefits, the visible consequences, attending to the pursuit of justice? The shadows in the allegory are mere shadows, mere appearances not in the sense that there is purported to be a greater reality in some world literally beyond this one, but rather in the sense that such shadows are mere externalities, visible only, as it were, when one is blinded to the fact of human finitude. Prometheus teaches us all sorts of reasonable, practical skills—especially skills that can be quantified—but these skills altogether do not bind us together in cities. They are the kinds of skills and the kind of knowledge that provide purpose and hopefulness only when we turn a blind eye toward death, human mortality. They are the kinds of skills that produce visible consequences—in another dialogue Socrates names such tangible Promethean benefits as wealth, nobility, fine clothing, and healthy body[6]—but such externalities pale in importance in view of death. Utilitarianism and consequentialism—Prometheus is suggested here to have been the patron saint of Athenian sophists, Socrates' lifelong opponents—cannot bind us fully together. And, by contrastive implication, true political wisdom—whatever it is—must take death more fully into account. Doing right, pursuing justice in this political world, will defy utilitarian considerations, and the benefits of political wisdom may be visible, as it were, only from the perspective of death.

Of course Socrates' death provides the background for much of the cave allegory—this is no great secret nor any great insight into the hidden workings of the text. The underworldly imagery of the scene surely borrows from Orphic sources, including the Homeric *Nekyia*, and constitutes another of the many *katabaino* (descent) scenes that run from the beginning to the end of the *Republic*, providing the main dramatic motif for the book as a whole.[7] Once again (as with the opening dialogue in the *Pireaus* with the now-dead Cephalus) we find ourselves in Hades, and our cavelike existence can be so construed.[8] But the point of this deathly casting cannot be, as the Straussians have insisted, mainly to issue a warning to would-be Socratic philosophers that their lives may be imperiled if they attempt to bring justice down from the heavens.[9] Rather, the Promethean tenor of the allegory suggests that Socrates' accusers, Promethean-Pythagorean[10] prisoners all, were at the time more dead than Socrates. I do not believe Plato constructed that deathly irony simply to perpetrate an elaborate compensation fantasy or simply to enforce some invidious distinction between the prisoner's ignorance and Socrates' supposedly superior insights. There must be more to this complex story than assigning blame, issuing warnings, and privileging philosophy.

Indeed, the allegory invites us to look at all of human existence from the perspective of death (which, after all, is the only distinctly mortal perspective).[11] And from that vantage the question for the philosophically inclined becomes: Why pursue politics or justice or goodness when humans are, as it were, already dead?[12] In the allegory the one stick figure who breaks free and beholds the light outside the cave meditates on precisely this question (516c-517a). Such a person no longer covets the prizes and honor and power that humans confer upon themselves, and he would agree with Homer that it is better to follow the plow of an indigent serf "than be king over all of these exhausted dead" (*Odyssey* 11.489-90). At this point, such a person has not yet turned around and reentered the cave. But Socrates was a person who had, as it were, reentered the cave. He continued to engage his fellows though he strongly suspected them to be know-nothings, and he remained in Athens to the end, despite all. This, then, is the main question posed by the allegory: What is the nature of the vision, what kind of person is it who sees the shadows as shadows, who sees the rewards of this world as paltry, who is well aware that all human endeavor ends in death and yet can rededicate himself/herself to this cave of ours, nevertheless?

Visibility is a motif that recurs throughout the *Republic*,[13] but is most apparent in the two main allegories of enlightenment, the divided line and the cave scene. If the light outside the cave is supposed to supplant the Promethean fires (517b), what is the nature of this light? I suggest that we readers have interpreted this light far too rigidly, gazing too uncritically at its image on the page in front of us while we search for some secret Gnosis that holds the key to Plato's cryptic cosmos.[14] Such mesmerizing stares have yielded time and again the standard "Platonic" interpretation: that Plato literally believes in transcendental entities called Forms that somehow hover metaphysically above us and to which only a hyperrationalism may gain epistemological access. Instead I want to propose that Plato invokes the vision of the essential *eidos* as a sustained play upon the theme of external (i.e., visible) consequences, which serves his overall project of begging the question of (and ever deferring any answer to) whether the pursuit of justice brings tangible rewards (especially in view of death).

Once alerted to this possibility—namely that Plato's famous Forms are a literary device playing ironically upon the theme of consequentialism—then we start to notice textual evidence supporting such a view.[15] The term *eidos* itself, as Eva Brann has argued, apparently is ironic, for it combines in one term both the aspect of visibility and invisibility—an intelligible "look"—the "sight" of something that cannot, properly speaking, be seen.[16] The questions surrounding these two main allegories all involve the quandary of how one can "see" justice though it eludes our normally shortsighted grasp. The text employs all sorts of visual devices to convey the difficulty involved in conceptualizing justice in a world in which the pursuit of injustice literally pays better. Socrates, for instance, tries to explain that the light of true justice, to those who have seen it, is "higher," "larger," "sharper," "brighter." In the cave section he remarks that it is very difficult for the ordinary person to see beyond the cavelike "shadows" of justice,[17] and by contrast the person who "sees" a different kind of justice will look ridiculous to the cave dweller (517e). I don't believe the main point of this invidious comparison is to enforce some ingrained, intractable distinction between those who see and those who can't or between sensible and essential realms; rather, the comparison emphasizes how difficult it tends to be to commit to seemingly remote notions of justice. Indeed Socrates insists in the cave allegory (518c) that the power of learning inheres in everyone's soul. But then he subtly upbraids those who choose in fact not to follow this vision: "It's as if," he says mockingly by way again of highly visual imagery, "we couldn't turn our eye from the dark to the bright without turning our whole body around" (518d).[18] Sight alone evidently will not suffice to convince most persons to dedicate their lives to the pursuit of justice. Therefore we must, as it were, try to turn the whole "soul" and the "eye of the soul"[19] toward the vision of justice, and then back around toward the cave.

Virtually every passage in the cave allegory attests to the great difficulty inherent in the attempt to convince persons to commit themselves to the pursuit of justice. Leading persons up to the proverbial light is, Socrates quips, like trying to lead them out of Hades and up to the gods (521c). And in a second, equally lighthearted analogy, Socrates says that the turning of the soul toward the light is not like the chance spin of an oyster shell from the dark side to the light side (521d). (The choice rather is arduous, the result of human deliberation, not mere happenstance.) Moreover, even once they are turned toward the light, such enlightened figures would prefer to linger in these upper regions and are liable to refuse to return to the cave. Hence they must be compelled to return; otherwise justice might never rule, for no right-thinking philosopher, Socrates remonstrates, would ever willingly descend. The purpose of these barbs, I submit, is to sting *us* with a critical commentary about our common worldly practices, for we humans tend to resist "seeing" for ourselves the greater significance of the pursuit of a "common good" (520a). Those readers who peruse these passages in search of hidden metaphysical information—as if Plato's ulterior point is to lay out a textual obstacle course whose challenge is met only by those epic readers whose exegetical skills are truly heroic—are maybe missing the point (as it stares them right in the face, I want to add).

Socrates insists that the road to philosophy's perch is narrow and steep. People are so disinclined to walk this path by themselves, he ventures, that it's as if a winch (521d, 521e, 523a) is required to lift the soul up toward the light. Socrates then elaborates on the many steps along this difficult way. A would-be philosopher must be well trained in gymnastics and poetry (521e). He or she must be able to count and to calculate. In a series of exchanges with Glaucon—*all* of which play upon sight themes in describing the process of philosophic education[20]—Socrates defends calculation as a skill contributing to the faculty of perception, which involves judging distances and depths (523b). Glaucon eagerly jumps in to demonstrate his own spatial acuity: "You obviously mean things seen at a distance or drawn in perspective" (523b). Socrates rebuffs him mildly with a pun: "You haven't quite hit the mark."[21]

Socrates' attempt to explain the peculiar vision belonging properly to the "eye of the soul" continues. Ordinary sight and ordinary sense impressions do not order themselves into intelligible classifications such as "large" or "small" (523c-524d). The faculty of understanding,[22] which operates separately from, as it were, the realm of visible impressions, must supply these classifications. Certain studies, such as mathematics, geometry, and astronomy, help to train this faculty, which then helps turn the soul toward the higher regions. Plato not so subtly seems to remind us that he is again deliberately playing upon sight metaphors: "Each of us has in his soul an organ blinded and ruined by other pursuits, though more worth preserving than ten thousand eyes" (527e). Socrates shifts attention from two-dimensional plane geometry (528b) to the study of three-dimensional solids,[23] and a discussion about the particular relevance of astronomy follows. This discussion, I suggest, is crucial for the proper appreciation of the famous Forms.

Socrates earlier had passed over the discussion of solids—which would have helped Glaucon's understanding of "depth" perception—and instead skipped directly to a discussion of astronomy, which, he notes, is the study of solids in motion. Earlier Glaucon had praised the study of astronomy on the grounds that it makes the seasons, months, and years more perceptible, which benefits the activities of farming, sailing, and soldiering (527d). Socrates had gently chided him for his "vulgar utilitarian" appreciation of astronomy, and now Glaucon wants to make amends. In his new praise for astronomy, Glaucon, evidently looking up in the air, remarks, "I think anyone can see that astronomy forces the soul to look up and leads it from things here to things there" (529a). Socrates expresses his disapproval over this claim and adds that some earnest philosophers treat astronomy in a way that actually turns the soul's gaze "downward." He rebukes Glaucon for his literalism: "How nobly you seem to take the study of things above!"[24] He even mocks him: "I'll bet if someone leaned back and tried to learn something by staring at the patterns on the ceiling, you'd think he was contemplating with intellect instead of his eyes" (529b).

Look up, blink down, lie on your back, stare at a book—the study of justice ultimately defies all of these shortsighted approaches.[25] The proper study of astronomy should treat the heavens as an aesthetic model, and no more than that (529e). And the study of music as a way of apprehending a greater sense of harmony should be taken with great reserve. Socrates mocks the Pythagoreans who struggle endlessly to measure audible sounds as a way of understanding greater harmony and justice (531c). All of these people—astronomers, mathematicians, musicians—don't quite get at justice (531d). Even mathematicians aren't very "sharp" at dialectics (531e). Plato's point in distinguishing so starkly in this section between the visible and the intelligible need not be that he wants to privilege the latter as if such a realm literally exists. To jump to that conclusion is to read the book in much the same way that Glaucon stared up at the stars. To be sure, Plato wants us to disengage our sensibilities from our immediate surroundings, and he lures us on with the image of a higher, brighter, better, truer realm. But he places so many qualifications around this upper realm and insists that its apprehension is so extremely elusive that we must at the least call into question our own first assumptions about what he means. He carries his exclusionary criteria, for those who can see properly, to the point of parody. Dialectics should be a joy unto itself, but very few humans will devote the necessary time and discipline to it (535c). Older men, in fact, are no longer receptive to learning (536d), so Socrates will start with the young; though the youth aren't ready to appreciate dialectics either, and they must be trained for thirty years (readers often seem to take these passages about age merely as down-to-earth practical advice). At one point in this discussion (536b-c) Socrates breaks in and admits that he is making himself look ridiculous because he is speaking far too seriously about philosophy, having forgotten that they have been talking playfully all along.

Readers at this point should also take this reminder to heart. Many of our serious professional commentators today, however, simply look past these remarks about playfulness and dismiss the frequently sportive character of the dialogue as a whole. Philosophy, they seem to hold, ought to be grave and ponderous, and the point of Socrates' dissembling—if they detect it at all—supposedly must be to reinforce indirectly the supramundane essentiality of the Forms. Somehow, after all of these twists and turns, ups and downs, thrusts and parries, puns and jests, images and allegories, questions and more questions, Plato is made out to be a hyperrationalist and manic metaphysician. If you think hard enough and squint long enough at his book, you supposedly stand a chance of communing with the Forms. Maybe, however, such a reading represents not the ultimate faithfulness to Plato but the ultimate victimization, a result of Plato's extended ironization of those who abide by a consequentialist ethics, even those who take consequentialism to an otherworldly extreme.

I propose rather that the Forms function in the *Republic* as yet another visual device, albeit one that helps put our notions of visibility into perspective. This light supposedly outside the cave serves as an aid to the imagination and to the understanding, a heuristic device, a foil to our normal affairs that helps us get, as it were, an outside look at ourselves. But I want to insist that the *Republic* through and through is about politics, not metaphysics; that the main drama centers upon the act of returning to the cave, not the ascending out of it. The light is a ruse, a mere image, a setup, and Plato admits as much. The constant play upon visibility in the text certainly supports an antiutilitarian, anti-Promethean reading of the cave, but Plato's apparent insistence that the alternative source of light remains difficult if not impossible to grasp undercuts the standard "transcendentalist" view of the Forms. The notion of an elusive *eidos* somewhere out there heavenward continues to play upon our need for visible rewards; it keeps us enthralled and reading; it is the ultimate extrapolation of the idea of consequentialism, and yet at the same time contains a sustained spoof thereof. We in the cave require tangible rewards and visible benefits for our efforts, and we have a hard time imagining anything outside the cave. At numerous points in the *Republic* Plato equates the "shadows" in the cave with wealth (though the shadows also stand at times for honor, reputation, gain, and in general all of immediate reality). A commitment to politics and to political community, on the other hand, requires that one look beyond one's nose and beyond the concern for immediate payoffs; a commitment to such an elusive, seemingly abstract concept of political justice requires that one be able to entertain a "big picture" on worldly affairs. But such a vision is hard to grasp—which is a polite way of saying that people generally choose *not* to look this way (the point is not that they are inherently stupid). Plato's portrait of us humans here in the cave is indeed funny (and not just a little sad as well): little stick figures ever resistant to an expansive outlook that suggests that there may be more to life than Prometheanism. Unwittingly, we live our lives now as if we were already in Hades, already dead, and the shortcoming of the Promethean ethic is that it must ignore the fact of our mortality. Plato wants to convince certain souls of the importance of reentering the cave though such a life may well look like a living death. But note: He never proves the existence of the Good anywhere in the *Republic*, he continues to beg the question of the nature of the light at the end of the tunnel, he is reluctant to lay all of his cards on the table, he dodges, he hedges, he forwards deliberately specious or contradictory or fallacious arguments, he writes a thoroughly unconvincing book if the point of it all is to show that justice pays better than injustice. Maybe the commitment to political justice requires a supreme sense of irony, because—dare we say it point blank?—the Forms and particularly the Form of justice do not, and never will, exist as such. The light is *only* metaphorical.

The *Republic* overall is the story of a series of attempts to convince Socrates' interlocutors, Thrasymachus, Glaucon, and Adeimantus, about the importance of pursuing justice, put to Socrates in the form of the question, Does a life of justice pay better than a life of injustice? Socrates tailors his arguments to address the respective concerns of each of his three respondents. Thrasymachus early in the book, after taking up the discussion where old businessman Cephalus and his son Polemarchus leave off, demands in effect a *quantifiable* answer to the justice question—something like the number twelve—and Socrates eventually in the dialogue supplies Thrasymachus with such a number: 729. The just man, Socrates computes, is 729 times happier than the unjust man. To the attentive reader it becomes clear that Socrates' mathematical arguments are mock (though it may well be that justice indeed delivers, as it were, a "greater" happiness of sorts).[26] Glaucon early on challenges Socrates with the dilemma of the ring of Gyges and the Helmut of Hades, both of which evince his concern for visible consequences in general. Much of the *Republic*, including the central line and cave allegories, is pitched to Glaucon, though Plato repeatedly alerts us readers that such images are just that, images.

Adeimantus' query—overlooked in most of the secondary literature—represents the toughest nut to crack. He presents Socrates with the challenge of a true Helmut of Hades, thus extending Glaucon's worldly concern for visible consequences into a realm of the invisible (*aides*), a veritable afterlife. What if the gods don't exist or don't care, he asks—why, then, pursue justice in this world? What if there is no otherworldly benefit to seek or retribution to worry about? As I read it, the final allegory, the Myth of Er, represents Socrates' response to Adeimantus (though the section is addressed explicitly to Glaucon). In this final Hades scene, Socrates seems to respond simply by denying the premises of Adeimantus' question. Essentially he contends that the gods do care. Socrates paints a big cosmological vision and weaves a fantastic tale of underworldly reward and retribution, involving an elaborate scheme of reincarnation. The bottom line in all of this: Good actions in this life will be rewarded in an afterlife, bad will be punished. And humans have the capacity to decide between the two, and thus should seek the knowledge to be able to distinguish between good and bad (618c).

All but the most credulous readers scratch their heads after reading the fairy-talish Myth of Er. Can Plato really be serious? Has he gone off the deep end? Some commentators have contended that the ending is just plain bad, and they wish it away. A few die-hard Platonists still insist that Plato means what he says here, but their numbers are diminishing. We might take a cue from the young Karl Marx, who was one of the first to contend that the Myth of Er was a spoof of sorts.[27] Don't believe that Plato has gone evangelical, Marx proposes. Plato doesn't really believe in this eschatological scheme, nor has he betrayed the spirit of Socratism (not in the sense of rationalism but as open-ended inquiry). Like Socrates, Marx argues, Plato here is being ironic.

We can gather our own evidence insinuating that Plato is being something less than straightforwardly sincere in his presentation of the Myth of Er, this Pythagorean phantasmagoria. A tip-off is that the entire section conspicuously contains self-referential contradictions, many of which call attention to the act of writing. The entire myth, for instance, is presented in an obvious mock-Homeric mode of writing—which is a bit unsettling especially since Socrates has just dismissed artistic representation at several removes from the truth, and Homer is named as the chief culprit of such a form of writing. Why admonish Homeric poetry and then pile on the allusions to the *Iliad* and the *Odyssey*? And, if one remembers, most of the poetic talk to be banished in the city involves talk about Hades—yet here in the Myth of Er we descend once again into the nether regions. Why, for that matter, end a book supposedly about a poetry-free philosophic education with a colossal superpoetic myth? Plato's coy presence seems to be with us.

The sight metaphors continue throughout the Myth of Er—indeed the myth presents the biggest image of all. The myth retells the telling of a story about an infernal traveler—Er—who has returned to tell his tale about the whole cosmos, having witnessed in the underworld "a sight worth seeing" and "a spectacle."[28] One of the main reasons to descend into the underworld, we are told, is to learn that one must remain faithful to the pursuit of Goodness, and even in Hades one shouldn't be "dazzled by riches" and other evils (619a). Er recounts the fates of souls that he saw in Hades, and two in particular—Orpheus and Odysseus—seem juxtaposed as polar examples. Orpheus and Odysseus were also infernal travelers, they both had seen death and then returned to the world. Orpheus descended to retrieve his lost love but he became embittered after his failure, and he foreswore all love of women thereafter. Amazons tore him apart (several versions of the story go), and his dismembered head floating on the water transformed into a singing swan. In the underworld Er sees that Orpheus, who chose first, chose the life of a swan, for he still hated women and wished not to be conceived and born of a woman (even though his original descent into death was out of love for a woman). The story suggests that he thus got what he deserved—a nonhuman life.

Odysseus drew the last lot, but it turns out that he would have picked the same soul had he chosen first—even though it was the least attractive life to the others. The significance of his choosing the life of "an ordinary citizen" has been interpreted by Straussian commentators to mean that one should avoid politics, but I don't believe that that reading is textually justified. Instead, Odysseus was a person who, like Orpheus, suffered and knew death, but, unlike Orpheus, he still affirmed ordinary human life. The difference between Odysseus' past worldliness and his newfound worldliness is that, remembering his previous struggles, he is now cured of ambition and eschews the badges of honor. Odysseus had some difficulty finding this life (unglamorous as it appears), but once he sees it, he chooses it gladly.[29]

Odysseus' ironic fate seems to accord with the anticonsequentialist, anti-externalist vision of happiness and reward that the book has been indirectly promoting all along. Such seemingly uneventful rewards will not be appreciated by others, and they bring happiness only to those who know suffering and death and yet are able to withstand the cynicism that death might otherwise counsel (whereas the embittered Orpheus became the victim of irony). Still, the myth ends on a grand flourish, an ostensible paean to consequentialism of a sort, stating that those who hold ever to the upward way and practice justice will indeed win "the prize for justice," like victorious athletes who collect their spoils.

What this mystifying finale means isn't obvious, though we at least know that Socrates has supplied Adeimantus with an otherworldly answer to his question concerning otherworldly matters. But the exact nature of this eternal reward ("both here and in the thousand-year journey we have gone through") isn't very clear, and actually Socrates has only begged Adeimantus' original question (if the gods don't care, then we don't know why the pursuit of justice is to be recommended). To the suspicious reader, I suggest, the ending—an underworldly extravaganza—looks inflated and contrived, and deliberately so. Just as Marx contended, it seems as if Plato wanted us, the readers, to see through the otherworldly designs that Socrates presented to his interlocutors. Plato subverts his own text (and we don't need a professional deconstructor to intervene and do it for us). Where does that leave us, then, if the Myth of Er, as the kicker to this strange book, doesn't convince us about the relative benefits of pursuing justice—and in fact seems deliberately to fall short of any such proof? Maybe the answer is an answer left by default: From the perspective of death, perhaps there is no good answer, no good reason, to pursue justice (especially in light of the consequences and the paltry rewards).

That's the key: The book is supposed to fail to convince us on the level of argument—and shame on those generations of readers who have chosen instead to flatter themselves by discovering "fallacies" in the arguments rather than crediting Plato with a slyly self-deprecating pedagogy. Those who continue to quarrel about whether philosophers should actually rule or not are missing the magic of the book. Nor can the point be that the reader ought to try to emulate or approximate the dramatic acceptances of the various characters, Thrasymachus, Glaucon, Adeimantus. Rather, the book fails, and there is a lesson implicit in that failure. The images of the book undermine themselves, so that we are invited or prodded into questioning the visible designs of the book, seeing through the arguments and allegories, identifying them as specious or mock (though important lessons may still be conveyed via such designs). Under the conditions sketched—namely that human life ends in death—no book can convince you to pursue justice in this world of ours. Truly the visible sketch of political justice on the page in front of you is preposterous—the Straussians are probably right about that—and it is unlikely that even an elaborate scheme of otherworldly rewards and punishments will persuade you otherwise.

Still, the book leads us on. It cannot all be for naught. This dazzling book cannot be simply an esoteric mockery of the pursuit of justice, a setup to ward off any effort in that direction. For instance, despite our skepticism regarding the quasi-religious details that make up the story of the Myth of Er, we nonetheless can appreciate the idea behind Odysseus' homecoming. We do, in reading this book, get a glimpse of a bigger picture (as it were) about the importance of justice, we do sense an oblique rationale for pursuing justice, even though we've conceded that no concrete rewards may accrue to us for our efforts. We want to continue. But once we have dismissed consequentialism as an admirable or persuasive grounding of our pursuits, transcendentalism offers no viable alternative, either. The ultimate secret revealed to the philosopher who ascends may well be: There is no light outside the cave, the Forms don't exist, there is no transcendental "reason" for seeking justice. The book throws a bone to those readers who desperately crave such hard and fast answers. The book in effect says: If you need arguments, here they are. If you need numbers, designs, myths, fictions, lies, a theory of Forms, here they all are. If you need a self-help book convincing you about the importance of justice, here it is. But the book is ultimately pitched to the reader who sees through such arguments, numbers, and myths, and who perversely presses on with the interpretive challenge.[30] In the face of death, no arguments will suffice for convincing us to pursue justice in this world. In view of the nearly inescapable fact that the pursuit of injustice probably does pay better, there is no cute turn-of-the-intellectual screws that will automatically change your mind. In such a world, a world in which there is no good reply to give to the resident cynic-sophist, the dedicated individual will have to convince himself or herself about the benefits of pursuing justice. How is one to remain dedicated to this world if that is all there is? No one can tell you. You must turn yourself around; a book can't do it. And silly little Forms won't suffice, either.

The *Republic* teaches us to look to ourselves, finally, for "reasons" or noble fictions to help convince us to continue seeking justice in this world—or, rather, to accept that no such discursive reasons are possible given the circumstances. I realize that some of my readers at this point might object, contending that my presentation resembles Tertullian or Sartrean existentialism: "I believe, *because* it is absurd." My answer to that charge is that the above "ironic" reading of the *Republic* departs from traditional existentialist accounts because it does not presuppose or offer or seek a new "authenticity" as a ground for existence. And the whole purpose of seeking to return to the cave is *intersubjective*: How is it that we might remain dedicated to a notion of the common good, to justice for the sake of others, in light of our radical skepticism, cynicism, and fatalism? The project is finally political, not strictly personal: For now we sense that what really holds a city together are these numerous acts of common striving. The book teaches aspiration (but without a clear end in sight). And the magic of the book is that the subliminal dialogue which Plato carries on with us readers can actually help to create this mutually reinforcing poise, of readers and writers engaging in a common pursuit toward the good. The odd result is that this book can create an ironic community (based on nothing more than a work of fiction): For a community of seekers *is* a community of sorts. That notion of community is, however, a far cry from the traditional reading of Plato according to which Plato allegedly seeks to impose uniform, universal standards upon a manipulated populace[31] (such a reading sadly caricatures the *Republic*, but generations of readers have accepted that read, which derives from Aristotle's original cheap-shot critique). Nor do I see that community as necessarily closed and invidious (for human mortality is a profoundly democratic condition). Instead, the book encourages a provisional embrace of the aspiration toward community by way of dialogue and questioning, ever mindful of death. Know thyself, and remember thy mortality.

Why dedicate yourself to others when that effort probably won't get you anywhere? Doesn't might make right? Why be good? The *Republic*, despite appearances, offers no real answer to these questions—at least not in the traditional sense of an answer. To the extent that he answers, Plato answers only by begging the questions, but in the process he helps disabuse the reader of his or her need for such answers. The *Republic*—to put it too programmatically—offers no program as such. It offers no set rationale. Throw away the image of philosopher-kings. Throw away the image of tripartite souls. Throw away the numbers game. There's no Form of the Good, no out there, no up there, no thereafter. We all live in a cave. We all shall die. Politics—if it is to work at all—requires irony.

This reading will be resisted. Much, so very much, has been invested in a literalist Plato through the ages. Entire books are still written today about the *Republic* in which irony is never mentioned or is even systematically denied (funny how irony unnerves some people). To be sure, a literalist read helps to allay our metaphysical anxieties. We can be comforted rather with our hopeful belief that rational self-interest is the very key to life and holds the modern secret to a viable politics. We can put Plato into a neat box. It throws us off, however, to think that the ancients might have been two steps ahead of us. Even the postmodern deconstructors, who sometimes present themselves as brokers in irony, can't quite seem to accept the idea that individuals such as Plato might already be complexly ironic in their writerly ways. That may be why Plato must be their fall guy, their straw man, Derrida's demon.

A rehabilitation of Plato would mark the beginning of an attempt to rethink the relationship between irony and politics. Traditionally these two lives—the life of irony and the life of politics—have been regarded as opposites (Richard Rorty's voice is only the latest to make this claim). The ironist, it is said, defies all formula, deflates all good intentions, derides all noble purposes. He is a master of the noncommital pose, and he delights in dashing all hopes for redemption. The politician (or the political philosopher), on the other hand, must be a believer in the cause. He or she must be earnest, must be resolute, must be committed—to humanity, to justice, to truth. These two lives are fundamentally at war with one another. Our contemporary postmodern pragmatists—such as Rorty—lately have been trying to teach us how to relinquish our cultural yearning for ultimate redemptions and justifications (Prometheanism more or less works, they say), and they view Plato—and the entire Western tradition—as the source of the problem. But perhaps Plato was well ahead of his time, and maybe his critics today might learn something from his early efforts to build a politics on the basis of irony. Even if objective dispensations of justice are not forthcoming, and political commitment does not in fact make sense in light of death, the alternative need not be simply to lower our sights and to abandon our vision.[32] Under conditions such as these, it may well be that only an ironic return to the political world, in pursuit of justice, can bind us together and allow us to fare well in these strange lives of ours with each other.

> For the life of irony having no reserve and weaving itself out of the flux of experience rather than out of eternal values has the broad, honest sympathy of democracy, that is impossible to any temperament with the aristocratic taint. One advantage the religious life has is a salvation in another world to which it can withdraw. The life of irony has laid up few treasures in heaven, but many in this world.
>
> —Randolph Bourne, "The Life of Irony"

NOTES

1. Or writing over speech, depending on whether you ask Eric Havelock or Jacques Derrida. See Havelock, *Preface to Plato* (Cambridge, MA: Belknap Press, 1963); Derrida, "Plato's Pharmacy," *Disseminations*, trans. Barbara Johnson (Chicago: University of Chicago Press, 1981), pp. 61-172.
2. A few commentators have recently attempted to venture beyond Strauss's dramatic reading of Platonic irony. They want to emphasize that the allegedly esoteric negativity of the drama *does* lead us to think, in a way, for ourselves or to make philosophy our own enterprise (and not merely to reject the political pursuit of justice). Such readings, though, still view Platonic irony as an instrument to reinforce a consequentialist truth, which all too often simply echoes Strauss's initial claim about some natural order of rank among readers or about the need for a protected elite. Surely the highest wisdom conferred by the study of philosophy must be something a bit more profound than the self-centering claim that the pursuit of philosophy constitutes the highest and wisest pursuit. See Drew A. Hyland, "Taking the Longer Road: The Irony of Plato's *Republic*," *Revue de Metaphysique et de Morale*, Vol. 93, No. 3 (July-Sept., 1988), pp. 317-335; Charles L. Griswold, Jr., "Plato's Metaphilosophy: Why Plato Wrote Dialogues," *Platonic Writings, Platonic Readings*, ed. Charles L. Griswold, Jr. (New York: Routledge, 1988), pp. 143-167.
3. I do not mean to play into Derrida's hand here, as if I were oblivious to his elaborate critique of "logocentrism." My position rather is that Derrida shares (maybe even borrows without proper attribution) Plato's concern

that readers continue to pose questions of texts and not presume that written meaning is stable and unitary. Derrida, on my account, has tried to exaggerate the distance between himself and Plato precisely because their projects are so similar. What else can explain Derrida's failure to address Plato's irony? Cf. Albert Cook, "Dialectic, Irony, and Myth in Plato's *Phaedrus*," *American Journal of Philology*, Vol. 106, No. 4 (Winter, 1985), pp. 427-441.

4. First, there is the evident paradox that the *Republic* is a *written* dialogue. Then, several references raise, at least implicitly, the question of writing: the letters of the individual and politics (368d, 402a); the baskets of instruction books by Orpheus and Musaeus (364e); the sketch of a city in words (369a); the question of the writings of the poets (e.g., 380a).

5. For the connection to the Aeschylus myth (and much more), I am indebted to Eva T. H. Brann and her fabulous essay, "The Music of the *Republic*," *St. John's Review*, Vol. 39, No. 1-2 (1989-1990), pp. 1-103. Brann also mentions irony in connection with the descent motif, and in general observes playful aspects of the *Republic*, all of which help us "to remind ourselves that while Socrates is speaking to Glaucon, the dialogue itself is speaking to us" (p. 96). Where we part, I might suggest in brief, is that she emphasizes the esoteric music of the *Republic* and I emphasize the mock-visual aspects; she traces the *katabaino* moments mainly to Hermes' descent, whereas I tend to emphasize Orpheus' descent.

6. *Gorgias* 524d.

7. In addition to the opening Pireaus scene, the cave allegory, and the Myth of Er, the Ring of Gyges (359d), the divided line (511b), and the Cap of Hades (612b) are *katabaino* stories. See my *Political Returns: Irony in Politics and Theory from Plato to the Antinuclear Movement* (Boulder, CO: Westview, 1990), pp. 103ff.

8. 521c, 534d.

9. The Straussian "ironic" reading of the *Republic*, which regards the pursuit of justice in this world more or less as a joke, seems to make far too much of this one passage (517a-b) as the basis for an interpretation of the entire book.

10. Clearly Plato conflates Aeschylus' cave with Pythagorean imagery. Brann contends that Socrates in *Philebus* (16c) intimates that Pythagoras is the true Prometheus.

11. It should be noted (but I haven't noticed this observation in any of my reading about the famous censorship of the poets) that the banned poetry in the *Republic* is poetry primarily about death and stories about Hades (386-388c). Socrates says that people should instead commend Hades, and not fear death, because otherwise people will not be sufficiently dedicated to fighting. This strikes me as another gentle ironization of people who are motivated mainly on the basis of a consequentialist ethic.

12. Here I think Plato has already anticipated and responded to Foucault's themes of the "death of the author" and the disciplining power of the prison.

Plato's ironic play on the Pythagorean notion of imprisonment and bodily death makes Foucault's twentieth-century insight seem pedestrian.

13. See Desmond Lee's excellent notes on visual imagery. Desmond Lee, ed. and trans., *Plato: The Republic* (New York: Penguin, 1974), pp. 312 n. 2, p. 314 n. 1, p. 315 n. 4. James Robert Peters warns against attending exclusively to visual imagery, but I don't think he considers the possibility that the visual devices can serve an ironic reading. "Reason and Passion in Plato's *Republic*," *Ancient Philosophy*, Vol. 9, No. 2 (Fall, 1989), pp. 173-188.

14. The contemporary critique of "gazing" and "ocularcentrism" seems to preclude an appreciation of Plato's irony. See Martin Jay, "In the Empire of the Gaze: Foucault and the Denigration of Vision in 20th Century French Thought," *Postmodernism: ICA Documents*, ed. Lisa Appignanesi (London: Free Association Books, 1989), pp. 49-87.

15. Brann points out that Plato never supplies us with an explicit account of the Good. "The Music of the *Republic*," pp. 50, 56.

16. Ibid., p. 48.

17. Socrates mentions that fighting over shadows is the cause of civil war (520d), and later he refers to Helen of Troy as a phantom (586c). Elsewhere he likens the pursuit of wealth to a two-dimensional shadow (587d).

18. Jowett senses irony in this analogy. B. Jowett and Lewis Campbell, eds., *Plato's Republic: The Greek Text*. 3 vols. (Oxford: Clarendon Press, 1894), Vol. 3, p. 322.

19. Those who asseverate that Plato privileges "mind over body" seem to be reading this passage as if it contained no hint of irony. Cf. John Clardy Kelley, "Virtue and Inwardness in Plato's *Republic*," *Ancient Philosophy*, Vol. 9, No. 2 (Fall, 1989), pp. 173-188.

20. 522e-523b. "Do you *see* what I *see* in this learning?" "It seems to be one of the studies we're *looking for* . . ." "Observe how I distinguish the things that lead up there from the ones that do not and agree or disagree so we'll *clearly see* . . ." "*Show* them . . ." "I will if you *watch* . . ." (my italics).

21. Jowett senses irony also in this passage. *Plato's Republic: The Greek Text*, Vol. 3, p. 330.

22. Later (533e), Socrates says that they shouldn't haggle over this word for the faculty of understanding.

23. Plato makes a similar shift from two-dimensional to three-dimensional figures at 587e. For a discussion of this passage, see *Political Returns*, p. 127.

24. Jowett points out that those who conceive "nobly" of things above are said in the *Timaeus* (91d) to be destined hereafter to enter on another life in the form of birds. *Plato's Republic: The Greek Text*, Vol. 3, p. 339.

25. Too often commentators presume that this antivisibility motif serves merely to enforce a distinction between the sensible versus intelligible worlds, as if the intelligible exists in some straightforward sense. While the irony of the dialogue, to my mind, detracts from such an interpretation, neither is its

function simply to subvert or mock entirely a visionary glance (as some readers of irony would have it).

26. See my *Political Returns*, pp. 124-128.

27. Karl Marx, *Karl Marx, Friedrich Engels Collected Works* (Moscow: Progress Publishers, 1975), Vol. 1, pp. 489-500.

28. Note that all three of the major *katabaino* scenes involve "spectacles" (327b, 515d, 619e). As I argue in *Political Returns*, what unifies these spectacles is not the visual imagery of up- or downward worlds but rather the concept of *returning* to the political world.

29. The Myth of Er contains a seldom-noticed indication of Plato's idea of gender justice. Several of the souls transmigrate from animal to human or human to animal, but several others, apparently disgruntled with their worldly gender assignments, now experience a change in genders. On the basis of this vignette, I think Plato is far from ignoring the significance of gender, and I don't think he is simply satirizing such concerns; but he seems by implication to be recommending a quiescence of sorts with respect to gender complaints.

30. If I seem to be borrowing an esoteric/exoteric distinction as a rough basis for interpretation, then I want to recast that distinction in terms of choice (cf. 617e) rather than one's natural endowment of *nous*. Hence if an elite is formed, it is a self-selecting elite: Everyone in principle has the possibility of making such a choice (cf. 518d).

31. Certainly the passage (619d) on the soul who came from a well-governed state (which owed its goodness to habit and custom and not philosophy) would militate against such a conclusion. Also the fact that the souls represent a great variety of lives overall, rather than conforming to a single mold.

32. Drew Hyland announces that the *Republic* is an "anti-utopian" work, because it "teaches us that the conditions for perfect justice are neither possible nor desirable." While much of this essay is insightful, especially in amending Strauss's understanding of irony, Hyland wants to foreclose all estimable political possibilities and to maintain that that foreclosure is compatible with philosophic irony. That final conclusion, I believe, still borrows too much from Strauss. Hyland, "Taking the Longer Road," p. 333.

2

"Shall Jonathan Die?": Swift, Irony, and a Failed Revolution in Ireland

John Traugott

Irony and political philosophy would not seem to be congenial modes of thought. It is nevertheless an unlikely historical conjunction of the two that I have now to discuss, and I would even go so far as to suggest that this instance may give rise to reflection on their possible mutual interest. The subject I bring to mind is the *The Drapier's Letters* (1724) by Jonathan Swift, the greatest ironist and satirist in our language, a work that attempted nothing less than the creation of a new polity in Ireland through a revolution by means of irony alone.

Political philosophy presupposes at least the possibility of communal action according to a collective opinion of "truths" and the dependability of common language. Irony to the contrary is a blood-sucking operation; the ironist is a vampire, and the relation between a vampire and his victim and accomplice-to-be is traditionally taken to be a perversely erotic one. These strange metaphors for the process of irony are Kierkegaard's.[1] The ironist's emptying out of meaning from linguistic formulas of thought by which we live, and for which we may die, may, if all goes well with his subversive rhetoric, infect us with an anguishing sense of nothingness. But just because irony is disintegrative and debilitating, we are drawn to the ironist, supposing that this vampire must have in store inviolable meanings, unknown to us but for which we yearn so as to fill the emptiness he has left us. Kierkegaard begins his discourse by putting on stage his idea of an inveterate and incurable role player, Socrates (as distinct from Plato), in the aporetic dialogues,[2] and the *Concept* is in fact a long gloss on this protean figure over whom no one has thrown a net. Alcibiades' serious joking in the *Symposium* about penetrating this ugly windbag of a satyr, who has, he supposes, a secret wisdom and beauty, sets the tone of this play. He resembles, says Alcibiades, the Silenus figures you can find in the statuary shops that open to reveal within golden gods, images of virtue. Crawling into Socrates' bed, hoping to exchange his beauty for the satyr's wisdom, all desire, as though bitten by a serpent in heart and soul, alas, he wears out the night fruitlessly. At least he amuses Socrates, who gives his friend instead a taste of his irony: If you hoped to have my wisdom for your beauty, truly you must see in me some rare beauty of a kind infinitely higher than any I see in you; and therefore you will have greatly the advantage, gold for brass, but look again, sweet friend, and see whether you are not deceived in me. This Silenus, says Kierkegaard, has no golden god within. The ironist's mode of thought is only negative; he does not possess the truth that he seems to promise. A solecism is required here: The ironist can only make us "know" what is not. The entire set of dialogues of the *Symposium* is in Kierkegaard's view Socrates' sometime attempt to find absolutism, though discovering only wind, and even the attempt is undercut by Socrates himself as he rings in the comedy of Aristophanes and Alcibiades. Yet, as Socrates alone knows what is not and can by his irony bring others to know it, this genius of his, it turns out, is an unsuspected golden treasure, a gift of freedom from delusion and the possibility of a new beginning. The apprentice ironist rids himself of the blather of received opinion that he once spoke as the dummy of the state's ventriloquism. Irony bestows upon him the subjectivity of personal life. He can hope to know himself. It is the beginning of consciousness.

In considering the political dynamics of Swift's irony, it should be borne in mind that Swift and Ireland were a very strange conjunction. Except for crucial political anomalies, which Swift gaily exploited, Ireland was very much a mercantilist colony in the early eighteenth century under like constraints in manufactures, agricultural production, exports, and imports—for the good of empire, it was naturally assumed by the English parliament—that obtained in the American colonies. But the anomalies, though assiduously soft-pedaled by the English government, were far more striking to a person like Swift who was looking to make mischief. At the same time that it was a colony, de facto, Ireland constitutionally was a separate kingdom with its own king (in the same person with the English king, though in the course of the *Letters* Swift dares to imply that this is not a necessary condition), its own parliament, its own established church, its own aristocracy, and of course its long and bitter history, going back (for the ascendancy) to the incursions of the Norman English in the twelfth century. Was it just a conquered country? Effectively it was since the bloodless Glorious Revolution of 1688 in England and the bloody triumph of the new king, William III, over James II at the Battle of the Boyne in 1690, but it had been conquered many times in earlier convulsions after the establishment of Norman overlordship—Henry VIII's assumption of the kingship in 1540, the plantations of Elizabeth in Ulster, and the submission of Gaelic chieftains to English law and suzerainty, the depredations of Cromwell, and finally William's destruction of the Irish Catholic forces who thought they were defending the English monarchy. But in fact none of these conquests was quite final. No sooner were the conquerors settled in their new rights and lands than in each case they tended to become, in various measures, Irish patriots. And of course there was English constitutional and common law upon which they could build their pretensions. A further anomaly was that by the penal laws of William and Anne two-thirds of the population, the professing Catholics, were deprived of most civil and religious rights, not to mention confiscation of the major part of their lands. For the most part in Europe the sovereign's religion was his people's religion, and no nonsense. Penal laws depriving religious nonconformists were a matter of course. Gaelic Irish were expected to conform to English law, custom, and religion. As most of the "old" English remained Catholic after the Henrician reformation, penal laws were not in theory meant to separate the races. In law a papist, whether of English or Gaelic descent, had only to take communion in the Church of Ireland to enjoy the same civil rights as English Anglicans, but here there was more than a touch of hypocrisy since few efforts were made by the government to encourage conversion as tenure of confiscated lands depended upon the papists remaining papists. The condition of the lower-class Catholics was so appalling that Swift proposed in one of his terrible ironies, *A Modest Proposal*, that the kinder and more economic thing would be that gentlemen should roast or stew Irish babies for their suppers. Nevertheless, in Swift's time a good many Irish landlords and people in commerce and in law had at least nominally gone over to Church of Ireland. That produced only another source of suspicion and antagonism. In short, Irish politics provided sufficient galling anomalies and ambiguities to feed Swift's ironic provocations.

Swift as a Church of Ireland priest had no sympathies for the Catholic religion—he had experienced at firsthand the last spasms of the wars of religion in Ireland—but he had profound sympathies for the cruelly deprived Catholic people and hatred of their oppressors, his own class. As dean of St. Patrick's he was himself of course, willy-nilly, part of the oppressive establishment. To have advocated either the emancipation of Catholics or partial restoration of their lands would have been tantamount to treason. Not the least of the skill of his irony in rallying "the Whole People of Ireland" consists in skirting these poisonous realities of Irish culture, or co-opting them for his own design.

The occasion of the *Drapier's Letters* was a tempest in a teapot. The king, George I, liked to please his mistresses by permitting them various kinds of pillage of treasury monies or extortions from postulants for official favors. He had made a gift to a favorite, the Duchess of Kendal, of a patent to coin half-pence for Ireland. As she was expected to do, she peddled the patent to the highest bidder, an obscure entrepreneur, William Wood—obscure until Swift made him notorious. Naturally the gentlemen of the Irish parliament, not having been consulted, were aggrieved by this insult to their dignity. The complaint was that the coinage would draw scarce gold and silver out of Ireland. In any case, to their way of thinking they ought to have had their fingers in the pie. Robert Walpole, the great first minister, later suggested to the Irish lord chancellor, a magnate whose estates originated in the Cromwellian confiscations of Catholic lands, that the real offense to him and his kind had been that the government had neglected to cut them in on the booty. Walpole had a nose for booty.

It was nothing to the king, and indifferent to Walpole, this hullabaloo raised by Irish gentlemen in their ridiculous parliament over their supposed constitutional rights. Rights? Walpole, who always had a firm hold on reality, was astonished that they could forget that their pretensions depended on English military power. Let them be good Protestant servants of the king, look the other way when his prerogative was concerned, especially if bedroom politics were involved, and amuse themselves by thinking up new laws against Catholics. Let them not forget that they were to do the king's business, not clog it through their peevish wounded vanity. This was the class Swift despised—his own—slaves to the English, slavedrivers to the papists.

> I know not how it comes to pass (and yet perhaps I know well enough) that slaves have a natural disposition to be tyrants; and when my betters give me a kick, I am apt to revenge it upon my footman; although perhaps he may be an honest and diligent fellow. I have heard great divines affirm that nothing is so likely to call down an universal judgment from heaven upon a nation as universal oppression; and whether this be not already verified in part, their worships the landlords are now at full leisure to consider. Who ever travels this country, and observes the face of nature or the faces and habits and dwellings of the natives,

will hardly think himself in a land where either law or religion or common humanity is professed.[3]

Thus, savoring all these sordid realities of the situation, which he knew from his long friendships in the highest circles, Swift saw his opportunity to enter the fray against the coinage with his *Letters* in the guise of a simple-minded but honest draper of Dublin who could see the obvious and would say it plainly to his people. His intentions had little to do with the complaints of the Irish parliament, whose grand pretensions he despised as little more that the bad faith of colonial agents of the English ministry.

In the first letter, "to the tradesmen, shop-keepers, farmers, and country-people," Swift had three ironic ploys: (1) to address the timorous common people on their own level and shame them into joining the battle by teaching them a thing or two about ironic ways of attacking tyrants with impunity; (2) to rub raw the resentment of the great landlords, entrapping them in their own preposterous postures, reminding them of their truckling to the English ministry in return for license to pillage their country, thus indicting them before the ordinary people; (3) to elaborate the figure of William Wood, into a sinister, vulgar, brutal shyster, so that he would become a national scape-goat in the evolving comedy. But something far more daring was also in process here—slowly, by ironic innuendo, this scapegoat was to become a surrogate for the king and his first minister, Walpole. Swift was just skirting sedition.

When the common people caught on to these ploys, realizing that they had a clever propagandist on their side who could say what he didn't say, they would enter the game and their character would perforce be changed. With the sophistication of irony would come the subjectivity of personal life. The echoes of acceptable opinion that suffused their lives would become ridiculous to them, opening the possibility of discovering a new political language. The Drapier's identity was not long in being guessed—he was not to be found, as he advertised, at his shop in Fishmantle Street—but the name of the great dean of the Cathedral of St. Patrick was spoken only *sotto voce* and entered into the conspiracy of the new-made ironists of the town. The evolving scenario Swift was writing ad hoc had a large cast of characters— ordinary people, disenfranchised papists, the great landlords of the Irish parliament, Walpole, his ministry, the viceroy, and the king, including his mistresses—all of whom it was his intention to maneuver into playing parts in his game of power that had nothing less for its goal than a feint toward revolution.

Every ironic utterance involves three persons: the first, the ironist, echoing received opinion, says what he hates to hear, but with a rhetorical twist
that makes strange his banal talk; the second, the would-be sophisticate,
catching the strange ring of the familiar echo, makes league with the ironist
so as not to be thought the third person, who, perceiving nothing, thinking
nothing, knowing nothing, is comforted to hear repeated the official banality.
Doubtless irony owes its original impulse to snobbery, but its philosophical
claim is to open the whole process of communication, first to doubt, and then
to rethinking. It remains, however, a mental activity of conscious elitism.
Irony, being only negative, Kierkegaard says, cannot give a positive; it
cannot set forth a thesis. Irony is a determination of subjectivity. It is the
way, not the truth. I would say that irony delivers only one message
concerning the text: "Not this, which by irony has been now emptied of
pretended meaning, but something else. You may wish to try to find out
what." With irony the subject is negatively free. One does not, however,
always wish to be free. How often is talk necessary to fill space or merely to
return the ball or to assure one's respondent that one is not dangerous. Such
empty signifiers are not entirely a matter of vulgar palaver. They may infect
the most serious "communication." Again, in Kierkegaard's view of Socrates, they are common even in philosophers who speak with the authority of
a daimon. At the end of the *Theaetetus*, after a long investigation of
"knowledge" with his pupil, Socrates has to say that all he has been able to
do is show Theaetetus that he has brought forth nothing but wind. "But if,
Theaetetus, you should ever conceive afresh, you will be all the better for
this investigation, and if not, you will be soberer and humbler and gentler to
other men, and will be too modest to fancy that you know what you do not
know. These are the limits of my art."[4] The function of the *irony* of the
Drapier's Letters is certainly to awaken the Irish people from the narcotized
condition in which the colonial rhetoric of the state has put them. His art
teaches them that through irony and its incitement to subjectivity they are
free to think what they can think. The absolute of majesty, the sanctity of
colonialism, dissipates into wind.

If the purpose was in the first instance to enroll these common people in
a conspiracy to block the currency of this new coinage, in itself a seditious
act, the Drapier's strange opening gambit is the key to Swift's ironic larger
purpose, to change mean people into free thinkers with solidarity in their
immediate political purpose, by promoting them from the third person, the
vulgar unknowing, to the second, the would-be ironist learning the uses of
irony from the first person, the ironist, thus imparting to them a giddy sense
of power in being able to defy the rhetoric of repressive authority with

impunity. In effect the hoi polloi would come to see themselves as the elite. He begins by berating them as nerveless and slavish helots: *"It is a great Fault among you, that when a Person writes with no other Intention than to do you Good, you will not be at Pains to read his Advices* . . . It is your folly that you have no common or general Interest in your View."[5] And so it goes: You don't know or inquire or care who are your friends and who are your enemies. It is enough to discourage anyone from endeavoring to do you good. You fly in his face for his pains. You are likely to betray him. However, here are the plain facts.

There follows a description of Wood. How did such a mean dealer get his Majesty's seal to coin so great a sum of bad money to dump in this poor country? We are far from the king's court, nobody to speak for us, though we have a great number of Irish lords and squires who spend their lives and fortunes in England, aping the English. Here begins Swift's long rhetoric to get the underclass to know that the Irish landowners are as much their enemies as the English. This Wood knows where to give money. The innuendo touches on the bribe Wood has given the king's mistress and the king's use of Ireland as a store to loot to gratify his favorites. It touches as well on the protest of the Irish lords, for as the *Letters* go on it is Swift's implied opinion that their protest is only to raise their market to be bought off. The king was deceived. He is a good king and, if he knew the truth of it, would withdraw the coinage. The irony thickens, skirting treason, but read rightly by the second person daringly compromises the king. Our House of Commons has made several *fine speeches* against the coinage, showing it was a wicked cheat, but Wood acts as if he is a better man than our whole parliament. How deftly he works underhand with English friends to get an order that the coinage must be received by the Irish. Here Swift opens another innuendo, that the first minister, Walpole, is seeing to the king's sordid bedroom accounts, as of course he was, for the king and Walpole understood one another. The minister had once ventured to mention the word "corruption," as some called it, in the court. The king replied blandly that he supposed Mr. Walpole was also paid for his recommendations. In subsequent letters, the theme of Wood's skulduggery is expanded:

> Observe this impudent Hardware man turning into ridicule the direful apprehensions of a whole kingdom, priding himself as the cause of them, and daring to prescribe what no king of England ever attempted, for sure there was never an example in history of a great kingdom kept in awe for above a year, in daily dread of utter destruction, not by a powerful invader at the head of twenty thousand men, not by a tyrannical prince (for we never had one more gracious),

or by a corrupt administration, but by one single, diminutive, insignificant mechanic.[6]

Wood, who can be ridiculed and scorned in safety, begins to metamorphose into an ironic surrogate for the whole English and Irish administration, king and first minister, and in the shadows, the Irish landlords and parliament. "Good God! Who are this wretch's advisers? Mr. Wood will oblige us to take his trash? We will shoot Mr. Wood through the head, like a highwayman or housebreaker. It is no loss of our honor to submit to the lion, but who . . . can think with patience to be devoured by a rat?"[7] Wood's contemptible character and contempt for Ireland is offered up as a sacrifice of which the powers-that-be can avail themselves if they wish to escape the turmoil in Ireland now developing under Swift's tutelage. Otherwise, as it is difficult to understand how a rat like Wood can engage the powers of a gracious king and great and incorruptible first minister on his behalf, the answer that the first minister is notoriously corrupt and utterly ruthless and that the king is a callous German autocrat dipping into the Irish till to pay off his German whore comes easily to mind to intensify Irish unrest. The rhetoric of majesty is emptied out by irony. The ordinary Irish people reading these letters can begin to conceive themselves a power free to think what it would be treason to say.

It is now time for instruction from the Drapier on how to resist the coinage without incurring punitive action by the English overlords. A great joke has changed the political landscape. They have only to join the joker to be something more than they were and to make the landlords and the English hegemony something less, while the protective coloring of professed respect for both remains in place.

The Drapier keeps the irony rooted in the actuality of ordinary Irish lives, and that actuality has been remade into a farce, the scenario of which they all, along with their talented friend the Drapier, can think of themselves as the writers. Comedies are written as a fantasy of triumph, to make dire troubles come out right, an eventuality that cannot be counted on in real life. Suppose that a swaggering soldier comes to your market or alehouse and offers Wood's money and threatens you if you do not take it. What do you do? You demand ten times the price of the goods, twenty pence for a quart of ale instead of tuppence. For the brewer will not be paid in such money, or if he is such a fool, the farmer will not take it from him because he knows that his rents must be paid the squire in good and lawful money, for if Squire Conolly has sixteen thousand pounds a year in rents for a half year he must have two hundred and fifty horses to bring that rent in Wood's halfpence (which if accepted will soon be the only currency in Ireland) to his cellar for stowage, to say nothing of the bankers who would need twelve hundred horses to carry forty thousand pounds in ready cash which they must have for their payments. There will not be a silver sixpence left in Ireland and not enough horses to move Wood's trash. And then the gentlemen of estates for want of payment in silver, the only lawful money, would turn off their tenants, the farmers, and run the whole country into sheep, needing only a few miserable cottagers, and whatever silver remains they will send to England for safekeeping.

Here Swift enters upon a new theme, that of law, for by law only silver is lawful money that must be accepted. Just to put the matter on the ground of law will now bit by bit open to a clear revolutionary challenge to England by turning back upon the government its perversion of the constitutional limitation on monarchy guaranteed by the Glorious Revolution and indeed by far more ancient provisions of the English and Irish constitutions. But at this point that is Swift's secret irony, which will slowly unfold its seditious and treasonous meanings as solidarity among the ordinary people develops. The law governing money will become the constitution governing Ireland and England and the common law, all evolving from the twelfth century. It is as well another swipe at the Irish landlords in the warning that if Wood's coinage passes, the landlords will take what silver they have left to England to live as absentee landlords, turning off their tenants and making sheepwalks. As everyone knew, this process had started long before Wood's coinage and was owing to rapacious landlords who would see their tenants starve rather than give up trying to cut a figure in London. Thus with this little reminder Swift serves notice to the landlord class that he intends to mock their bad-faith protests against Wood's coinage so as to raise the spirits of the common people.

The law of England, he says, gives the king all the mines of gold and silver but not of other metals. Then he begins to dig, painstakingly, for he is only a Drapier, after all, with no Latin, into the Acts of Parliament going back to Henry IV, and he finds that no subject is obliged to take any money which is not gold or silver, much less are they obliged to take "those vile half-pence." "Therefore, my friends, stand to it one and all: refuse this filthy trash. It is no treason to rebel against Mr. Wood. . . Our gracious prince (the King) hath no such ill advisers about him; or if he does, yet you see the Laws have not left it in the King's power to force us . . . Therefore you have nothing to fear." And then he rings in Scripture and God to validate the law—"these half-pence are the accursed thing, which as Scripture tells us, the Children of Israel were forbidden to touch."[8] This is no ingenuous piety but an ironic joke, for God, having forbidden them to touch Wood's coinage, will now confirm the Drapier's legal research, and then in the fourth letter approve revolution.

The Drapier then sets about to dig out constitutional law from buried tomes going back to the twelfth century on the authority of England over Ireland to coin money or do anything else. As this law is explicated to prove that the coinage must be wrong, the ironic counterpoint is that one can simply refuse to accept any purported action of king and minister which appears not to accord with the law. This is to turn English constitutional pretensions, which after the Glorious Revolution were of the first importance in the political mythology, against English colonial depredations. This idea of Swift's, ironically to use law against pretensions to law as though there must be some mistake that these good people, king and ministers, could be believed to do anything against law, is allegorized two years later in *Gulliver's Travels*, in the third voyage. There, the Flying Island (England), actuated by magnetic force, attempts to subdue the Lindalinians (Dublin, Ireland) by hovering low over them, blotting out their sun until the country dies, but the Lindalinians had built magnetic towers at the four corners of the town so that the island would be helplessly attracted and fixed if it descended over the town. If that happened they were determined to kill the king and change the government. Magnet traps magnet, law traps pretension of law. The passage was suppressed by the printer as politically dangerous.

With each successive letter the irony deepens. Wood becomes an increasingly scabby scapegoat, speculation about his favor with Walpole becomes more and more edgy, praise for the graciousness of the king and insistence upon his having been mislead by his advisers in propagating the coinage becomes more strained. The Drapier's pretense of being an ignorant, unlettered shopkeeper, "without help of books," becomes comical as he delves into centuries of tomes of the law (either in Latin or French). He puzzles over the meaning of "limited monarchy" as well as can be done by "so mean a man" as himself. He even questions whether the most fundamental law by which the English parliament arrogated to itself the right to legislate for Ireland can be correct. It is as though he can't believe his ears that the English king and ministry and parliament should say that Ireland is a colony. He elaborates a history that makes of Ireland across the travails of six centuries "an imperial realm." Is it true or false? That is the wrong question. History or myth, it is the premise and condition of national identity and dignity. The lowly, scarcely literate Drapier has somehow become a scholar of law, a historian, a logician. As they take to themselves Swift's jokes, a gaiety infects the common people so used to servility; suddenly—a dream of power—they are told how to resist English hegemony with the impunity irony offers. They have only to adopt the Drapier's ironic manner, laying on praise and obeisance for his Majesty, while making the implied association of Wood and the sordid and rapacious bedroom politics of king and minister an insolent popular comedy. Everyone in the street is an insider, a voyeur in the royal bedroom. The voyeurs find a new solidarity. A national political consciousness is born. The letter ends with a burst of comedy that is clearly Swift all but unmasking the Drapier to draw round him the whole populace.

> I was in the case of David, who could not move in the armor of Saul; and therefore I rather chose to attack the uncircumcised (Wood, I mean) with a sling and a stone . . . For Goliah had a helmet of *brass* upon his head, and he was armed with a coat of mail, and the weight of the coat was five-thousand shekles of *brass*, and he had greaves of *brass* upon his legs, and a target of *brass* between his shoulders. In short he was like Mr. Wood, all over *brass*, and he defied the armies of the living God. Goliah's conditions of combat were likewise the same with those of Wood: If he prevail against us, then shall we be his servants. But if it happen that I prevail over him, I renounce the other part of the conditions; he shall never be a servant of mine; for I do not think him fit to be trusted in any honest man's shop.[9]

Swift was accused by Archbishop Boulter, the primate of Ireland, installed by Walpole to keep tabs on political malcontents, and particularly on Swift, of raising the mob. Swift answered, "I raise the mob? If I raised my little finger, they would tear you to pieces!" Walpole in a weak moment entertained the notion of bringing Swift to England to try him for sedition. He was told that it would require ten thousand soldiers to get him out of Ireland. Irony was on the verge of creating the national identity announced in the fourth letter, "To the Whole People of Ireland." Clearly this letter broaches revolutionary principles, without irony, but still hedging round the powers-that-be with ironic obeisance.

First of all it is addressed to the "whole people," farmers, tradesmen, and landlords, and, implicitly, the dispossessed Catholic majority, in compliance if not in solidarity with the ascendancy. Wood and his hirelings of the press had accused the *Drapier's Letters* of being a papist plot to overthrow the government. The fear of Catholicism was not entirely paranoia and prejudice. The penal laws against Catholics in England were mainly observed with graceful negligence, and Catholics, remembering the pains of the religious wars, were content with this sort of temporizing. Alexander Pope, though a Catholic, could move with honor and ease in the highest circles, and the attacks of journalistic hooligans upon him as a papist were only grist for his poetic mill. This civilized demeanor was hardly the case in Ireland. The revocation of the Edict of Nantes by Louis XIV and the continuation of cruel persecutions of Protestants well into the eighteenth century gave English colonialism in Ireland the excuse (often specious) it needed to refuse amelioration of the laws confiscating for obedient Protestants the greater part of Catholic lands. French incursions in Ireland, and the threat of them, continued to terrorize Protestants, while the Stuart Pretender, with English and Irish Jacobite henchmen, held an exiled court legitimized by France. Walpole himself thought he saw papist and Jacobite miscreants lurking everywhere, and he and the Irish ascendancy looked on Swift as tainted by his friendships with Jacobites and Tories swept into oblivion a decade earlier by the accession of George I. Almost no one in the ascendancy was likely to temporize with Catholics. Swift's disgust with the humiliation and economic degradation of Catholics by Irish Protestants, who salved their resentment of English colonialism by whipping papists, was enough to feed their suspicions. His propaganda for political change in Ireland could miscarry at any moment if Wood's accusation that it was a papist plot gained credence. Without excluding Catholics as part of the "whole people," the *Letters* have to disavow any active role for them. Nevertheless, in various ways, their presence as willing supporters of Swift's agitation is acknowledged. They were a considerable commercial and agricultural element in the "whole people." Catholic baiting by Protestant toadies was inconsistent with the aim of the *Letters*. In any case we do not lack Swiftian outbursts of rage and pity for the cruelty visited upon Catholics by the ascendancy. It was "on the teachings of Swift" that Grattan in 1780 declared Ireland an independent kingdom, emancipated the Catholics, and so terrified the landlords that after twenty years of increasing Catholic insubordination following on the emancipation the Irish parliament, exclusively made up of Protestant landlords, voted for union with England and the abolition of its own legislature (1800). The Anglo-Irish "nation" was dead and buried.

An organic metaphor runs through the letter "to the whole people." The body politic has its parts and constitution, its disease and corruption, its care and physician, and its despair and death. The Drapier appoints himself as the physician able to cure Irish despair. Esau came fainting from the fields, at the point to die; is it any wonder that he sold his birthright for a mess of pottage? A people long used to hardship lose by degrees the very notion of liberty, and from lowness of spirit, accept impositions laid on them by a stronger hand as legal. Weak people are frightened and fear the king's prerogative without knowing what it is; they fear to be called papists, to be thought ripe for rebellion, and ready to shake off dependency of Ireland upon the crown of England. These calumnies are the only recourse left to the dog Wood. And then once again the Drapier trots out professions of unexceptionable loyalty to the king, complimenting him on his respect for English constitutionalism—this to disarm him in prologue for the impeding argument for the rights from nature, God, and country justifying the end of Irish dependency as a colony and of putting Ireland constitutionally on the same footing with England. Moreover, he knew very well that dependency was the security of the landlord class, and without a doubt he wished to injure them in the eyes of the people.

The rumor planted in London newspapers to frighten the timorous Irish was that the lord lieutenant (viceroy) was being sent over to dissolve parliament and, if necessary, pour Wood's brass molten down Irish throats. To this Swift has gaily comic and ironic reassurances: Are we to believe that so little a creature as Wood could find credit enough with the king and his ministers to have the lord lieutenant scurrying over to Ireland about his errand? Moreover, says the Drapier, I calculate that there being a million and a half Irishmen and fifty million of Wood's coins, two molten coins to each dose, every person would have to swallow seventeen doses and that would require fifty thousand operators, allowing one operator to each person. Still further, the great first minister, Mr. Walpole, *must* be opposed to Wood because he is said to be a *wise man*, pursuing the best *interests* of the king and of *personal integrity* above all corruption. This was irony squared, for Swift knew that the new viceroy was indeed to be Wood's errand boy to pull the king's and Walpole's chestnuts out of the fire. Besides, "Walpole" was almost a synonym for "corruption" throughout England and Ireland. To boot, Swift hated the man. On the edge of lèse majesté, the streets of Dublin began to pass the joke around as the wit of the town. Pusillanimity was changing to arrogant gaiety.

But here Swift had as well a much deeper and far more daring vein of lèse majesté to mine with his irony. This little tempest in a teapot in Ireland was as well a marginal skirmish in the games of empire on the large European stage. John, Lord Carteret, the new viceroy, whom Wood was setting up in the London press as the agent sent to take the bluster out of the Irish, was well known to Swift. In the court of Queen Anne, Swift had been friend, adviser, and propagandist to the Tory ministry of Harley and Bolingbroke. There, Carteret was a young courtier who struck everyone as a person of exceptional promise. Witty, learned, noble, he was just to Swift's taste, and a feast of mutual flattery developed between the two, though, Swift always feared, with more than touch of condescension on the part of the aristocrat. Far from flying blind when he advises the populace not to stew about what

Carteret will do once he reached the bog of "wretched" Ireland, Swift knew very well the European political games affecting English policy in the Baltic from Petersberg to Hannover and with France, in which Carteret figured first as a brilliant ambassador to Sweden at the age of twenty-nine and a few years later as ambassador to France and secretary of state for the southern department in the privy council, where he became Walpole's chief rival for the king's favor. Each had a key to the royal bedchamber, Walpole having bought the thin Protestant mistress, the Duchess of Kendal, who had sold the coinage patent to Wood, and Carteret the other, the fat and Catholic Countess of Darlington. Carteret had a further advantage: He could speak fluent German to the king, who had no English, while Walpole had to content himself with a demotic, nearly unintelligible Latin with the king. Carteret was altogether too fine for Walpole, a rough Norfolk squire, who decided he had to finish off this charmer. Opportunely, Walpole's spies, who were everywhere, had learned that Carteret, to make trouble for Walpole, had spread among the Irish lords the story of Wood's bribe to the Duchess of Kendal for the right to coin the half-pence for Ireland, which provoked the ruckus that Swift exploited. Walpole had a refined revenge: He persuaded the king to appoint Carteret viceroy so as to settle the scandal, thinking that if Carteret temporized with his friends in Ireland, Swift among them, he would lose the king's favor, or if he succeeded in making the coinage pass, the credit would redound to himself as policymaker.

Now Swift planned to exploit this enmity. When he told the Irish people that they had nothing to fear, he was obviously counting on Carteret's secret sympathies to protect him personally and his struggle with Walpole to lead him to aid and abet Swift's efforts surreptitiously to bring about a radical revision of the English colonial policy in Ireland. He was convinced that only such a revision, effectively home rule, would save Ireland from a catastrophe. And of course he was right, as subsequent history shows. He was, however, treading on the edge of treason, and he knew there was no help to be expected from the Anglo-Irish aristocracy. By his lights their pretentious parliament was a craven and venal rout of pomposities, "unclean spirits" (Mark 1:26): "Let them rave of making laws;/ . . . Let them dabble in their dung,/ Let them form a grand committee,/ How to plague and starve the city;/ Let them with their senseless quills/ Scribble senseless heads of bills,/ We may, while they strain their throats/ Wipe our asses with their vote" ("The Legion Club"[10]). Meanwhile the common people lived in "filth and nastiness upon buttermilk and potatoes, without a shoe to their feet; or a House so convenient as an English hog-sty to receive them." What was left? Irony, to create a national political consciousness by turning the snobbery of irony upside down for solidarity among the people in contempt of their rulers, both the English and their collaborators, the Anglo-Irish landlords.

The Drapier published his fourth and truly revolutionary letter on the day Carteret arrived in Ireland to assume the viceregality (October 22, 1724). Swift had already sent Carteret copies of the Drapier's earlier letters. Carteret was a month answering and Swift sent him a peevish rebuke, as though he expected better treatment from an old friend. Carteret answered graciously and ironically, with a slight whiptail of a warning: "I am convinced by the kindness of your reproaches . . . that you still retain some part of your former friendship for me, of which I am the more confident from the agreeable freedom with which you express yourself. . . ."[11] Now came this notice to Carteret of what he could expect upon his arrival:

> My lord, we are here preparing for your reception, and for a quiet session under your government; but whether you will approve of the manner I can only guess. It is by universal declaration against Wood's coin. One thing I am confident of, that your Excellency will find and leave us under dispositions very different, toward your person and high station, from what have appeared to others (September 22, 1724).[12]

The letter is ironic and calculatedly overbearing but measuredly affectionate and deferential, both an appeal to an old friend and a half-expressed warning of dangerous adventure. And so the two wits were quits, but both must have wondered how matters really stood between them.

Carteret, having lost his game with Walpole, was now in Swift's scenario to enter on a new game in Ireland, perhaps making trouble for Walpole by letting the agitation against the coinage run on. By now everyone in Dublin knew that the Drapier was Swift; Carteret knew it; both he and Swift, however, continued the charade as though neither knew this Drapier. That was to allow Carteret room to maneuver. The ironic stage was set: The Drapier plays loyal subject of George I, King of Ireland, but purveyor of subversive innuendos about the King of England. Carteret, Swift thought, might play loyal servant of the king while ironically keeping up with Swift the fiction of the Drapier and maneuvering the situation to a recasting of Irish politics vis à vis England. All this dancing would be nonsense to a reality professor like Walpole.

A surprise was in store for Swift. Carteret went straight to the privy council, harangued them about "Swift's pamphlet," and then issued a proclamation for the arrest for sedition of the "author" (carefully not naming Swift) of the "wicked and malicious" tract by M.B. Drapier. But M.B. Drapier would not be found in his shop in Fishmantle Street, as Carteret well

knew, and no one went to the deanery of St. Patrick's to find Swift. And no
one in Dublin would go to the castle to denounce Swift as the author. All
was going, after all, as Swift had more or less calculated, or so he hoped. He
could look like a martyr without actually being one. After the proclamation,
Swift sent out his emissaries on the streets of Dublin to pass around among
the people a passage from I Samuel 14:45: "And the people said unto Saul,
Shall Jonathan die, who hath wrought this great salvation in Israel? God
forbid: as the Lord liveth, there shall not one hair of his head fall to the
ground, for he hath wrought with God this day. So the people rescued
Jonathan, that he died not." It became a password repeated by rote throughout
Dublin. A bold stroke, more ironic comedy to screw up the pitch of gaiety
and solidarity, all but a direct challenge to majesty. For Carteret the worry
would have been that Swift would become so giddily arrogant as to cast off
the ironic cloak of the Drapier and stand trial so as to polarize the community.
Carteret wanted Swift to know that that would violate the rules of the game.
He sent a warning by way of the archbishop: "I told his Grace that no man
in the kingdom how great and considerable he might think himself was of
weight enough to stand a matter of this nature."[13] The pamphlet, he said, was
so seditious and treasonous as to require the viceroy to bring the author to
justice. Still pretending not to know the author, he sent word by the archbishop to the "author" that he would arrest him and bring him to trial in
England. But this may only have been Carteret's way of putting Swift on
notice that the two of them must play out a delicate game and no false moves.
Walpole was one to manage crises, usually by some form of bribery; he did
not provoke them. He was quite capable of brutal action, but only when the
consequences would not impede business. He had decided to take Carteret's
advice to find a solution. Without any doubt, however, the "treasonable"
passages in Swift's fourth letter, carefully marked by Carteret for the privy
council, would have put him in jeopardy had not Swift and Carteret had the
requisite finesse to play out their ironic games with one another. What were
these "seditions" and "treasons" and how did Swift cloak them in irony so
as not to force the issue upon the government?

His Majesty graciously has told us that he would grant the patent for
coining money only as it is agreeable with the practice of his ancestors. But
as Wood's coinage is not agreeable to the practices of the past, and his
Majesty is a lawful monarch, and the law obliges no subject to take money
that is not silver, and he as a wise monarch governs the realm as God governs
the world, by settled laws, he cannot mean to do something that is not in
accord with law; but if the law allowed him to compel us, which it does not,
we would yield because we know from experience what the English would

like to do to us, though we are their fellow subjects. But even if the king was sending the viceroy to compel us to submit to the fraud of this sharper Wood, how would he prevail upon a parliament that could bribed only with Wood's worthless half-pence? Therefore I have proved to you, my fellow subjects, that the king has no desire to impose this unlawful coinage on us. However, I am almost tempted to wish that this project of Wood's might succeed so that all our absentee landlords who spend Irish money in England would have to come home and live with us as beggars, naked and starving. Thus Swift elaborated the ironic comedy.

Now as to Lord Carteret, he is a gentleman of great goodwill. It is true, indeed, that other viceroys have been able to carry points of terrible consequences to this kingdom with *dinners* and *burgundy* and encouragement to busy ourselves with some further acts against popery—but these were methods for corrupt times. Lord Carteret would have none of this.

All this buffoonery is a surreptitious compliment to Carteret, the man, but for the viceroy, an insult to his masters the privy council and its habits of buying off Irish aristocrats with a dinner and burgundy and a smile and a threat. A further thought—if Wood's coinage passes we will be rid of the English, no more money, no more exploiters, no more of their cast-offs sent over to fill up our vacancies and take our sinecures, ecclesiastical, civil, and military. What Englishman would leave to come here to be paid in Wood's half-pence? At last, they will stay where they are and we will be left alone in our beggary. Peace at last. Dependency (i.e., in effect, the colonial exploitation of Ireland) is founded on an illegal assumption by the English parliament and privy council of the right to legislate for Ireland, despite our parliament and our ancient constitution as an imperial realm equal to England under our king, the King of Ireland. If he happens to be at this time the same person as the King of England, we could, if the Pretender came to the throne of England, prevent him from becoming the King of Ireland. Little wonder that Carteret marked this passage as treasonous, for under cover of a sort of joking irony, it clearly raises the specter of Ireland having the right to choose its own king, in short, plain rebellion.

Swift then pushes the argument into the open: It is true that the English parliament has assumed the power of binding this kingdom by laws enacted there, but government without the consent of the governed is the definition of slavery. The remedy is therefore in the hands of our own people. By the laws of God, of nature, of nations, and of your own country you are and ought to be as free a people as your brethren in England.

But then an ironic retreat from this "seditious" tocsin of liberty: I beg leave to tell Mr. Wood that he is guilty of a great indiscretion by causing so honorable a name as that of Mr. Walpole to be mentioned in his support. In a paper of his contriving, it is said that Mr. Walpole will cram his brass down our throats and that we must either take these half-pence or eat our brogues. And in another we read that some great man has sworn to make us swallow his coin in fireballs. What vile words are these to put in the mouth of a great councillor, in high trust with his Majesty, and looked upon as a prime minister. This is not the style of a great minister. Swift then calculates how many torturers would be required to shove fifty million half-pence melted into fireballs down the throats of a million and half Irishmen. Where would they find them? It must be a spurious report. But I will now demonstrate, beyond contradiction, that Mr. Walpole is against this project of Mr. Wood and is a friend to Ireland: He is a wise man and an able minister and has the true interest of the king at heart. And as his integrity is above all corruption so is his fortune to temptation. My dear countrymen, we are safe.

Subversion, rebellion, identification of Wood with the king, and Walpole: That is burden of the savage indignation and the heady comedy of this irony, so brilliantly done, so successfully toying with lèse majesté, so heartening to the fearful that for the moment at least it was a new world. Subsequent events were less stirring. Walpole took Carteret's advice and withdrew the patent. Wood vanished as scapegoats are meant to do. Swift had worked his most brilliant ironic stroke in the final raucous praise of Walpole, with all its Aristophanic stage props—brass, brogues, fireballs, millions of upturned throats, bustling torturers, the whole operation supervised by this bungling swindler, Wood, for here was an escape hatch ready fabricated for the clever first minister. He had only to kill off Wood, withdraw the patent with a gracious speech from the throne implying that had the king only known, et cetera, and the whole hullabaloo was finished.

Everything was as it had been. Swift's constitutional pretensions for Ireland went glimmering into the heavenly orbit of utopias. One supposes—because that was his method of resolving sticky political dilemmas—that a certain amount of largesse was spread about among Irish grandees by Walpole, but in any case all was quiet. Midleton, the Irish lord chancellor, had been appalled by Swift's letters and now could pretend not to know him. He knew, as Walpole knew, that accommodation was the only possibility for the Anglo-Irish ascendancy if they wished to preserve their privileges. They were after all not a nation but a garrison. So far as I know Swift is the only political agitator in history to employ irony as a strategy to change a government, though some of Shakespeare's and Stendhal's figures could give sketches of the uses of irony in politics.[14] It would require, it seems, as it did in Ireland, a discontented people, a government of constitutional pretensions and tyrannic intentions, and a skill at irony not far inferior to Swift's. What Swift accomplished was to transform an elitist literary form with philosophical bearings into a popular movement in which ordinary people, who wouldn't have known what the word "irony" meant, could think of themselves, once they caught on to this way of speaking dangerous thoughts with impunity, as superior to their oppressors. They became in this strange way the elite; they were, so to speak, the playwrights of this comedy. It was a world upside down in which a slavish people suddenly became savvy to political games and machinations, to say nothing of having the scales fall from their eyes as they looked on majesty. How could they not have felt the elation of solidarity, the thrill of political consciousness? The elation was, however, momentary, the solidarity illusory, the political consciousness hopeless.

For Swift we must suppose there were very different considerations. He knew intimately the games of politics; he knew that the rules were juggled by ultimate power so that he could not win.[15] His resolution *manqué* by way of brilliant irony was finally reduced again to a tempest in a teapot. W.E.H. Lecky, the great Irish historian, wrote that Swift had created the political consciousness of the Irish people, to bear fruit in the next century; but when Lecky saw that Swift's teachings would mean the end of Anglo-Irish hegemony, he regretted his enthusiasm for them and suppressed his chapter on Swift in his *Leaders of Public Opinion in Ireland*.[16] A real revolution destroying the Anglo-Irish nation (so-called) did come, as Lecky feared; and we would have to communicate with Swift's ghost to know whether he thought his ironic sedition of 1724 was a success or failure.

In the end Carteret's finesse came to the aid of Walpole's political savvy and relieved him of an annoyance. Carteret was subsequently a very popular viceroy who knew how, Swift said later, to bind Ireland's chains more genteelly than any viceroy before him. Carteret and Swift took up again something of their old pleasure in one another's wit. Carteret probably saved Swift's skin, but it would have been a utopic fantasy on Swift's part to imagine that he could change the course of empire with Carteret's help against king and ministry, for however much he scorned Walpole, however disappointed he may have been in his own career, Carteret was absolutely loyal to the system. However, utopic fantasies run through Swift's writings, always exploded by irony, to be sure; but the mixture of his yearnings for the ideal with ironic negativity is exactly the condition Kierkegaard identifies as the ironic soul and which he discusses at length in his treatment of the actuality of Socrates. Swift, incidentally, was much attracted to Socrates, including his parody in Aristophanes.

The impossibility of Swift's "revolution" returns us now to Kierkegaard's *Concept of Irony* and to one of his fundamental arguments, that irony cannot but be absolutely negative. Irony empties out the received notions and clichés by which political life is controlled, by which the dummy is ventriloquized by the state; but philosophically it questions the linguistic constructions—the reality of abstractions, the security of definitions, the significations of signs, the predications of the persons ("I" and the others)—by which we think we communicate. Saying what is not, it opens the mind to the anguish of having to say what is. That, to say the least, is a very onerous burden. It is true that the momentary declaration of independence of Grattan's parliament of 1780 invoked Swift's name, but by then consciousness had evolved to the point that the Anglo-Irish could think of treating Catholics as fellow citizens, and the shibboleths of that moment recall Swift's address to the "whole people." It was also, however, a delusionary effort, and today Irish nationalists would look upon it as a moment of bad faith because the reality was that the ultimate "nation" was buried in the mainly landless Catholic population. Arguably the agitation of Parnell for home rule in the late nineteenth century owed some of its energy to the words of Swift. At least Ireland's greatest poet, William Butler Yeats, could write in 1935 in the poem "Parnell's Funeral," "Through Jonathan Swift's dark grove he [Parnell] passed, and there/ Plucked bitter wisdom that enriched his blood." Yeats had created a myth of an independent nation drawing its strength and genius from the melding of the Anglo-Irish and Gaelic traditions, and the passion of Swift was somehow to pass into the desire of the state. Yet I think Swift would not have quite understood such talk. The consciousness his irony was to inspire was skeptical as to the right thinking of the real (as opposed to the mythic) state. Ironically, then, Swift's one "positive" effort in his ironic vein, the politics of the *The Drapier's Letters*, was in the end as negative as the utterly skeptical purely literary works such as *A Modest Proposal, Gulliver's Travels,* and *A Tale of a Tub*. The ultimate negativity of the irony of *The Drapier's Letters* might indeed have been a bitter wisdom for Ireland, and might still be could it empty out the ages-long political rhetoric of Ireland and permit, as Kierkegaard says is the function of irony, a new beginning. Swift was certainly the ironist Kierkegaard envisages, a predicateless man, in one mask or another, playing games, a philosopher *and* a comedian. The ironist must be capable of playing all roles. Being negative, irony is not a state of mind that easily tolerates the absolute, though, Kierkegaard insists, it always yearns for it; otherwise, all pretensions to truth would not inevitably come into question. It is the way, not the truth, says Kierkegaard, parodying John 14:6: "Jesus saith, 'I am the way, the truth, and the life.'" Irony is the condition of the authentic life. If so, it is not likely to lead to the violent newfound (and soon lost) faiths of revolution. Rather, it would be something like the truth to think of Swift's irony, as Kierkegaard thinks of all irony, as making possible a "revolution" in consciousness.

NOTES

1. Søren Kierkegaard, *The Concept of Irony, with Constant Reference to Socrates*, trans. by Lee M. Capel (Bloomington: Indiana University Press, 1965).
2. Treated in the section "The abstract in the early Platonic dialogues culminates in irony," chap. 1. The dialogues taken up are *Symposium, Protagoras, Phaedo*, and *Republic*.
3. Jonathan Swift, "A Proposal for the Universal Use of Irish Manufactures," in *Prose Works of Jonathan Swift*, ed. Herbert Davis (Oxford: Basil Blackwell, 1948), vol. 9, p. 21.
4. Plato, *Dialogues of Plato*, trans. B. Jowett (New York: Random House, 1937), vol. 2, p. 217.
5. Swift, "A Letter to the Shop-Keepers, Tradesman, Farmers, and Common People of Ireland," in *Prose Works*, vol. 10, p. 3.
6. Swift, "A Letter to Mr. Harding the Printer," in *Prose Works*, vol. 10, p. 19.
7. Ibid.
8. Swift, "A Letter to the Shop-Keepers," pp. 11-12.
9. Swift, "Some Observations . . . to the Nobility and Gentry," in *Prose Works*, vol. 10, p. 48.
10. Swift, *Poems*, ed. H. Williams (Oxford: Clarendon Press, 1937), vol. 3, p. 817.
11. Swift, *Correspondence*, ed. H. Williams (Oxford, Clarendon Press, 1965), vol. 3, p. 214.
12. Ibid.
13. Cited by Herbert Davis, ed. *Prose Works*, vol. 10, p. xxi, from *State Papers*, vol. 384, p. 63.
14. For very interesting speculation on the possible uses of irony in politics, see John Seery, *Political Returns: Irony in Politics and Theory from Plato to the Antinuclear Movement* (Boulder, CO: Westview, 1990).
15. The court games the king of Lilliput runs to keep his ministers in order, in which Flimnap, the champion rope dancer, has seemed to many to resemble Walpole, are a brilliant treatment of politics-as-game. See my discussion of it in "The Yahoo in the Doll's House," in *English Satire and the Satiric Tradition*, ed. Claude Rawson (Oxford: Basil Blackwell, 1984).
16. W.E.H. Lecky, *The Leaders of Public Opinion in Ireland* (New York: D. Appleton, 1872).

3

Goethe:
The Politics of Allegory and Irony

Jane K. Brown

On the question of Goethe and politics, the verdict is generally negative. Although the poet served for some fifteen years in a variety of responsible positions on the Privy Council of the Duchy of Weimar (as, for example, minister for mines, roads, war, finance, as well as various cultural functions), and although he was the lifelong friend of the Duke of Weimar, he was often regarded as unpolitical. His political stance has tended to be dismissed or, alternatively, excoriated as reactionary.[1] In all fairness to the scholarship, there have been well-meaning reasons: those who cast the poet as the cultural father of Germany's Second Empire routinely located him on Olympian heights; others trying to rescue him from this and later exploitation repeated the gesture, ironically defeating the purpose of their own discretion. Goethe and irony has been a somewhat healthier topic: since World War II it has become generally recognized that he was an ironist of great sophistication, certainly in his later years, and probably all along.[2]

As a poet who was also actively engaged in government, Goethe is a pivotal figure for exploring the question of politics and irony, for he reveals the complex interaction between political and aesthetic concerns during the European transition from feudal to modern state. Initially Goethe's irony enables him to appropriate the rhetoric of power in court masque, even though he was marginal to the system at a marginal court in an age when courtly power was only questionably grounded. As extended by Goethe in the 1790s under the impact of Kantian idealism, ironic representation comes ever more itself to ground political power. This complete blending of the aesthetic and political realms is suggestive in the extreme, but difficult to conceive in concrete terms, and indeed Goethe never formulated any mature political theory. Instead, he expressed himself with sketches of utopias and allegories, veiled in ever more complex ironies.

Hence I would like here to develop not Goethe's theory of politics, but his literary practice of politics. Goethe on politics is rather like Jane Austen, an equivalent writer in the conservatism, critical attitude, and extreme discretion of her political expression. I would like, however, to go beyond recent work on Austen, which has shown the political positions implied by particular allusions, subject matter, style, and plot structure.[3] I will argue that for a German of Goethe's background and upbringing politics was by nature a strictly personal affair (at least until the first or second decade of the nineteenth century). Because, further, of his position at court, he was heir to certain forms of court drama that make his writing on political issues more openly allegorical than Austen's.[4] As a result, political discussion takes the form of ironic allegory, which evolves into a practice of ironic and self-conscious representativity for both the poet and for the politician as well.

I

Germany was politically backward in the eighteenth century; hence a German figure reveals particularly clearly the political transition that England and France made much more gradually. The most striking aspect of this backwardness for our purposes is that German politics was still largely a family affair. Goethe was born in 1749 into a "Germany" that consisted of some three hundred separate territorial states or free cities, often minuscule—the total population of the two duchies ruled by the Duke of Weimar, for example, numbered only 100,000 in 1785.[5] Most Germans lived under the more or less benevolent despotism of the "Landesvater," of whose court they were hangers-on or petty officials, whom they served as a tradesmen, or, if they were peasants, whose hunts they unwillingly hosted. Residents of the fifty-one free towns and of various small towns only nominally under the control of some princeling were ruled by paternalistic coteries or outright patriciates.[6] In either case the right to participate responsibly in political life depended on the accident of birth; most Germans, regardless of level of wealth, achievement, or education, had no political voice, and were effectively children of the state.

If one happened to be born into an urban patriciate, as Goethe was, political activity would still be perceived in family terms, for the patrician belonged to a small clan of influential families that controlled a very restricted realm (36,000 souls in Frankfurt am Main). Since his grandfather was the mayor, Goethe experienced almost literally the period's central metaphor of political authority: the ruler is father of his country. Although Goethe's father did not participate in the local hierarchy into which he had so carefully married, the failure stemmed from a perceived personal insult, not from a reasoned decision to eschew political activity. Consider also how Goethe describes in his autobiography, *Poetry and Truth* (*Dichtung und Wahrheit*), his allegiance during the Seven Years' War, when he was ten: "And so I too was for Prussia, or rather, for Fritz: for what did we care about Prussia? It was the personality of the great king that impressed everyone" ("Und so war ich denn auch preußisch gesinnt oder, um richtiger zu reden fritzisch gesinnt: denn was ging uns Preußen an? Es war die Persönlichkeit des großen Königs, die auf alle Gemüter wirkte").[7] It is thus built into Goethe's earliest perceptions that personal and political motivations are congruent.

What we would have to call international politics involved only the clan of royal families that ruled Europe. During the Seven Years' War Goethe's grandfather supported Austria and France, his father, Prussia. Although the personal disagreement poisoned the atmosphere in the family for several years, the autobiography gives no hint that the views of either could affect the outcome, or even the impact on the residents of Frankfurt, who were helpless before powers much greater than themselves.[8] Furthermore, despite the political aversion of Goethe's father to the French, from January 1759 until the end of May 1761 the French commandant Count Thoranc was billeted in the Goethe household, where his courteous hosts seconded his strong interest in local painters and turned the house into an atelier for contemporary German art. And Goethe took full advantage of the French language theater brought by the occupiers—for he had, of course, been thoroughly trained in French at home. At the personal level we see cultured individuals who share interests independent of political allegiance or activity, at the political level events operating independently of personal communities. In the autobiography we do not see larger events such as the war—and this failure to see is willed. It cannot be attributed to the perspective of the ten-year-old's memory, because Goethe undertook extensive research to bolster his memory elsewhere in the book. Later Goethe would consistently evoke the French Revolution with the image of a thunderstorm: an event of this scale is a phenomenon of nature operating according to its own laws,[9] not a political event in the terms of Goethe's world at all.

From Goethe's arrival in 1775 until the end of the Wars of Liberation, there can have been little in his personal experience in Weimar to change these patterns of perception. He entered this town of some six thousand residents (twenty-five hundred of whom were connected with the tiny court!) as the favorite of the eighteen-year-old duke, joined the Privy Council (three members), and received a patent of nobility in 1782 exclusively on the basis of this personal relationship. Indeed, the patent of nobility was not necessary for the fulfillment of his duties as minister, but was to make it easier for the Weimar court to enjoy his social talents—the duchess could not play cards with a member of the middle class, regardless of her admiration for Goethe's personal gifts. Everywhere in such a small government the line between political and personal was impossible to draw—are factions in an organization of this scale political or personal? Is the decision to balance the budget by reducing the military force from eight hundred to under two hundred political or personal, when the only function of the force is to provide the duke a hobby?

Politics is thus not a matter of systems, structures, and institutions, as it already was in the Anglo-French sphere. Either subrational in its personal manifestation of one big not-so-happy family, or beyond human rationality as an inescapable natural phenomenon, politics is subject in neither aspect to systematic action, nor even to rational analysis. In this respect it resembles nature, for Goethe disliked analytic procedures in science also (he is famous for a lengthy polemic against Newton's theory of color). He preferred instead detailed observation, description, and organization of perception. One can expect to find the same in his relation to politics—observation, sophistication about the preconditions of both observation and observability, and strong reservations about the possibility of action, for the larger political sphere, like the larger natural sphere, cannot be subject to action.

In Goethe's works about the French Revolution, then, politics is conceived exclusively either in terms of relations among individuals or in terms of major disasters such as weather or fires. Two comedies from the early 1790s, *Hubbub* (*Die Aufgeregten*) and *The Citizen General* (*Der Bürgergeneral*), present miniature German provincial versions of the revolution in which family relationships are center stage. In the two best-known works about the revolution, *Conversations of German Emigrants* (*Unterhaltungen deutscher Ausgewanderten*, 1794/5) and *Hermann und Dorothea* (1797), this is still the case. In the first a group of noble refugees flee their estates on the French side of the Rhine; the revolution is kept at a safe distance from the action, apart from their political disagreements, which, however, they agree to suppress in the interests of civility, and apart from the general tension resulting from this repression. *Hermann und Dorothea* deals with the passage of French refugees at a safe distance from a small German town untouched by the disturbances; a young man from the town eventually brings home one of the refugees and marries her into safety. In both works one can find echoes of Goethe's personal experiences growing up in Frankfurt: the conflict between his father and grandfather over the Seven Years' War is repeated in *Conversations*, while the hero of *Hermann und Dorothea* carries vivid memories of the mood in which his grandfather returned from city council meetings. Based as they are on experience, these works are more realistic than many works that seem to raise political issues more directly, such as the noisy, paranoid dramas of the German *Sturm und Drang* movement.

Politics seems, in this view, to fall into two spheres, the personal and the impersonal. The personal sphere is subject to control in the form of social interaction, thus by the normal social virtues of civility, manners, effective social bearing—of which irony often forms a part. The larger sphere is subject to no such control, it must be suffered. Nevertheless, the opposition is not simple: for the same social virtues that enhance personal intercourse make life under extraordinary circumstances livable. Events may be beyond individual control, but reaction to events is not; in this respect all political action is personal, for our only defense against political cataclysm is individual manners.

II

If Goethe's whole experience of politics, like that of most Germans of his day, was personal rather than institutional, the rhetoric available to him for political expression as a poet was highly formalized in the institution of court masque. Masque had evolved as the supreme Renaissance expression of the person-focused courtly system, which had already decayed in Goethe's time and was to disappear altogether. I would like to analyze some of Goethe's early efforts in this genre to show how the discrepancy between the rhetoric of masque and the actual power structure necessitated the introduction of irony, then show how this new dramatic mode carried over even when Goethe went beyond the masque to other forms of political expression.

Goethe was not only government minister during his early years in Weimar but also chief court entertainer. All members of the court shared in lightening the boredom of the ruling family by playing cards, attending assemblies, participating in excursions, reading aloud, whatever. But the chief burden of more formal dramatic entertainments—and amateur theatricals were extremely popular in the period—fell inevitably on the leading poet at court, who might be a local schoolmaster or perhaps tutor to a member of the royal family. Both of these were the case in turn before Goethe arrived in Weimar. Goethe's oeuvre includes some fifteen court masques written for specific occasions, usually the birthday of the duchess, as well as *Singspiele* (plays with songs) written for amateur performance at court. He wrote, in addition, numerous prologues, epilogues, and dramatic interludes for the professional theater company resident in Weimar from 1791 on. Although he filled no government offices after 1788, except for supervision of museums and collections, and direction of the Weimar court theater, Goethe continued to receive a high annual salary from the duke. He was, for all practical purposes, a salaried court poet, a position that carried with it specific generic strictures.

By its very nature court masque, a genre that dates from the Italian Renaissance, is concerned with politics. Stephen Orgel has shown how Renaissance masque both reflects and reflects upon the power structure of the court.[10] Weimar was hardly to be celebrated in the same terms as the Stuart court. Furthermore, in Stuart masque the visible hierarchies of the masque and audience mirrored allegorically the invisible hierarchies that organized the cosmos, but by Goethe's time the cosmological underpinning had largely crumbled, leaving the form unanchored, and its political implications, therefore, unconvincing. The high points of the tradition are represented by figures such as Ben Jonson and Milton; to judge by Goethe's critique of court festivities in the fourth book of *Wilhelm Meister's Apprenticeship* (*Wilhelm Meisters Lehrjahre*, 1795/6), it had fallen on evil days indeed by the mid-eighteenth century. Goethe complained more than once about the frivolity of the tasks into which he was pressed.[11] In writing court masque, therefore, Goethe faced the difficulty that the power relations underlying his masques were but a shadow of those that underlay the beginnings of the tradition in the Renaissance.

Nevertheless, the three-page "Masque of Winter," written to celebrate carnival in 1781, shows how, even in the service of vanity, he dealt with problems of both the court and the age. It is a simple processional masque whose characters are Sleep, Night, Dreams, Winter, Gambling, Wine, Love, Tragedy, Comedy, Carnival, Study, and a group of carnival figures from around Europe. Each character speaks only once. Despite the limited space for dramatic development, the masque addresses the need for community at court, particularly in the royal marriage. The duke and duchess were both under twenty at their arranged marriage in 1775, and of dramatically different temperaments; not until 1783 did they produce an heir, a pressing matter for the stability of such a small court. The masque moves from isolation to community through a change in linguistic patterns. The first seven characters (almost half the text) speak exclusively in terms of dichotomies such as sad or happy, feared or loved, frighten and give pleasure, come together or flee, giving or taking, young and old.[12] In the midst of this group Winter asserts that his function is to join the members of the audience together: with Tragedy (number eight) joining starts to take place, for her language proceeds beyond oppositions to oxymoron—"Tears are joy, pains pleasure," she says.[13] Comedy continues by eliminating opposition altogether: "I make them laugh, that is better and that is more."[14] Carnival repeats the word "more" three times in the next six lines, and her maskers speak always in pairs, not as individuals. The masque has now moved dramatically from isolated individuals to a community of maskers who, in their different national garbs, nevertheless all represent the same carnival spirit.

The need to interpret the theme through linguistic patterns reveals an indirectness of expression foreign even to allegory. If the ruler is no longer convincingly the representative of divine power on Earth, mythological equivalences of figures at court are absurd, and the poet can only represent his concerns even more indirectly than the Renaissance allegorists. His allegorical figures no longer represent members of the court, they only talk about them or to them in veiled fashion. Indeed, Goethe seems to be aware of this problem. Winter explains that they are all there to while away the long winter evening—gambling, drinking, love, theatricals, and carnival are the obvious activities the court turned to, carnival being the choice of the moment. Thus at the first level this masque is about itself and shows the audience its own self. It thereby paradoxically repeats the same boredom faced by the court on a daily basis and to be dispelled by this very masque. It does not reflect the power of the court or its place in a larger hierarchy, as the Stuart masque does, but simply the court in a mirror with no larger context. Thus the masque not only confronts its audience with the problem of its own lack of political function but also reveals an ironic self-awareness. Allegory that no longer glorifies is irony. In the last speech a figure named Study, played by Goethe, praises himself for having written up "all our wittiness" so comprehensibly. With this self-deprecating gesture Goethe protects the masque from a pretentiousness inappropriate to the very modest progressive court of Weimar.

Indeed, Goethe had to thread a perilous path between pretentiousness and triviality. *Lila*, a play first written for the court in 1776, demonstrates the difficulties attending allegory in court politics. This odd little operetta has always been understood as a masked appeal to the duke and duchess for better mutual understanding. It deals with a melancholy woman who, after certain "political" (note the personal use of the word) gossips have mistakenly reported her husband's death, now believes that her friends, family, and husband are imprisoned by a demon and that those who appear before her are dangerous ghosts. Goethe, in the role of Dr. Verazio, whose name suggests "truth," cures her by having all of her family stage a play in which he, as a magician, assists her to free everyone from the demon.[15] In 1782 Goethe reverted to this fairy-tale theme of lifting an enchantment to dramatize once again the need for cooperation in the ruling family in a pantomime and ballet about the recovery of eternal youth. The local situation is translated into romance and fairy tale, the vehicle of court masque. Fairy tale is much less pretentious than mythology or even than the allegories of the "Masque of Winter." It has, however, seemed trivial to every generation after the immediate audience of the first performance, for whom the allegorical meaning evidently rescued the significance.[16]

When romance was adopted as appropriate material for court masque in the early seventeenth century, it was taken seriously. In the immediate wake of Tasso and Ariosto romance was the modern successor of epic, and as such had every claim to significance. By the late eighteenth century neoclassicism had acclaimed tragedy the serious genre par excellence; opera, now the dominant dramatic carrier of romance themes and materials, was considered trivial and not great art. Fairy tales performed before the court in Weimar, therefore, could not assert the same seriousness as fairy tales performed before the court of James I. We confront here an analogous problem to the impact of secularization on court masque. Had the court in Weimar not recognized the irony in Goethe's casting as "Dr. Truth," it would hardly have demanded a repeat performance, as it did. Irony, like significance, rescues the allegorical vehicle from its own triviality. Goethe seems clearly to have understood from his earliest days in Weimar that effective allegorical statement and, therefore, effective political statement would be possible for him only in an ironic context.

The allegorical masques of Christoph Martin Wieland, Goethe's immediate predecessor as court poet in Weimar (and also an important author of romances and novels), form an instructive contrast. Wieland was a master of Rococo self-deprecating irony; by making his classical divinities and romance figures speak like eighteenth-century courtiers, he rescues his masques and operettas for the court from pretentiousness. But unlike Goethe he builds in no moments of self-reflection. Instead stage and audience remain completely separate. In *Aurora*, for example, written for the birthday of Karl August's mother Duchess Anna Amalia, Diana, Aurora, and Amor interrupt their own lovemaking and sleep to prepare a birthday celebration for the duchess; Amor asserts in all seriousness that he cannot inspire love for the duchess in the hearts of her subjects because she has already done so on her own. The masque is graceful flattery. Similarly, *The Choice of Hercules (Die Wahl des Herkules)*, a didactic operetta written to celebrate the seventeenth birthday of Karl August, ends with an exhortation to the duke to love virtue and be a good ruler; the operetta mirrors what his tutor would like him to be, not what he is. And unlike the Goethe texts we have considered, Wieland's masques do not address problems at the court, at best only the hypothetical problem that Karl August might prefer pleasure to virtue. Since he mirrors the court itself neither explicitly nor implicitly, Wieland denies himself the opportunity for Goethe's self-reflexive irony.

In the 1780s Goethe turned his attention to the international situation, but the court masque form continued to structure these more ambitious works.[17] Whether we consider the works that openly deal with the French Revolution, such as *Hubbub* or *Hermann and Dorothea*, or the great "classic" plays such as *Iphigenia in Tauris* or *Egmont*, whose political significance must be sought by interpreters,[18] all are dogged by an arbitrary, even visionary happy ending that has seemed unconvincing to generations of readers. *Hubbub* ends a provincial German version of the French Revolution with a farcical nighttime garden scene reminiscent of the end of *The Marriage of Figaro*; *Egmont* ends with a dream vision of its dead heroine as the goddess of freedom, in response to which Egmont marches off to his execution as if he were winning a battle. Even the earliest critic of the play, Friedrich Schiller, complained of this "somersault into opera," while many later critics have been unwilling to acknowledge Egmont's heroism or political competence. Similarly the engagement that ends *Hermann and Dorothea* has struck some readers as naive, if not smug.[19] These endings are disturbing because the texts are more realistic (verisimilar in the neoclassical sense) than the masques and operettas of the preceding decade, but they still end with the resolution and order typical of all forms of allegorical drama based on romance.

Goethe evidently recognized the difficulty readers were having with his happy endings, for two texts uncover the formal origin of these visionary endings. *Conversations of German Emigrants* ends not in the realistic aristocratic circle of refugees in which it begins, but with a fantastic fairy tale entitled "The Fairy Tale" ("Das Märchen"). This fairy tale is in fact a sophisticated version of "Lila": a princess named Lilie is freed from an enchantment by a snake, some will-o'-the-wisps, and an old man with a magic lamp; with her the whole land is redeemed. Thus *Conversations* moves from realism to an allegorical happy ending. *The Natural Daughter* (*Die natürliche Tochter*, 1803), Goethe's "vessel for his thinking about the French Revolution,"[20] was to have been the first play in a trilogy based on the memoirs of Stéphanie de Bourbon-Conti (1798), who claimed to be an illegitimate princess of the French royal family. This play, already much less realistic than its source, covers the story of Stéphanie through her kidnapping to prevent her legitimation. Although Goethe sketched out two plays about her return to public life, he never wrote them, but instead in the same year wrote fragments of another play, *The Throne of the Lions* (*Der Löwenstuhl*), about the return of a different daughter of noble blood to a father who simultaneously recovers his throne, now stylized in terms of the sixteenth century and romance. When Goethe took up this play again ten years later, he recast it as an opera with bizarre magical effects. Thus in both these works, the happy ending is explicitly associated with a move to romance mode.

If the irony in the earlier masques derived from their self-reflexivity, in these works it derives from endings that cannot be taken quite seriously. The ending of *Hubbub* seems downright silly, and when Hermann says "Now what is mine is more mine than ever," there is reason to worry about smugness.[21] There is considerable irony at the end of the "Fairy Tale," as the citizens of the newly redeemed world scramble on the ground for gold scattered about by the departing will-o'-the-wisps, and the final scene of *The Throne of the Lions*, in Goethe's draft, involves suits of armor coming to life in what is surely a savage comment on the Restoration mentality already becoming evident in 1813.[22] Goethe's move to make the conventions more explicit in these last two works shows that their resolutions are neither naive nor exclusively self-destructive. Goethe's irony arises from an instability in point of view that allows the poet simultaneously to mean and not quite mean what he says, to engage in "very serious jokes" ("sehr ernste Scherze," as Goethe would later describe the ironies of *Faust II*).

Thus, if the family imagery in Goethe's representation of politics derives from his personal political experience, the allegorical romance mode of his representation derives from the institution of court masque. Goethe himself (in *Götz von Berlichingen* of 1773) and many of his contemporaries, Schiller foremost among them, had turned to Shakespearean models for a new mode of political expression in drama. One of the more remarkable achievements of Goethe's conservatism, however, was his return to the institution of court masque. Through ironic distancing he revitalized the court masque so successfully for the eighteenth century that it remained the form of choice for his dramatic analysis of politics.

III

Beginning in the 1790s, Goethe became interested in problems of representation, and his irony became increasingly associated with self-conscious reflections on the political manipulation of representations. As an allegorical mode, masque renders power relations visible. This was a large part of its appeal to the Stuart court, and also to Goethe, for whom sight was the primary sense. Already in *Lila* the difference between how things appear to the heroine and what they really are is a central problem, and *Iphigenia in Tauris* (1787) turns at the end on political intrigue (secret plans to escape on the basis of lies) transformed into open, truthful statement. But in *Egmont*, completed after *Iphigenia* though published the same year, and on a more explicitly political topic, Goethe's concern shifted to the effectiveness, more than the truthfulness, of what is seen. Here the concerns of the nineties are first adumbrated.

Egmont's identity is the central question in Goethe's play about the hero of the Dutch resistance to Spain. Almost every scene presents a different version of who this person is: he is the great military leader celebrated in ballad and broadside, the inspiring leader of soldiers, the personable aristocrat, the model of the latest Spanish fashions, loyal supporter of the Spanish regent, fomenter of intrigue against Spanish rule, friend of iconoclasts, easygoing and unselfconscious lover of life. Ironic inconsistency reaches its symbolic height at the center of the play, where Egmont goes to visit his middle-class beloved wearing a cloak to hide his Spanish court finery. After he has dramatically revealed his splendid court costume, he insists that the "real" Egmont is not the public Egmont in Spanish garb but the private, indeed secret, lover. This assertion, however, is contradicted by the structure of the scene, which makes the cloaked, secret lover of melodramatic convention the one we see first and the splendid Spanish Egmont the inner one to be revealed. Furthermore he says the real Egmont is the one who embraces Klärchen, which indeed we see him doing, but in his Spanish court costume. As he marches off to his execution, he appears on stage finally as the great hero of the ballads. It is never settled whether Egmont is an intriguer or a sleepwalker, but it is beyond doubt that he is an effective leader because of his splendid appearance and his well-publicized war record. Somehow the

most "real"—or the most effective—Egmonts in the play are the most
publicly visible ones, not the secret plotters. He is, finally, an allegory of the
values that will eventually free the Netherlands from Spain.

At this abstract level then the play concerns not individuals but the state,
just as the masques and plays examined above did. Political drama of the sort
Goethe is now writing is peopled not by real individuals but by typical
individuals. The corollary of this statement is that political action is achiev-
able not by individuals but by figures who can present themselves successfully. Politics thus depends no longer on birth, position, or even power, but
upon capacity to represent. Thus in the "Fairy Tale" of 1795 the king receives
three symbolic objects as he ascends the throne, the sword of power, the
wreath of wisdom, and the scepter of "appearance" or "seeming" ("Schein").
Goethe realized very early what European regimes rediscovered in their drift
toward democracy in the course of the nineteenth century, that effective
government demands successful cultivation of the trappings of power.[23] And
with this insight we have moved from reflections on modes of writing about
politics to modes of political action.

The politics of seeming arises in part from a significant shift in aesthetic
sensibility around 1790. If the aesthetics of the 1770s had valued the
individuality and inner essence of the perceiving subject, a newly emerging
aesthetics, to which Goethe was a major contributor, placed higher value on
the impersonal representation of the object. This aesthetics of objectivity in
Goethe is normally dated to his journey to Italy (1786-88).[24] The first version
of it coalesces in the essay "Simple Imitation of Nature, Manner, Style"
("Einfache Nachahmung der Natur, Manier, Stil"—1789), where Goethe
distinguishes the three levels of artistic activity identified in the title. Simple,
faithful imitation of objects can lead to great art but is in itself limiting: "It
is easy to see that a capable but limited talent could treat pleasant but limited
objects in this fashion (i.e., simple imitation)" ("so sieht man leicht, daß eine
zwar fähige, aber beschränkte Natur angenehme, aber beschränkte
Gegenstände auf diese Weise [d.h. einfache Nachahmung] behandeln
könne").[25] True style, highest of the three categories in the title, demands
faithful representation based not only on accurate imitation but also on the
more subjective generalizing and organizing capacity identified as "manner." Style, or great art, rests "upon the most profound fundaments of
knowledge, upon the essence of things, insofar as that can be known in visible
and graspable forms" ("auf den tiefsten Grundfesten der Erkenntnis, auf dem
Wesen der Dinge, insofern uns erlaubt ist, es in sichtbaren und greiflichen
Gestalten zu erkennen," ibid., p. 297). Style thus goes beyond the literally
real and present to something more general, more truly objective. But in this

respect it is the same kind of representation we have been considering in the masques and in *Egmont*. To the extent that political representation can be assimilated to such a concept of aesthetic representation, it does not degrade but rather ennobles political activity.

In the course of Goethe's friendship with Schiller (1794-1805), this concern for the objectivity of art would grow in both poets to insistence on the absolute autonomy of the work of art. It was influenced by the intensive study both poets had devoted, independently, in 1790 and 1791 to Kant's *Kritik der Urteilskraft*, which had just appeared and where the concept of "aesthetic disinterest" is developed. This concern for aesthetic autonomy has been equated to strict political neutrality, but I think extreme discretion better describes both Goethe's and Schiller's position.[26] When the introductions to Schiller's periodical *Die Horen* and *Conversations of German Emigrants* ban political discourse from their agendas, this has less to do with neutrality than with the defense of an aristocratic political viewpoint. For they ban such discussion explicitly in the interests of discretion and good manners, a code of behavior clearly and recently of courtly origin, indeed the heart of courtly "seeming" or representation of self. Goethe's political practice and his analysis of politics thus come together in the controlled civility of his works of the 1790s.

The "Fairy Tale" blends aesthetic and political "seeming" almost indiscriminately. When the king is invested with his royal powers at the end, he receives the wreath of wisdom from the statue of a king made of gold, the scepter of seeming from a silver one, and the sword of power from one of bronze. The silver king, "seeming," is the most beautiful and elaborately decorated of the three. He cannot, furthermore, feed the light of some admiring will-o'-the-wisps (they live on gold), but willingly reflects it and allows his beauty to be enhanced by it. The statues not only provide the political powers of the king, but they are also each identified with one of the three estates of France; the seeming of the silver king is thus political and aesthetic simultaneously.

The same is true for the many other elements that "seem" or "shine" ("scheinen"). Will-o'-the-wisps begin the process of redemption. Besides their shining, they have only two qualities: good humor and courtly manners. They express their goodwill by scattering shining gold pieces about wherever they go; they produce this money by eating gold, and their gold pieces are eaten in turn by the central mediating figure in the tale, a green snake, who starts to shine with their light and eventually turns into the shining bridge of gemstone that unites the previously divided land. The will-o'-the-wisps behave like courtiers (a political quality), give form to the gold they eat (an aesthetic quality), and return the gold to circulation as coin (political again). The snake similarly transforms the gold into an object of beauty (gemstone) and also into a symbol of political unity (bridge) that restores circulation to the blighted land. A shining magic lamp carried by a wise old man—a stand-in for Goethe—is also central to the process of redemption. It transforms stone into gold when it shines alone, wood into silver, and dead things into precious gems. The value it generates is both economic and aesthetic. At the same time the old man, who is never without his lamp, directs the process of redemption. Seeming in the "Fairy Tale" is aesthetic, political, and social simultaneously.

Henceforth "Schein," or representativity, as I will call it, remains central to Goethe's concept both of aesthetic and political power, although the connection did not always remain as seamless as in the "Fairy Tale." The final step in the development I have been charting from the ironic representation of politics to politics as representation can be seen in the allegorical prologue to the opening of the Weimar court theater on September 19, 1807. Weimar had been sacked a year before by the victorious French after the battle of Jena and Auerstedt; in this prologue Goethe celebrates the return of the duke and duchess to their city and the recent Peace of Tilsit. The prologue is thus also a court masque. The goddess of war and then a fugitive woman dramatize the miseries of the late war, once again imaged as a thunderstorm, but at the end of the scene the name of the duchess suddenly appears in the sky as a sign of hope. The scene changes to a throne room where Majesty and Peace celebrate the return of peace and order. At the end they turn to the duchess in the audience and declare her return the embodiment of the return of peace and order they have just been celebrating. In effect, then, the figures in the masque extend their meaning from themselves to the duke and duchess sitting in the audience; the masque has turned the rulers themselves into representative figures and symbols. In the Stuart and Caroline masques the royal spectators and the representation mutually validated one another by their relation to the cosmic context; here the representation validates the royal figures by taking them into itself. In the "Fairy Tale" the king was invested with the symbolic attributes of the three kings, one of which was seeming. But the prior existence of the three kings connects them to tradition. Here the duke and duchess are invested with and by symbols that have only just come into being on the stage. They derive their legitimacy only from the aesthetic seeming, not from some prior existing order. The irony of aesthetic discourse not only makes it possible to represent politics, but it now makes it possible for politics to be.

It would be possible to pursue the theme of "seeming" through much of Goethe's later work. Bernhard Böschenstein has argued convincingly, for example, that the real tragedy in *The Natural Daughter* is the divorce of seeming from essence.[27] As late as 1831, the year before he died, Goethe was exploring the dangers of political seeming divorced from valid essence in Act IV of *Faust II*, where Mephistopheles employs the mere appearance ("Schein" again) of fire and cascading water to defeat an enemy army.[28] Seeming can also be pursued through Goethe's conduct of his own life as he increasingly turned himself into a public monument for his contemporaries and for posterity. It is, perhaps, this profound awareness of the power of appearances that made him so skeptical of democratic institutions.

It remains to ask after the relation of Goethe's seeming to Jürgen Habermas' discussion of the transformation of "publicity" ("Öffentlichkeit") in the eighteenth century. In *Strukturwandel der Öffentlichkeit* Habermas argues that "public" refers to the ruling group, the government, into the eighteenth century, and he analyzes Goethe's discussion of aristocratic cultivation of appearances and manners in *Wilhelm Meister's Apprenticeship* as a late example of this understanding of the term.[29] The development of bourgeois society brought with it, Habermas shows, a transformation in the concept of public: public is now the unassembled agglomeration of private citizens critically debating affairs of state. As part of this development the concept of "public opinion" emerges in the late eighteenth century; concomitantly the category of the aesthetic, earlier in the service of the public representativity of the state, becomes privatized.

Against this background Goethe's insistent efforts to aestheticize political discourse in literature are not simple conservatism. His irony infuses the subjective point of view, the private, into the traditional forms of aristocratic public representativity. He does, to be sure, preserve elements of the older social forms, but at the same time he also adjusts the older forms to new circumstances, and thereby mediates between past and future. Goethe saw that the old mode of a power justified by its status as representation of supernatural order was dead, but he also saw the limitations of the new ideology defined by Habermas of a public that engages in critical discussion—witness the babbling of the mob in the scenes at the imperial court in Act I of *Faust II*. The moments of self-consciousness and irony in Goethe's use of the traditional forms for representing power rescue his stance from anachronism.

The skepticism of *Faust II* suggests that Goethe himself moved beyond the optimism of his politics of seeming at the turn of the century to delineate the less conciliatory politics of a postdemocratic age. Indeed, just how an ironic politics might function in the real world is not clear. It seems to be another of the typically impossible syntheses that underlie all romantic thought—irony and dialectics are after all the two romantic structures for relating irreconcilable opposites. As Goethe knew from his efforts as theater director in Weimar, and from the increasingly perplexed reception of his own works from the mid-1790s on, the capacity to read appearances ironically and to recognize the proper relations between appearance and essence was—and always would be—anything but widespread.

For Goethe, then, the connection between irony and politics is complex, evolving, and profound. There seems no question that Goethe claims a political role for the poet at least from the time of his arrival in Weimar; initially he conceives this role as that of adviser in the context of a political system that is essentially personal. Tradition, genre, and court manners all combine to make the basic mode of advising allegorical in the most traditional sense—more or less traditional characters and situations represent equivalents closer to home. In this context irony functions to rescue traditional allegory from the dangers of triviality and irrelevance in a secularized society. This allegorical mode carries over, we have seen, from Goethe's court masques into his classical dramas of the late 1780s. The nature of his allegory becomes more generalized: characters and situations appear more individual and verisimilar, yet at bottom still represent types and abstractions. And even outside the realm of the masque allegory remains fused with Goethe's characteristically self-reflexive and self-undermining irony, which is never univocal. Thematically his concerns shift more to the larger, impersonal political realm, but his advice as poet remains essentially the same as that tendered in the more personal context. At the same time his earlier ironic practice is now thematized in reflections on the nature and function of representation, of which political representation is one aspect. Thus in the later 1790s we observe a transition from formal to thematic, from irony to aesthetic representation. Goethe's ultimate blending of the closely related tropes of allegory and irony—both involve saying other than what one means, the first seriously and the second, in Goethe's case, with unclear or ambivalent intent—makes the political role of the poet now equivalent to the poetic role of the politician. The poet is no longer simply the wise personal adviser or tutor to the ruler, but in a much more profound sense the creator of power. Power itself is recognized not to be an essential phenomenon that the poet transmits to the ruler by representing it to society; instead it comes into being through its very representation. Thus Goethe's importance lies not in any theory but in the way his development—in resistance to the dominant trends of the period—reveals how the modern understanding of power emerged.

NOTES

1. These attitudes have begun to change in recent years. See especially Dieter Borchmeyer, *Höfische Gesellschaft und französische Revolution bei Goethe. Adliges und bürgerliches Wertsystem im Urteil der Weimarer Klassik* (Kronberg: Athenäum, 1977).
2. See, for example, Ehrhard Bahr, *Die Ironie im Spätwerk Goethes: "...diese sehr ernsten Scherze..." Studien zum Westöstlichen Divan, zu den Wanderjahren und zu Faust II* (Berlin: E. Schmidt, 1972).
3. See Warren Roberts, *Jane Austen and the French Revolution* (New York: St. Martin's Press, 1979) for the first; David Monaghan, *Jane Austen: Structure and Social Vision* (New York: Barnes and Noble, 1980) for the second; Marilyn Butler, *Jane Austen and the War of Ideas* (Oxford: Clarendon, 1975) for the last two.
4. Austen critics avoid this word but compare the implications of "it is largely through manners that Jane Austen works out the question of social morality and power" (Monaghan, *Jane Austen*, p. 10), or "Jane Austen's achievement is to naturalize a didactic tradition" (Butler, *Jane Austen*, p. 167).
5. Information on the political, economic, and social situation in Germany in Goethe's time is drawn from W.H. Bruford, *Germany in the Eighteenth Century: the Social Background of the Literary Revival* (Cambridge: Cambridge University Press, 1935) and *Culture and Society in Classical Weimar: 1775-1806* (Cambridge: Cambridge University Press, 1962). These are still the standard accounts in English on the topic.
6. The distinction between what I am calling "coterie," a group to which all citizens in theory have access, and a patriciate derives from Mack Walker's *German Home Towns: Community, State, and General Estate 1648-1871* (Ithaca, NY: Cornell University Press, 1971), p. 60. In this brilliant and authoritative analysis of German town life, Walker emphasizes the extreme paternalism of the democratic town governments, which he describes as "avuncular" and governed by "joint uncles" (p. 57).
7. *Aus Meinem Leben: Dichtung und Wahrheit* (Part 1, Book 2), *Gesamtausgabe der Werke und Schriften*, Vol. 8 (Stuttgart: Cotta, 1952), p. 58 f.
8. Like most cities in the later eighteenth century, Frankfurt had outgrown and mostly pulled down its old city walls.
9. Cf. Bernhard Böschenstein, who refers to the "negative Naturgesetzlichkeit" of politics, "Die Bedeutung der Quelle für Goethes 'Natürliche Tochter,'" in J.W. Goethe, *Die natürliche Tochter. Mit den*

Memoiren der Stéphanie Louise de Bourbon-Conti und drei Studien von Bernhard Böschenstein (Frankfurt am Main: Insel, 1990), p. 330.

10. *The Illusion of Power: Political Theater in the English Renaissance* (Berkeley: University of California Press, 1975).

11. Cited in *Goethes Sämtliche Werke: Jubiläums Ausgabe*, Vol. 9 (Stuttgart: Cotta, n.d.), p. 435 f.

12. Cf. Ernst M. Oppenheimer, *Goethe's Poetry for Occasions* (Toronto: University of Toronto Press, 1974), pp. 81-84.

13. *Gesamtausgabe der Werke und Schriften*, Vol. 3 (Stuttgart: Cotta, 1959), p. 1281.

14. Ibid.

15. The plot described here is really Goethe's revision of 1788; in the version performed at court the roles of wife and husband were reversed. Apparently staging the version Goethe published later would have violated court decorum by being too obvious. Once, however, the situation had ceased to be court politics, it was acceptable even to publish the version that corresponded so closely to the personal situation.

16. *Lila* was revived with new music in Berlin in 1818; Goethe took no interest in the performance and was not surprised that it failed. See Hans Gerhart Gräf, *Goethe über seine Dichtungen*, Part 2, Vol. 3 (Darmstadt: Wissenschaftliche Buchgesellschaft, 1968), pp. 320-25.

17. After 1783, with a healthy heir and a second son, the ducal marriage ceased to be a political problem, even though the relationship did not particularly improve; around this time Karl August began his futile diplomatic efforts to preserve the status of the tiny German states caught between Austria and Prussia. Goethe was skeptical of such efforts from the very beginning: They belonged to the category of natural phenomena that could not be impacted from such a human-scale standpoint as Weimar. Disillusioned with the possibilities of political action even at the level of Weimar, he resigned his government offices and turned exclusively to intellectual and cultural pursuits.

18. See, for example, Dieter Borchmeyer, *Die Weimarer Klassik: Eine Einfuhrung* (Kronberg: Athenäum, 1980), pp. 104-30.

19. See especially Frank G. Ryder and Benjamin Bennett, "The Irony of Goethe's *Hermann und Dorothea*: Its Form and Function," *PMLA*, Vol. 90 (1975), pp. 433-46; and my response in Jane K. Brown, "Schiller und die Ironie von *Hermann und Dorothea*," in *Goethezeit: Studien zur Erkenntnis und Rezeption Goethes und seiner Zeitgenossen. Festschrift für Stuart Atkins* (Berne: Francke, 1981), pp. 203-16.

20. *Tag- und Jahreshefte 1799, Gesamtausgabe der Werke und Schriften*, Vol. 8 (Stuttgart: Cotta, 1959), p. 1025.

21. *Gesamtausgabe der Werke und Schriften*, Vol. 2 (Stuttgart: Cotta, 1950), p. 603.

22. The same motif recurs in *Faust II*, Act IV, as explicitly Mephistophelian.

23. This is the lesson above all of Eric Hobsbawm and Terence Ranger, eds., *The Invention of Tradition* (Cambridge: Cambridge University Press, 1983).

24. I have discussed the origins and implications of this shift in "The Renaissance of Goethe's Poetic Genius in Italy," in *Goethe in Italy, 1786-1986*, ed. Gerhart Hoffmeister (Amsterdam: Rodopi, 1988), pp. 77-93.

25. *Gesamtausgabe der Werke und Schriften*, Vol. 16 (Stuttgart: Cotta, 1961), p. 295.

26. Borchmeyer, *Die Weimarer Klassik*, pp. 179-87.

27. "Goethe's *Natürliche Tochter* als Antwort auf die französische Revolution," *Die natürliche Tochter*, passim, especially p. 348 f.

28. *Faust*, 10710-61. Cf. my analysis of the aesthetic implications of this episode in *Goethe's Faust: The German Tragedy* (Ithaca: Cornell University Press, 1986), pp. 225-30.

29. Jürgen Habermas, *Strukturwandel*, I, 2, Exkurs; Habermas, *The Structural Transformation of the Public Sphere: An Inquiry into a Category of Bourgeois Society*, trans. Thomas Burger and Frederick Lawrence (Cambridge, MA: MIT Press, 1989), pp. 12-14.

4

Comedians of the Ascetic Ideal: The Performance of Genealogy

Daniel W. Conway

The lawgiver himself eventually receives the call: *patere legem, quam ipse tulisti* [submit to the law that you yourself legislated].

—Friedrich Nietzsche, GM III:27[1]

Introduction

The turn to irony, a gambit familiar to literary critics, has in recent years become attractive to political theorists. Despite its supposedly corrosive influence on political commitment—as identified, for example, by Socrates' accusers—irony has emerged as the last resort for those who no longer believe the various metanarratives that have collectively defined our peculiar historical identity. In a "postmodern" age marked by the alleged theoretical shipwreck of both liberalism and Marxism, irony preserves the domain of political theory for those who would otherwise be obliged to abandon it.[2] But what does it mean exactly for a political theorist to embrace irony? Does the ironic turn amount to anything more than a cynical surrender to nihilism?

Political theorists who turn to irony often acknowledge the legacy of Nietzsche, whose philosophical hammer has crushed our foundational aspirations and littered our world with fallen idols. Despite the current enthusiasm for Nietzschean irony, however, the precise nature of Nietzsche's bequest remains unclear. It is somewhat ironic that Nietzsche, whose writerly strategies have virtually defined the compass of contemporary irony, says very little about irony per se. He professes his "love of irony, even world-historical irony" (EH:cw 4), but nowhere offers an account of irony or of his strategy for deploying it. Obviously influenced by the Romantic irony of the brothers Schlegel, he nevertheless acknowledges no debt to their transcendental buffoonery.[3] His reticence may be partially attributable to his belief that irony has been restrictively confined to rhetoric and tropology. In his own writings, Nietzsche successfully transplanted irony from the relatively hermetic environs of tropology into the fertile soil of philosophy, where it bloomed to inform his entire critical project.[4] As we will see later on in more detail, Nietzsche believed that irony is particularly well suited to moral pedagogy, as a means of neutralizing the formative influence of teachers on students.[5]

Ostensibly following Nietzsche's lead, contemporary, "postmodern" ironists train their sights on the bloated, obsolete idols of modernity. Having taken to heart Nietzsche's critique of foundationalism, ironists flirt instead with historicism and nominalism, routinely deconstructing any stray claims to objective validity. Ostensibly empowered by Nietzsche's pronouncement of the "death of God," ironists declare war on all gods in miniature, even proclaiming the death of the "author."

Despite their apparent, and often avowed, allegiance to Nietzsche, however, many contemporary ironists enjoy the distinctly un-Nietzschean luxury of exempting themselves from their own irony. The irony of these wayward heirs of Nietzsche is ultimately self-reverential—and therefore conservative—in scope.[6] This artificially limited—and so unironic—deployment of irony issues in the smug self-assurance that ironists know something that others do not, even if it is that there is nothing to know. These would-be Nietzscheans thus betray their problematic debt to Socrates, for whom, Nietzsche insists, "irony [was] an expression of revolt [and] of plebeian *ressentiment*" (TI 2:7). The insight into the contingent construction of all authority has consequently become a source of authority for professional deconstructors, and the insight into the bankruptcy of all metanarratives the source of metanarrative authority for postmodern critics in general.

By enacting a self-reverential irony, these contemporary Nietzscheans reproduce in their own critical strategies the same methodological error that Nietzsche attributes to the "genealogists of morals" who preceded him. These "English psychologists"—Nietzsche mentions Rée, Buckle, and Spencer by name but probably means Hume and Mill as well—habitually confused their own morality with morality itself, and consequently exempted nineteenth-century English morality from their otherwise promising historical investigations. Reading their own pet categories (e.g., utility, custom, sentiment) into the whole of human history, they immodestly situated themselves at the pinnacle of moral evolution. This "English" approach to genealogy is not only anachronistic but furthermore projects onto the screen of history (and thus eternalizes) its practitioners' own peculiar self-misunderstandings. The English genealogists assiduously searched for (and claimed to find) *reasons* in themselves and in those whom they studied, mistakenly assuming in both cases that these reasons ultimately explain why people act as they do. Their ignorance of their own morality ensured their continued ignorance of the history of morality.[7] Nietzsche's predecessors and progeny thus share a kindred pride in their own "objective" authority, and consequently adopt critical strategies that are self-reverential in scope and design.

In the twilight of the idols, however, we must beware of resurrecting the dead gods even as we proclaim their demise. Before philosophers can successfully implement any post-Kantian critical strategy, they must disavow their remaining vestigial authority and surrender their final, self-reverential stronghold—even at the expense of jeopardizing the very project of critique: "This pride *has* to be humbled, this evaluation disvalued: has that end been achieved?" (GM I:2). Unlike most Nietzscheans, Nietzsche does not understand his signal insight into the "death of God" as freeing him (or anyone else) from relying on "gods" as guarantors of meaning. Nietzsche's "insight" is simply that, and thus reflects his unique historical destiny: Although apprised of the "death of God," Nietzsche can neither trust nor renounce his metaphysical yearnings for objectivity, God, and Truth.

In order to neutralize these ante-postmodern yearnings, which he acknowledges but cannot quell, Nietzsche must enact nothing short of a self-referential irony, an irony so thorough and corrosive that it obliterates altogether the privileged authority of the philosophical critic. Unlike those contemporary Nietzscheans whose own authority conveniently eludes their otherwise potent irony, Nietzsche deliberately and preemptively invalidates any privilege that might accrue to him as a physician of culture.[8]

In an attempt to enact this self-referential irony, Nietzsche deploys a diverse array of critical strategies that are designed to undermine his intermittent claims to philosophical authority. Yet Nietzsche also realizes that these supposedly destabilizing critical strategies are themselves authorized and set in motion by Nietzsche the philosophical critic. The success of these self-referential strategies would paradoxically reinforce our sense of the formidable authority originally invested in them. The ensuing enhancement of Nietzsche's authority as the originator of these critical strategies would consequently offset any diminution in his authority as the target of these strategies. Nietzsche's apparent entrapment in a vicious circle leads many of his readers to conclude that his "deconstruction" of authority should have culminated in the termination or abandonment of his critical project.[9]

Nietzsche hopes to escape this potentially vicious circle by deploying a complex, self-neutralizing critical strategy: genealogy. As we have seen, the practice of genealogy as a critical strategy is not original to Nietzsche; his English predecessors modeled genealogy on the "objective" sciences, thus failing (or refusing) to interrogate the genealogist's own role in executing this practice. Contemporary Nietzscheans often reprise this self-reverential failure, and their confusion surrounding their precise inheritance from Nietzsche points to a larger confusion concerning genealogy itself as a critical strategy.

Although Nietzsche is not the first philosopher to adopt the practice of genealogy as a critical strategy, he is the first to recognize and explore its performative dimension. As a performance, genealogy announces and exploits its own divestiture of objective authority, thereby "demoting" Nietzsche to the status of his other data. The ultimate authority of Nietzsche's critical strategies must reside elsewhere than in Nietzsche, and ideally will lie with his readers. His self-referential irony effectively shifts the burden of authority from him to his readers, thus dissolving—or rather exploiting—the vicious circle of authority.[10] His irony thus transforms the greatest perceived deficiency of his practice of genealogy—its failure to deflect self-referential challenges to its authority—into its crowning triumph.

Those contemporary ironists who would follow Nietzsche characteristically stop short of his greatest insight: Irony becomes political only when it consumes even the originary authority of the ironist. Rather than compromise his project, Nietzsche's penchant for self-reference establishes genealogy as the sole post-Kantian critical strategy suitable for deployment in the twilight of the idols. Genealogy marks our point of entry into the self-referential—and thus political—dimension of Nietzsche's irony.[11] His performance of genealogy furthermore furnishes an instructive example of the "comedy" that he proposes as the sole means of challenging the hegemony of the ascetic ideal. Nietzsche's performance of genealogy thus suggests an alternative model of political agency, for genealogy constitutes an ascetic strategy that he believes may prove (relatively) less harmful to us.

I

For more than a hundred years now, readers have scoured the pages of *Toward a Genealogy of Morals*, hoping to discover a teaching of liberation or redemption. Intoxicated by Nietzsche's empowering vision of the regeneration of "health" and the rebirth of "nobility," his readers have anxiously searched for (and occasionally claimed to find) *his* alternative to the ascetic ideal. But they have searched in vain. Everywhere Nietzsche turns, he uncovers institutionally inscribed evidence of the unchallenged dominance of the ascetic ideal; the historical and philosophical arguments of the *Genealogy* collectively announce the *complete* victory of slave morality.

Of course, Nietzsche talks a good game, tempting us with redemptive visions of an epochal revaluation of values. Yet he simply does not deliver. At the close of Essay II, for example, he invokes the powerful image of the "Antichrist and antinihilist," a "victor over God and nothingness" who, he confidently assures us, *"must come one day"* (GM II:24). But at this point he breaks off abruptly, deferring obscurely to "Zarathustra the godless" and resuming his obtrusive silence on the question of an alternative to the ascetic ideal. This disappointing aposiopesis punctuates Nietzsche's chronic failure to provide "serious" solutions to the problems he raises.

Nietzsche may not liberate us from our past, but he does introduce us to our enemies. The most dangerous enemy to beware when reading the *Genealogy*—save one—is Nietzsche himself, as resentful and manipulative as any ascetic priest. In his "review" of the *Genealogy*, Nietzsche acknowledges the pervasive duplicity of the book, advising prospective readers to approach it cautiously: "Every time a beginning that is *calculated* to mislead: cool, scientific, even ironic, deliberately foreground, deliberately holding off" (EH:gm). Nietzsche's avowed intention to manipulate his readers reminds us that his aims and our own are not always meet, that the genealogist's own agenda may often be downright cruel.

In alerting his readers to his own duplicity, however, Nietzsche also exposes the extent of their investment in his redemptive authority. His empty promises of redemption thus contribute to a rhetorical strategy designed to expose his readers as complicit in the nihilism against which the *Genealogy* warns us.[12] Self-reverentially exempting ourselves from Nietzsche's genealogy writ large, and thus ignoring its ominous message, we slavishly turn to him to redeem us from the legacy of slave morality. Distracted perhaps by Nietzsche's stirring rhetorical flourishes, we tend not to notice that he too labors in the twilight of the idols, consigned by his crepuscular destiny to a longing for redemption that he knows to be nihilistic. Nietzsche, in short, is in no position to redeem anyone.[13] Hence the more serious problem of self-reference raised in the *Genealogy* is not Nietzsche's but our own. *We*, who turn finally to Nietzsche for redemption, are our own most dangerous enemies.

But we should not allow our gratitude for this insight to allay our suspicions of Nietzsche; if anything, we should escalate our vigilance of his machinations. After all, Nietzsche's readers are not exclusively responsible for conscripting him as a prophet of redemption. Although the argument of the *Genealogy* discourages us from anticipating an alternative to the ascetic ideal, Nietzsche's rhetorical performance encourages us nonetheless that an alternative ideal is possible, and that he and Zarathustra will eventually lead us to it. While forcing us to read ourselves into the grim genealogical tale he lays out for us, he also encourages us to exempt him—our would-be redeemer—from the otherwise totalizing history of slave morality. We may be inclined to thank Nietzsche for exposing our redemptive investment in him, but we must bear in mind that he deliberately cultivates this dependence in us and that he will parlay any ensuing "gratitude" into an aggrandized authority for himself. Indeed, Nietzche's empty promises of redemption expose his own complicity with nihilism.

Nietzsche's entanglement in the slave morality he presumes to document obliges us to distinguish between his practice of genealogy and his performance of genealogy. In this former capacity, Nietzsche "scientifically" charts the evolution of slave morality under the unchallenged aegis of the ascetic ideal. In this latter capacity, he validates the conclusions of his investigation by foregrounding his own residual hopes for redemption. Nietzsche's practice of genealogy accomplishes the initial, and ultimately self-referential, interrogation of authority, while the latter foregrounds his divestiture of authority and accomplishes the duplicative gesture of re-authorization.[14] When turned against the genealogist, thus exposing the genealogist's own subjective interests and prejudices, genealogy consumes its own originary authority, but also illuminates its previously unacknowledged performative dimension.

Nietzsche's performance of genealogy thus corroborates the account of slave morality that his practice documents. Although he claims for himself no privileged authority, and furthermore calls into question all such claims, his performance nevertheless encourages us to confer upon him a trans-genealogical standing that somehow ensures his success where all previous philosophers have failed. If we refuse to exempt his performance from the findings of his practice, then we must be prepared to admit that Nietzsche's promises of redemption are as groundless and manipulative as those of any ascetic priest, and that his practice of genealogy is predicated on a similarly dubious authority. It is important to note that Nietzsche's genealogy of morals actually predicts (or implies) both his own complicity with slave morality and our willingness to exempt him nonetheless; that is, his performance of genealogy is perfectly consistent with his (de-authorized) practice of it.

Toward the end of his investigation of the ascetic ideal, Nietzsche finally entertains the question that his readers have long since formulated: *"where is the opposing will that might express the opposing ideal?"* (GM III:23). He quickly rules out science, the reigning god of modernity, for it embodies either "the latest expression of the ascetic ideal" or "the unrest of the *lack* of ideals, the suffering from the *lack* of any great love, the discontent in the face of involuntary contentment" (GM III:23). "Men of science" are not the free spirits Nietzsche seeks, for their signature faith in truth bears witness to their underlying belief that truth alone can redeem the human condition. This belief in turn betrays the conviction that the human condition stands in need of redemption, a conviction symptomatic of nihilism. For similar reasons, Nietzsche also disqualifies the "unconditional honest atheism" that has been so fashionable since the nineteenth century. A genuine alternative to the ascetic ideal must neither promise nor anticipate the redemption of the human condition.[15]

In an almost offhand remark, Nietzsche declares that "the ascetic ideal has at present only *one* kind of real enemy capable of *harming* it: the comedians of this ideal [*die Komödianten dieses Ideals*]—for they arouse mistrust of it" (GM III:27). This, the only answer Nietzsche provides to the most important political question raised in the *Genealogy*, is so strange and unsatisfying, especially in light of the rhetorical crescendo that builds up to it, that few readers can take it seriously. Nor does Nietzsche deign to shed any additional light on these mysterious enemies of the ascetic ideal.[16] He lavishes the orotund prose of the *Genealogy* on such pressing political topics as diet, the chastity of philosophers, and German music, but he never again mentions these enemies of the ascetic ideal.

Although Nietzsche nowhere explains how one becomes a comedian of the ascetic ideal, I suspect that he would deem any such explanation superfluous. If we understand "comedy" as the species of Nietzschean irony peculiar to genealogy (which is in turn only one textual strategy among many that Nietzsche deploys), then the *Genealogy* itself comprises an exemplification of the comedy Nietzsche recommends as inimical to the ascetic ideal. In order to appreciate Nietzsche's comedy, however, we must focus on his performance of genealogy, which in turn requires that we follow his practice of genealogy to its ultimate, self-referential conclusion. As a genealogist of morals whose critical strategy applies self-referentially, Nietzsche himself becomes a comedian of the ascetic ideal.[17] Nietzsche arouses our mistrust of the ascetic ideal by arousing our mistrust of *him*, as a purveyor of the ideal. In his performance of genealogy, he presents himself as a *Doppelgänger* of the ascetic priest.[18] Only the strong and healthy among us, Nietzsche believes, warrant the future of humankind. Hence "it cannot be the task of the healthy to nurse the sick and to make them well" (GM III:15), for the healthy would thereby risk contagion. The task of ministering to the sick and infirm consequently falls to the ascetic priest, a "physician" who is himself sick: "*Dominion over the suffering* is his kingdom, that is where his instinct directs him, here he possesses his distinctive art, his mastery, his kind of happiness" (GM III:15).[19] I see no reason, aside from our redemptive investment in Nietzsche, to exempt him from this hard truth, or to assume that he includes himself unequivocally among the healthy. Nietzsche, after all, is a self-proclaimed "decadent" who claims to have "resisted" the decadence of modernity (CW P).

Furthermore, virtually everything Nietzsche says about the ascetic priest applies equally well to himself as a genealogist of morals.[20] Like the ascetic priest, Nietzsche "alters the direction of *ressentiment*," exciting in his readers an affective enmity for the institutions of slave morality. Like the ascetic priest, Nietzsche hopes to assuage the *horror vacui* of the human will by providing an interpretative context in which suffering is justified. Toward this end, he fashions a "genealogy of morals" that catapults the reader back to a point of historical rupture, the consequences of which define our current plight. Nietzsche's genealogy thus attributes our current experience of nihilism to the machinations of a dimly historical figure, the ascetic priest. Like the ascetic priest, then, Nietzsche locates the source of our current suffering in "a piece of our past"; in order to explain the origin of guilt [*Schuld*], Nietzsche simply borrows and adapts the ascetic priest's account of the origin of the bad conscience [*schlechtes Gewissen*].

Most important, Nietzsche figures the ascetic priest as an *agent*, thus availing himself of the intentionalist categories and vocabulary he ostensibly seeks to discredit.[21] The *Genealogy* thus becomes Nietzsche's own priestly weapon, for it reproduces and exemplifies the precise interpretative strategy that Nietzsche imputes to the ascetic priest. The victory of slave morality, Nietzsche explains, is predicated on the currency of its enabling account of moral agency, its successful transformation of sufferers into sinners. Inspired to creative genius by his consuming *ressentiment*, the ascetic priest presides over the birth of the will, a metaphysical construct to which the slaves appeal in order to *blame* the nobles for their nobility. In a similar fashion, Nietzsche cleverly manipulates his readers into *blaming* the ascetic priest for their current plight and holding him responsible for the victory of slave morality.[22] For Nietzsche, then, the practice of genealogy is simultaneously a performance, for he recapitulates the logic of the slave revolt even as he documents it.[23]

But most readers find nothing comic in the self-referential implications of Nietzsche's *ressentiment*-laden critique of slave morality. How does the self-conscious production of yet another ascetic priest challenge the hegemony of the ascetic ideal? How does Nietzsche's comedy differ from the ascetic priest's own double gesture of exposure and self-concealment?

Nietzsche claims a compelling historical warrant for his comedy. Shortly after identifying the comedians of the ascetic ideal as its only enemies, Nietzsche invokes what he calls the "law of life": "All great things bring about their own destruction through an act of self-overcoming [*Selbstaufhebung*]" (GM III:27). As evidence of the execution of this law, Nietzsche cites the inexorable logic that governs historical Christianity:

> In this way Christianity *as a dogma* was destroyed by its morality; in the same way Christianity as *morality* must now perish, too; we stand on the threshold of *this* event. After Christian truthfulness has drawn one inference after another, it must end by drawing its *most striking inference*, its inference *against* itself; this will happen, however, when it poses the question "*what is the meaning of all will to truth?*" (GM III:27).

Nietzsche exposes the will to truth as the last vestige of historical Christianity, and thus as the final stronghold of the ascetic ideal.

Hoping to render the will to truth problematic, and thus hasten the preordained *Selbstaufhebung* of the ascetic ideal, Nietzsche and his "unknown friends" conspire to subvert the ascetic ideal from within. Their comedy supplies the embodied media through which the "will to truth gains self-consciousness," thus precipitating the suicide of Christian morality. By self-consciously deploying the methods and practices of the ascetic priest, Nietzsche hopes to induce the will to truth to undertake an unprecedented—and ultimately fatal—self-examination.[24]

But the *Doppelgänger* is not simply a *rôle* that Nietzsche plays for our edification. He *is* an ascetic priest, and his performance, though rhetorically enhanced, is genuine. Although Nietzsche's performance perhaps encourages us to exempt him from the terms of his genealogical narrative, his practice certainly offers us no justification for doing so. If we attend closely to the self-referential implications of the *Genealogy*, we see that Nietzsche warns us against *all* ascetic priests, *himself* included.[25] For example, his account of the inevitable *Selbstaufhebung* of the ascetic ideal challenges the ascetic priest's own metanarrative only insofar as it mirrors the latter. Nietzsche does not speak from the privileged external perspective of the physician of culture, but from within slave morality itself. He too is a creature of *ressentiment*, and he quite openly resents the victory of slave morality.

The sole difference between Nietzsche and the ascetic priest he describes lies in the performative dimension of Nietzsche's genealogy of morals. Unlike the ascetic priest, whom he identifies as "the actual *representative* of seriousness" (GM III:11), Nietzsche dramatizes (and comically exaggerates) his own priestly aspirations. Nietzsche orchestrates his performance of genealogy to draw attention to his own priestly motives, thus linking the genealogy of morals inextricably to the genealogy of Nietzsche. I do not mean to suggest, however, that Nietzsche enjoys full control over the performative dimension of genealogy, for although his performance comprises a rhetorical element supplied by him, it also comprises elements unknown to him. Note, for example, his shameless affectation of scientific objectivity, whereby he gains our support for his thinly veiled attack on Christianity. Even his carefully crafted preface manifests his own copious resentment: Therein he scores a hollow academic victory over Paul Rée, a former (and allegedly successful) rival for the affections of Lou Salomé.

By exposing along the way his own priestly aspirations, Nietzsche's genealogy effectively invalidates any claim he might (and does) make to the privileged authority of the disinterested scientist. Confessing his own implication in the historical crisis that his genealogy ostensibly addresses, he observes that "there is reason enough, is there not, for us psychologists nowadays to be unable to shake off a certain mistrust of ourselves . . . probably we too are still victims of and prey to this moralized contemporary taste and ill with it" (GM III:20). The aim of his comedy is to communicate this mistrust to us, and subsequently to extend this mistrust to the ascetic ideal itself. By preemptively sabotaging his own priestly agenda, Nietzsche hopes to preclude his possible conscription as a prophet of redemption.

Nietzsche's comedic performance thus arouses our mistrust of his evil twin Fritz, the earnest, Leipzig-trained philologist. The aim of Nietzsche's performance is to proclaim: *ecce homo*! Behold the genealogist, the comedian of science, for whom the will to truth is both indefensible and indispensible! Behold Nietzsche, the self-identified ascetic priest who dares yet to philosophize! And, finally, behold yourselves, unwitting seekers of historical redemption!

But does Nietzsche's comedy mark the emergence of a self-neutralizing species of ascetic priest, or the evolution of a more resilient strain of priestly mischief? If the self-implicating scope of genealogy fails to betray Nietzsche's priestly mischief, then genealogy would be exposed as a particularly insidious priestly strategy whereby Nietzsche pretends to take our side versus the ascetic priests. Having cleverly secured our trust, and encouraged us to drop our guard, Nietzsche would then accede to the station of superpriest. Readers would once again turn to him to redeem them from their need for redemption. We should therefore not grow too trusting of Nietzsche, for his priestly influence over us always mitigates the success of his comedic assault on the ascetic ideal; he does not (and cannot) acquaint us with all of his priestly aspirations. Even in comedy, he remains our most dangerous external enemy. If we embrace Nietzsche's genealogy of morals as potentially advantageous for us, then we must do so in spite of Nietzsche himself, whom we can no longer trust.

II

The performative dimension of Nietzsche's genealogy of morals inevitably draws our attention to its author: What kind of philosopher would deliberately pursue comedy, thereby forfeiting the substantial authority that would accrue to the physician of culture? This is certainly not the philosopher-king of Plato's *Republic*, for whom Socrates claims the privileged perspective of the Promethean benefactor. Although Nietzsche is as fond as Plato of casting philosophers as the architects of political redemption, he usually reserves this station for those mysterious "philosophers of the future" who will forcibly wring nihilism from the fabric of modernity.

From Nietzsche's other writings, we know that he imagines the "philosophers of the future" on the model of world-historical commanders, who will inaugurate a revaluation of values and legislate the social conditions of affirmation and nobility.[26] These "philosophers of the future," Nietzsche tells us, "will be free, *very* free spirits," "something more" than those "merely free spirits" who strive to perfect their comedy (BGE 44). Although the *Genealogy* does not discuss these "philosophers of the future" in any detail, Nietzsche does conclude Essay II by invoking his vision of a "stronger age than this decaying, self-doubting present," an age graced by a "man of the future, who will redeem us not only from the hitherto reigning ideal but also from that which was bound to grow out of it, the great nausea, the will to nothingness, nihilism" (GM II:24).

But if these redemptive lawgivers belong only to the future, then what are we to make of the "philosophers of the present," those self-deprecating genealogists who must stem the tide of nihilism until their successors arrive? Nietzsche begins Essay III of the *Genealogy* by charting the historical descent of the "philosophers of the present." This unflattering genealogy, however, only exacerbates our doubts about the redemptive powers of comedy. The philosophical type, Nietzsche explains, has survived and flourished only under the aegis and protection of the ascetic ideal:

> For the longest time philosophy would not have been *possible at all* on earth without ascetic wraps and cloak, without an ascetic self-misunderstanding. To put it vividly, the *ascetic priest* provided until the most modern times the repulsive and gloomy caterpillar form in which alone the philosopher could live and creep about. (GM III:10)

Nietzsche's genealogy of the philosophical type thus reveals that ascetic ideals have traditionally provided the optimal conditions under which a philosopher could achieve a supreme state of spirituality (GM III:7). As a consequence, the philosophical type has historically instantiated a species of ascetic priest, in whose guise philosophers have been obliged to conduct their investigations.

By implicating the philosophical type in the career of the ascetic priest, Nietzsche tenders a devastating indictment of the "philosophers of the past." In a description of the ascetic priest that is equally apposite to the "philosopher of the past," Nietzsche explains that

> He brings salves and balms with him, no doubt; but before he can act as physician, he first has to wound; when he then stills the pain of the wound *he at the same time infects the wound* . . . in [his] presence everything necessarily grows sick, and everything sick tame. (GM III:15)

In order to enhance their own political standing, philosophers have traditionally created the conditions of their own authority, deliberately cultivating an audience in need of the peculiar brand of priestly redemption that they alone can deliver. If Nietzsche is right, then philosophers have traditionally secured their own authority at the expense of humanity as a whole, promising redemption to those whom they have previously infected with the *need* for redemption.[27]

Nietzsche's genealogical survey of the "philosophers of the past" not only invalidates their various claims to a privileged authority, but also attributes to them the very deficiency—be it sin or sickness—they have presumed to redeem. Like the ascetic priests who figure so villainously in the *Genealogy*, the "philosophers of the past" were "physicians" who *were themselves sick* (GM III:15). As a consequence of their priestly heritage, philosophers have traditionally served as both the focal points of the political community and the most pathogenic elements within it. Although it is their privilege to legislate and maintain the ideals of the community, it is their historical destiny to poison these ideals and cultivate in the community an unhealthy dependence on themselves.[28] They establish the values whereby the community might flourish and thrive, but they also stunt the growth of the community.

As a document of Nietzsche's own pedigree, this genealogy of the philosophical type explains both why he cannot offer us redemption and why he will attempt to do so anyway. Like it or not, Nietzsche is a direct descendant of the "philosophers of the past," and thus inherits their priestly allegiance to the ascetic ideal.[29] Nietzsche's self-referential genealogy of the philosophical type thus reflects the distance that separates him, as a genealogist of morals, from the unknown lawgivers and commanders for whom he prepares this genealogy.[30] Rather than mount a direct assault on the ascetic ideal, Nietzsche and his fellow "philosophers of the present" are uniquely bound by their historical situation to resort to comedy. Although the epochal revaluation of values remotely motivates their performances, they are not "philosophers of the future" and must busy themselves with the preparations for a revaluation of values.

Despite its ostensibly deflationary assessment of the "philosophers of the present," Nietzsche's genealogy does not impute to them the grim seriousness of the ascetic priests. Straddling the intersection of past and future, the "philosophers of the present" embody a mutant species of the priestly type: They are part ascetic priest and part free spirit. The hybrid nature of these "philosophers of the present" (partially) accounts for the erratic and often self-compromising narrative of the *Genealogy*, which urges us toward "nobility" by slyly enslaving us to Nietzsche's self-serving distortion of history. Nietzsche knows that his readers are sick and that they are susceptible to his promise of redemption. He also knows that *he* is sick and that he will exploit for his own ends his readers' pathological need for redemption.[31] Yet Nietzsche also acknowledges a duty to legislate against the deleterious influence of all ascetic priests, including himself. This self-referential insight, which alone separates him from other ascetic priests, prevents him from pretending that he is somehow exempt from the priestly heritage of philosophers. *Qua* ascetic priest, Nietzsche cannot resist exciting our longing for redemption and thus further sickening us. *Qua* free spirit, however, he attempts to neutralize his own priestly aspirations by alerting us to the nihilistic ramifications of our own longing for redemption. "Philosophers of the present" too are lawgivers, but their unique historical situation demands that their legislations apply self-referentially.[32] By means of his comedic performance, Nietzsche negotiates between these two roles and thus distinguishes himself from other ascetic priests.[33]

If successful, Nietzsche's comedy transforms the greatest perceived deficiency of the *Genealogy*—its failure to identify a "serious" alternative to the ascetic ideal—into its singular triumph. Nietzsche's genealogy reveals a moral history and prehistory dominated exclusively by the ascetic ideal. No alternative ideals are currently available to us, for modernity lacks the "great health" that such an alternative presupposes (GM II:24).[34] The philosophers of the future may someday discard the mask of the ascetic priest, but Nietzsche cannot. He is a "philosopher of the present," and comedy is his only means of deflecting his own *ressentiment* and mitigating its deleterious effects. Breaking (albeit incompletely and irresolutely) with a millennia-long tradition of philosophers and ascetic priests, Nietzsche refrains from offering his readers a recipe for redemption. Despite the hopeful rhetoric that informs the performative dimension of his genealogy of morals, Nietzsche presents no alternative to the ascetic ideal. Comedy may be capable of harming the ascetic ideal and loosening its stranglehold, but it does not constitute an alternative ideal or goal. For all its novelty and promise, comedy remains an irreducibly ascetic strategy, a performance of self-directed violence.

Nietzsche's comedy is political not only in its preemptive, self-neutralizing capacity, but also in its exemplification of an alternative ascetic strategy, in which capacity it "harms" the ascetic ideal. The political ramifications of Nietzsche's performance in the *Genealogy* are obscured somewhat by his apparent ambivalence toward the ascetic ideal. He presents the ascetic ideal as responsible both for our current plight *and* for our prospects for overcoming it. On the one hand, the *Genealogy* reveals that our allegiance to the ascetic ideal has culminated in the *will to nothingness*, whereby we identify our greatest prospects for power and flourishing with the destruction of our own affective ties to life. Human animals will, if necessary, orchestrate their own self-annihilation, for even this goal is preferable to no goal at all (GM III:28). On the other hand, the *Genealogy* reveals that no alternative ideals are available to us, and Nietzsche seems reconciled to our continued reliance on the ascetic ideal: "All honor to the ascetic ideal *insofar as it is honest!* so long as it believes in itself and does not play tricks on us!" (GM III:27).

Although alarmed by the self-flagellation induced by the ascetic ideal, Nietzsche admits that the ascetic ideal "saved the will" and transformed man into an "interesting animal," "pregnant with a future." Under the aegis of the ascetic ideal, we have learned to experiment with ourselves and to exploit the plasticity of the human soul. Nietzsche thus sees in the power of the ascetic ideal the sole promise of our future: Now that we know what the ascetic ideal can do, he hopes to harness its power for less destructive ends.[35] The aim of Nietzsche's comedy is not to overthrow or replace the ascetic ideal (what could that mean to the author of the *Genealogy*?) but to modify the manifestations whereby ascetic practices are inscribed into the institutions of Alexandrian culture.[36] Nietzsche's comedy "harms" the ascetic ideal by changing its aspect, by challenging the dominant ascetic practices of Western culture and proposing alternatives. Whereas civilization necessarily demands *askēsis* in some form or another, Alexandrian culture has (almost) exclusively endorsed nihilistic and potentially mortal ascetic strategies. Nietzsche believes that the ascetic strategies most familiar to us, those responsible for facilitating our "evolution" from natural to human animals, have not only exhausted their usefulness but have also engendered the "will to nothingness" that permeates modernity and threatens our very existence. If we are to survive our present engagement with nihilism, we must somehow replace these obsolete nihilistic ascetic strategies with alternative (albeit equally ascetic) strategies.

As practiced by Nietzsche, genealogy enables us to determine the precise conditions of our historical situation and the particular relations that govern it; thus armed, we might more accurately assess the relative threat of the alternative ascetic strategies available to us. All ascetic strategies (which Foucault has helpfully classified as "techniques of the self"[37]) are, by their very design and purpose, harmful to some extent to the human animal, but certain ascetic strategies can perhaps prove less threatening to us in our specific historical situation. Although the ascetic ideal itself is simply unassailable, Nietzsche suggests that we can successfully implement (relatively) less destructive ascetic practices. For example, he argues that

> the most spiritual men . . . find their happiness where others would find their destruction: in the labyrinth, in hardness against themselves and others, in experimentation [*Versuch*]; their joy is self-conquest; asceticism becomes in them nature, need and instinct. Difficult tasks are a privilege to them; to play with burdens which crush others, a recreation. *Knowledge—a form of asceticism.* (AC 57, emphasis added)

The comedians of the ascetic ideal are those genealogists who relentlessly interrogate current ascetic practices and strategies and expose their relative dangers. But these comedians do not simply unmask the multifarious manifestations of the ascetic ideal; they are also "enemies capable of *harming* it." In Nietzsche's hands at least, genealogy not only diagnoses and exposes; it also opposes and resists. Nietzsche advertises the *Genealogy* as a polemic [*eine Streitschrift*], a work that is political not only (or primarily) in its practice and teaching, but also in its performance. The *Genealogy* offers no alternative to the ascetic ideal (for *askēsis* is definitive of the human animal), but in its performance of comedy, it exemplifies an ascetic strategy that may prove to be less threatening to us in our specific, genealogically illuminated historical situation.

As a comedian of the ascetic ideal, Nietzsche experiments *on himself*, self-referentially deploying an alternative "technique of the self" that might succeed in retarding his own decadence. In his performance of genealogy, he thereby instantiates his own sketch of "the genuine philosopher," who "lives 'unphilosophically' and 'unwisely,' above all *imprudently*, and feels the burden and the duty of a hundred attempts [*Versuchen*] and temptations [*Versuchungen*] of life—he risks *himself* constantly; he plays *the* wicked game . . ." (BGE 205). Nietzsche's performance of genealogy not only exemplifies one such experiment, but also invites us to conduct similar experiments of our own and "to play with burdens which crush others" (AC 57).

In proposing "knowledge" as "a form of asceticism," Nietzsche recommends genealogy itself, a critical strategy whereby one gains knowledge only at the expense of one's own authority, a method of historical investigation that (cruelly) invalidates the scientist's claims to objectivity. Genealogy itself, insofar as it comprises dimensions of practice and performance, represents an alternative ascetic strategy that may (temporarily) disable the will to nothingness and thus ensure our survival in the twilight of the idols.

Nietzsche concludes his genealogy of the philosophical type by dramatizing the inherent danger and indeterminacy of his self-referential strategy. He asks, "Has this many-colored and dangerous winged creature, the 'spirit' which this caterpillar [i.e., the ascetic priest] concealed, really been unfettered at last and released into the light, thanks to a sunnier, warmer, brighter world?" (GM III:10). Once again, Nietzsche indirectly responds to his own rhetorical question with an "answer" as gray as the genealogist's subject matter. If this metamorphosis has begun, then we need look no further for its signs than the *Genealogy* itself; the self-referential scope of genealogy marks the sole standard whereby Nietzsche can claim to have emerged even partially from the chrysalis of the ascetic ideal. The extent of this metamorphosis is presumably measurable in terms of the success of Nietzsche's comedy: Do his readers still look to him for redemption and liberation, or is his penchant for self-parody sufficiently contagious to loosen the stranglehold of the ascetic ideal? Have we too become comedians of the ascetic ideal?

To answer such questions, of course, we must voluntarily assume the burden of authority that Nietzsche's comedy has thrust upon us and thus acknowledge his successful enactment of a self-referential irony. Nietzsche himself can provide no standard whereby we might judge the success or failure of our genealogical experiments. Indeed, if Nietzsche's performance of genealogy is to inspire similar performances in us, then we can look to him no more for redemption. Yet we must also be careful not to take Nietzsche's comedy too seriously, nor (self-reverentially) to invest in it our residual hopes for redemption. It is crucial to Nietzsche's irony that his performances point *both* to redemption, for those inclined to seek it, and to the self-referential irony that I attribute to him. We can never know how seriously Nietzsche pursued the vision of redemption that provides the material for his comedic performance. The point of his performance, I take it, is that we need no longer care.

NOTES

I presented an earlier version of this essay to the American Political Science Association. I would like to thank Sara Blair, Bonnie Honig, and John Seery for their instructive comments. I would also like to acknowledge the generous support of the Oregon Humanities Center.

1. With the exception of occasional emendations, I rely throughout this essay on Walter Kaufmann's editions/translations of Nietzsche's works for Random House and Viking Press. Numbers refer to sections rather than to pages, and the following key explains the abbreviations for my citations. AC: *The Antichrist(ian)*; BGE: *Beyond Good and Evil*; CW: *The Case of Wagner*; EH: *Ecce Homo*; GM: *Toward a Genealogy of Morals*; GS: *The Gay Science*; TI: *Twilight of the Idols*. My references to *Ecce Homo* specify chapters via shorthand notation, denoting chapters by lowercase letters. In addition, I also use the following abbreviations: clever: "Why I Am So Clever"; destiny: "Why I Am a Destiny"; wise: "Why I Am So Wise." I designate references to the prefaces of these works with the letter P.

2. Ironists such as Richard Rorty, for example, know that liberalism is simply unjustifiable as a system of political organization, yet they continue to reap the benefits of conceptually bankrupt liberal institutions. Rorty attempts to consecrate the marriage of irony and liberalism in *Contingency, Irony and Solidarity* (Cambridge: Cambridge University Press, 1989).

3. For a reckoning of Nietzsche's debts to Romantic irony, and to the Schlegel brothers in particular, see Adrian Del Caro, *Nietzsche contra Nietzsche* (Baton Rouge: Louisiana State University Press, 1989), especially chapter 2; Ernst Behler, "Nietzsches Auffassung der Ironie," *Nietzsche-Studien* Band 4, 1975, pp. 1-35; and Ernst Behler, *Irony and the Discourse of Modernity* (Seattle: University of Washington Press, 1990), especially pp. 66-71.

4. Here I follow the suggestion of Behler ("Nietzsches Auffassung der Ironie"), who maintains that Nietzsche removed irony from the jurisdiction of the literary and reintroduced it into "the sphere of life [*die Sphäre des Lebens*]," where it had also been at home in classical antiquity (p. 7).

5. Nietzsche observes that "Irony is in place only as a pedagogic tool . . . its objective is humiliation, making ashamed, but of that salutary sort which awakens good resolutions and inspires respect and gratitude." *Human, All Too Human*, trans. R.J. Hollingdale (Cambridge: Cambridge University Press, 1986), p. 146. In a discussion of irony to which I am greatly indebted, Gregory Vlastos detects a similar moral agenda—the promotion of autonomy—in the ironic discourse of Socrates. *Socrates: Ironist and Moral Philosopher* (Ithaca, NY: Cornell University Press, 1991).

6. Self-reverential irony (a designation suggested to me by Professor Sara Blair) thus represents a species of what Wayne Booth calls "stable irony," for "once a reconstruction of meaning has been made, the reader is not then invited to undermine it with further demolitions and reconstructions." *A Rhetoric of Irony* (Chicago: University of Chicago Press, 1974), p. 6.

7. Perhaps the best example of this error issues not from the English psychologists but from the German philologist C.A. Lobeck, who "gave us to understand that all these [Dionysian] curiosities really did not amount to anything" (TI 10:4). Nietzsche believes that these "curiosities" *do* amount to something, but he does not believe that we gain access to the Dionysian via the *reasons* that Dionysian enthusiasts might give for their actions. According to Lobeck, these initially meaningless Dionysian "curiosities" were retrospectively invested with meaning by epigones who sought reasons for these seemingly pointless rituals. Lobeck accurately describes what *he* is doing, but he considers himself historically distanced from the reason-givers whose intercession he posits. Although the "original" Dionysian enthusiasts had no reasons for their actions—had Lobeck dared to consider this claim he might have scooped Nietzsche—Lobeck assumes that reasons alone enable historical explanation; so he posits these mythical reason-seeking (and reason-finding) intermediaries.

8. Nietzsche's self-referential irony perhaps represents an extreme species of what Booth calls "unstable irony": "the truth asserted or implied is that no

stable reconstruction can be made out of the ruins revealed through the irony. The author—insofar as we can discover him, and he is very often remote indeed—refuses to declare himself, however subtly, *for* any stable proposition, even the opposite of whatever proposition his irony vigorously denies." *A Rhetoric of Irony*, p. 240. Nietzsche's self-referential irony ultimately eludes the categories of Booth's taxonomy, falling somewhere between "unstable-finite irony" and "unstable-infinite irony." This "gap" in Booth's taxonomy is at least partially attributable, I believe, to his failure to discern a pedagogical, or political, dimension of irony. Behler (*Irony and the Discourse of Modernity*) acknowledges the self-referential scope of Nietzsche's irony, characterizing it as "a self-critical awareness of our linguistic embeddedness" (p. 112) that anticipates Derridean deconstruction. Behler's emphasis on the linguistic provenance of Nietzsche's irony tends to eclipse its strategic, or political, aims.

9. A kinder, gentler Nietzsche has recently emerged as the product of scholars who believe that Nietzsche's continued investment in a project of critique is rhetorical, misunderstood, overstated, or an aberration. Alexander Nehamas, for example, assures us that "Nietzsche . . . does not advocate and does not even foresee a radical change in the lives of most people. The last thing he is is a social reformer or revolutionary." *Nietzsche: Life as Literature* (Cambridge, MA: Harvard University Press, 1985), p. 225. See also Rorty, *Contingency, Irony and Solidarity*, especially chap. 5.

10. Gary Handwerk discerns a similar "ethical" project—the building of a "consensus" and "community" of readers—in the irony of selected nineteenth- and twentieth-century writers. *Irony and Ethics in Narrative* (New Haven, CT: Yale University Press, 1985).

11. If we insist that Nietzsche remained blind to the nihilistic currents within his own thought, then we are obliged to juxtapose his penetrating critique of modernity with an embarrassingly naive constructive agenda born of fantasy and delusion. Representative of this interpretative strategy is Alasdair MacIntyre's discussion of Nietzsche in *After Virtue* (Notre Dame, IN: Notre Dame University Press, 1984). MacIntyre contends that "it is in his relentlessly serious pursuit of the problem, not in his frivolous solutions, that Nietzsche's greatness lies" (p. 114).

12. Arthur Danto similarly acknowledges the cruelty of Nietzsche's rhetoric: "Someone who uses ascetic practices to kill asceticism is engaged in a very complex communication, supposing he is coherent at all, and he would be right that we are missing what is taking place when we merely *read the words*." "Some Remarks on The Genealogy of Morals," in *Reading Nietzsche*, eds. Robert C. Solomon and Kathleen M. Higgins (New York: Oxford University Press, 1988), p. 17. Danto views the Genealogy as a "therapeutic" book (p. 19), but assumes—mistakenly, I think—that Nietzsche exempts himself from the therapy he dispenses.

13. Nietzsche's insight into the nihilistic ramifications of his early thought is announced in the 1886 *Versuch einer Selbstkritik*, which he adds as a preface to the new edition of *The Birth of Tragedy*. The actual *Kehre* in his

thought, occasioned by his discovery of the (self-referential) problem of nihilism, occurs sometime between his completion of Part III of *Thus Spoke Zarathustra* in 1884 and his subsequent decision to add a parodic Fourth Part to his *Hauptwerk*.

14. Behler (*Irony and the Discourse of Modernity*) suggests that "As in the case of Nietzsche, [post-Nietzschean] irony is best conveyed in action, through performance, a kind of writing which in the mood of a joyful wisdom employs the logic of play and the rules of the game" (p. 103).

15. Tracy Strong has long maintained that Nietzsche's preoccupation with a politics of "transfiguration" or "redemption" vitiates his thought and that "at the end of Nietzsche's life . . . [he] comes to despair of the possibility of ever accomplishing such a transfiguration." *Nietzsche's New Seas*, eds. T. Strong and M. Gillespie (Chicago: University of Chicago Press, 1988), pp. 13-14. As I indicate in this essay, I believe that by the end of Nietzsche's sane life, he had long since acknowledged the nihilistic ramifications of his youthful longings for a redemption of modernity. Strong thus chronicles the despair of a Nietzsche whom Nietzsche himself had long since subjected to an unrelenting self-parody.

16. Nietzsche's sole previous reference to these comedians hardly inspires our confidence in their redemptive powers. In the previous section, he wonders "how many comedians of the Christian-moral ideal would have to be exported from Europe today before its air would begin to smell fresh again" (GM III:26).

17. Nehamas similarly maintains that Nietzsche presents himself as a comedian of the ascetic ideal, but Nehamas explicitly denies the self-referential scope of Nietzsche's comedy: "[To be such a comedian] involves the effort to reveal the inner contradictions and deceptions of asceticism, to denounce it, and yet not produce a view that itself unwittingly repeats the same contradictions and deceptions, for to repeat these is to fail to arouse mistrust in the ascetic ideal; on the contrary, it is to offer a demonstration that it is inescapable" *Nietzsche*, pp. 133-34.

18. Referring to himself as both a decadent and the opposite of a decadent, Nietzsche explains that "This *dual* series of experiences, this access to apparently separate worlds, is repeated in my nature in every respect: I am a *Doppelgänger*, I have a 'second' face in addition to the first. *And* perhaps also a third" (EH:wise 3).

19. Nietzsche's uncharacteristically insistent authorial cues in this section—"I insist that precisely this matter requires profound apprehension and comprehension"—perhaps attest to the self-referential scope of his sketch of the ascetic priest.

20. Note how well the following sketch of the ascetic priest describes Nietzsche himself: "The ascetic priest is the incarnate desire to be different, to be in a different place, and indeed this desire at its greatest extreme, its distinctive fervor and passion; but precisely this power of his desire is the chain that holds him captive so that he becomes a tool for the creation of more favorable conditions for being here and being man . . . the ascetic priest,

this apparent enemy of life, this denier—precisely he is among the greatest conserving and yes-creating forces of life" (GM III:14).

21. Much is made of Nietzsche's celebrated deconstruction of subjectivity and moral agency. Too often, however, Nietzsche's readers conclude that his deconstruction of moral agency frees him from his reliance on it, as if the insight into the social construction of the intentionalist vocabulary were in itself liberating. This reading effectively attributes to Nietzsche the optimism and belief in moral progress more properly associated with the Enlightenment. Nietzsche himself realized that his insight into the historical contingency of subjectivity did not in any way free him from this contingency or his reliance on it to describe the world.

22. Just as the ascetic priest blames the sick for their own bad conscience, so Nietzsche blames the ascetic priest for his moral interpretation of the bad conscience. According to Nietzsche, the suffering associated with the bad conscience is simply the price we pay for having renounced our natural instincts. Although no one is responsible for the existential suffering of the bad conscience, the ascetic priest is responsible for the surplus suffering engendered by his moral interpretation of the bad conscience. Nietzsche feels that his interpretation of the suffering of the bad conscience (as meaningless) is preferable to the more familiar, guilt-based interpretation of the ascetic priest; neither eliminates the pain of the bad conscience, but Nietzsche's would eliminate the surplus suffering of guilt.

23. Jeffrey Minson maintains that "the central dilemma for Nietzsche's ideal of genealogy" lies in the basic incompatibility of the "methodological starting point" of genealogy (viz. "the dissociation of origins and outcome") and Nietzsche's "moral-critical presumption" to deploy genealogy as a critical strategy. *Genealogies of Morals* (London: Macmillan, 1985), p. 77. If I am right about the self-referential scope of Nietzsche's irony, then Nietzsche is well aware of the dilemma Minson points out. He "solves" this dilemma, I believe, by conveying his "moral-critical presumption" via his performance of genealogy.

24. In his 1886 Preface to *Daybreak*, Nietzsche elaborates on his scheme to subvert Christian morality: "We too are still *men of conscience* . . . It is only as men of *this* conscience that we still feel ourselves related to the German piety and integrity of millennia, even as its most questionable and final descendants, we immoralists, we godless men of today, indeed in a certain sense as its heirs, as the executors of its innermost will . . . In us there is accomplished—supposing you want a formula—the *self-sublimation* [*Selbstaufhebung*] *of morality*." *Daybreak*, trans. R.J. Hollingdale (Cambridge: Cambridge University Press, 1982), p. 5.

25. It is difficult to confer a privileged epistemic status onto an author who begins, as Nietzsche does, by announcing that "We are unknown to ourselves, we men of knowledge—and with good reason. We have never sought ourselves—how could it happen that we should ever *find* ourselves? . . . So we are necessarily strangers to ourselves, we do not comprehend ourselves, we *have* to misunderstand ourselves, for us the law 'Each is

furthest from himself' applies to all eternity—we are not 'men of knowledge' with respect to ourselves" (GM P:1).

26. See, for example, BGE 42-44.

27. Nietzsche explains that "the priestly type . . . of man has a life interest in making mankind *sick* and in so twisting the concepts of good and evil, true and false, as to imperil life and slander the world" (AC 24). He later adds that "the priest desires precisely the degeneration of the whole, of humanity: for that reason, he *conserves* what degenerates—at this price he rules" (EH:dawn 2).

28. Hence Nietzsche's ambivalence to the comedians of the ideal: As transitional figures, they serve both to harm the ascetic ideal (GM III:27) and to pollute the intellectual atmosphere of Europe (GM III:26).

29. As he readily admits, "we godless men and anti-metaphysicians, we too still derive *our* flame from the fire ignited by a faith millennia old, the Christian faith, which was also Plato's, that God is truth, that truth is divine" (GS 344; cited in GM III:24).

30. See GM I:9 and BGE 44.

31. We must not allow Nietzsche's praise for the free spirits to obscure the all-too-human truth that the ascetic priest *too* is a lawgiver. "The slave revolt in morality begins when," under the direction of the ascetic priest, "*ressentiment* itself becomes creative and gives birth to values" (GM I:10). Slave morality may involve an "inversion of the value-positing eye" (GM I:10), but it remains legislative nonetheless.

32. Booth acknowledges a "supreme irony," suggesting that the "true philosopher lives in self-corrective dialogue." *A Rhetoric of Irony*, p. 275.

33. In the books following the *Genealogy*, Nietzsche renders thematic his own dual legacy as a "philosopher of the present." In *Ecce Homo*, he claims that although he is a decadent he is also "the *opposite* of a decadent" (EH:wise 2). In *The Case of Wagner*, he admits to his own decadence but claims that "the philosopher in him" has enabled him to "resist" this decadence (CW P). Although he does not elaborate on the terms of this resistance, we can probably assume that his comedy plays some role in it.

34. Nietzsche originally believed that art could provide the desired alternative to the ascetic ideal, and hoped that his *Birth of Tragedy* might catalyze a rebirth of tragic culture. Despite the apparent resignation of the *Genealogy*, Nietzsche there suggests that "art . . . is much more fundamentally opposed to the ascetic ideal than is science . . . To place himself in the service of the ascetic ideal is therefore the most distinctive corruption of an artist that is at all possible" (GM III:25). Nietzsche promises that he will "some day return to this subject at greater length," but it is not clear what later text(s) (if any) he might have had in mind.

35. Nietzsche argues, for example, that no logical necessity binds the ascetic ideal to our current practices of self-annihilation: "Man has all too long had an 'evil eye' for his natural inclinations, so that they have finally become inseparable from his 'bad conscience.' An attempt at the reverse would *in itself* be possible—but who is strong enough for it?—that is, to wed the bad

conscience to all the *unnatural* inclinations, all those aspirations to the beyond, to that which runs counter to sense, instinct, nature, animal, in short all ideals hitherto, which are one and all hostile to life and ideals that slander the world" (GM II:24).

36. This is not to say, however, that Nietzsche's ambivalence is easily dismissed: Despite his insight into asceticism as the founding principle of civilization, he nevertheless expressed an inconstant and flickering hope of articulating an alternative to the ascetic ideal. Although he proposes the ascetic ideal as *the* principle of civilization, as definitive of our species, he also speaks vaguely of an alternative to the ascetic ideal, even suggesting on one occasion that his *Zarathustra* provides such an alternative (EH:gm).

37. Foucault explains his interest in techniques (and technologies) of the self in an interview entitled "On the Genealogy of Ethics: An Overview of Work in Progress," collected in *The Foucault Reader*, ed. Paul Rabinow (New York: Pantheon, 1984).

Part II

CONTEMPORARY CONTESTATIONS:
FEMINISM, CULTURE, RESISTANCE, PLAY

5

Good Housekeeping:
Virginia Woolf and the Politics of Irony

Sara B. Blair

On the Grounds of my university, I recently had a conversation with a senior colleague who shares a number of my research interests. After a preliminary interchange, he asked me about my current projects. I explained that I was writing a paper on Virginia Woolf's essays of literary doctrine, and in particular on the importance of irony as a feminist strategy in those essays. To which my colleague replied, "I guess it will be a very short paper."

Umberto Eco and Stanley Fish have recently reminded us that there is always someone who will take ironic discourse seriously.[1] Although my colleague's response advertised itself as ironic, it nonetheless trades on particular critical canons, and thereby usefully raises a number of questions that have become central to my thinking about Woolf, reading the feminine, and the broadly political uses of irony as a narrative politics. How is it possible that two contemporaneous readers of Woolf could have incommensurable understandings of her project, as fundamentally ironic and as unremittingly "straight"? To what extent do her self-representations encourage constructive failures of consensus through the creation of "secret economies" or "double visions" that subvert their own governing premises, forestalling the reader's desire for totalizing narratives?[2] And in a theoretical culture still struggling to consider, after Foucault after Beckett, what matter who's speaking, what matter who's reading the ironic text; whose reading will institutionally or critically prevail?[3]

I insist on the signal failure of consensus involved in this scholarly interchange in order to direct such questions against current thinking about irony and about Woolf as feminist writer. In part, I would argue, Woolf's irony in these documents anticipates the response that would fail to acknowledge it, because it is a textually specific strategy; both a conservative and a "radical" instrument, it records the historical limits of Woolf's self-invention as female subject and author. Enacted in and against the patriarchal high culture she inherits, and out of which she speaks, Woolf's irony seeks to legitimate her narrative performances even as it challenges the institutions and practices it employs to bring itself into being. This is not to argue that Woolf's irony partakes of a more general, and genial, "undecidability" characteristic of the modern or modernist or postmodern text, nor is it to read Woolf's art of self-invention as a continuous play with the radical contingency of a subject always other to itself.[4] Instead, it is to make a case for Woolf's irony, in her most powerful essays of literary doctrine, as a feminist politics that draws on and revises its available resources: the tradition of the *eiron*—one she knew with scholarly if autodidactic rigor—and the canons of literary modernism.[5] Invoking these gendered fictions of authority ironically, Woolf writes herself viably into the reigning canons of Anglo-American high culture and purposively negotiates its structures of gender, class, and nation.[6] Out of historical necessity, she creates a critical genre that works against itself—not in reverence to the autonomy of the sign but in the context of the specific literary culture she engages and resists.[7]

To read Woolf's literary doctrine as ironic in this way addresses a number of larger questions. Most immediately, it helps account for the value of the institutional interchange recorded above. Woolf, in the tradition of the *eiron*, inhabits the structures of authority—and particularly of gender—that she challenges. Consequently, her texts create a dialogue with the "straight" reader, with significant results: She appeared in print in some of the most influential political vehicles of her day; was the first woman invited to deliver the prestigious Clark lectures at Cambridge; and has been taught, canonized, and engaged in the academy by readers strongly resistant to radical feminisms.[8] Yet the space created by Woolf's ironic gestures has nonetheless sheltered the historically disenfranchised, the female and working-class "outsiders" whom she struggles in literary terms to speak for and represent, as well as emerging feminist constituencies within the academy.[9]

To recognize this doubleness, however, is most emphatically not to claim for Woolf a power to sublate or transume her cultural resources; only by recognizing the continuity of her texts, as political performances, with the traditions they seek to undo can we fully account for their ironic complexity, their limits, and their creation of dialogue and intervention rather than consensus.[10] In large part, my colleague's double reading of Woolf is enabled by the textual dynamics of her irony, which measures and necessarily runs the political risk of being read straight, of perpetuating the institutions on which its own critical power is founded.[11]

In particular, it is Woolf's negotiation of the metaphysics of gender that creates these competing personae, voices, and texts. Accordingly, her self-representations enable useful contestations between, and within, feminist theory and theories of irony. On the one hand, the critical discourse of irony, across the traditions of rhetoric, analytic philosophy, and poststructuralism, has tended to reify, often with an astonishing lack of self-consciousness, the trope of irony as the "womanly" art.[12] Even in more attentively gendered readings, the figuration of irony in and through the "feminine" largely obscures the specifically feminist uses and potential of irony as a mode of performance.[13] Like many readers after de Man, who understand irony as the very condition of readability, those honoring a formalist tradition insist on gender as metaphor, and thus put gender as historical fact under erasure. Conversely, "irony" as a term in feminist literary criticism and theory is all too often synonymous with a vague "otherness," a form of difference neither historically situated nor accountable to the particular textual performances on which irony as a political gesture so meaningfully depends.[14] If contemporary readings of irony account more richly for the politics of Woolf's self-representation, for her literary doctrine as feminist performance, that performance also raises questions about irony as a critical discourse. To what extent does it depend on the suppression, through ostensibly ironic figuration, of forms of attention or engagement it seeks to privilege? In what sense can irony be construed as a feminist rather than a merely "feminine" activity? If irony necessarily implies the construction of gendered subject positions, what matter who speaks in the ironic voice?[15]

I propose to raise these questions through close attention to a representative essay familiarly known as "Mr Bennett and Mrs Brown." I choose this essay for a number of reasons: Its economy will indeed enable me to write a short, or introductory, paper, and it stands usefully for more widely read texts of Woolf's feminist doctrine. More important, the essay stages the problem of irony in virtually all aspects of its production and transmission. Originally delivered as a lecture to a literary society at Cambridge in May of 1924, it was revised and published three times during the following year, in journals with widely varying missions.[16] The multiple life of the essay encodes the remarkable force of its performative dimension, and particularly the force of its representation of the author as womanly *eiron*. Seizing on figures of the feminine that are foundational to high modernist doctrine, popular literary culture, and the rhetorical tradition of irony, Woolf naturalizes her own authority to speak transparently from a domesticated body and a distinctively female literary corpus. Yet even as she genders the literary tradition and the literary act, she works consistently and ironically against the essentialized authority she initially claims. Woolf thereby creates interventions within and through the historical conditions she employs as feminist resources. Read as an ironic performance, "Mr Bennett and Mrs Brown" genders the production of literary authority and of irony as a political resource. And, by recalling the historical dimensions of ironic discourse, it serves as a useful text to a postmodernity no longer at home in its own ironic history.

As its title would suggest, "Mr Bennett and Mrs Brown" most immediately concerns Woolf's vituperative journalistic battle with its eponymous hero, Arnold Bennett, who reigned throughout the 1920s as the foremost defender of Edwardian cultural politics. Their contention began with an initial attack by Bennett, in an essay entitled "Is the Novel Decaying?" All too clearly, he complains, the answer is yes. Singling out Woolf for censure, he attributes the fall of the novel to the designs of second-rate novelists, those "interested more in details than in the full creation of individual *characters*." The problem is exemplified by *Jacob's Room*, Woolf's most recently published, extraordinary novel-elegy; although "packed and bursting with originality," it creates "characters" who "do not survive vitally in the mind." Its rejection of traditional modes of characterization is "characteristic" of "the new novelists" associated with modernism, among whom Bennett cannot identify "any coming big" talents.[17]

If literary history has proven Bennett wrong, or at least wrong-headed, it continues to read his doctrine through the lens of formalism, obscuring the continuity of his formalist rhetoric with an essentialist politics of the "character" of the literary act.[18] His designs are more obvious in a contemporaneous work of social criticism, ostensibly sympathetic to women's suffrage but aptly entitled, in the possessive, *Our Women*. In that text, Bennett concocts a modern fairy tale whose "characters" embody the political consequences of his literary doctrine. For "Jack" and "Jill," happily ever after means the recognition that anatomy is destiny: "Every man knows in his heart, and every woman knows in her heart," Bennett sententiously declares, "that the average man has more intellectual power than the average woman." Women as subjects are essentially defined, for Bennett, by a "desire to be dominated," "in itself a proof" of their "intellectual inferiority."[19] No wonder, then, that women artists, including Woolf, fail to achieve the status of (or to represent) legitimate subjects in their own right; no wonder that, governed by the inexorable laws of biology, "'Women can't paint, women can't write.'"[20]

As Bennett's larger critical idiom suggests, his critique of Woolf as novelist is informed by fictions of gender, raised as questions about what counts, in the social arena and in the literary text, as a unified subject, as an authentic self, as a legitimate moral agent—assuming these entities to be naturally or biologically constituted. Rather than attack this assumption *prima facie*, Woolf plots a carefully ironic response to Bennett, appropriating the continuity of his formalism with larger political designs. At the head and center of her argument— which she initially imagines in private as "a paper upon Woman," "a counterblast to Mr. Bennett's adverse views"—she places a revised version of Bennett's own doctrine. Renaming her essay "Character in Fiction," she asserts that the definitive function of the novel *is* to "express character," to discover those universal, transhistorical human truths—"the spirit we live by, life itself"—that subsist beneath the surface of subjective experience.[21] The shift from Bennett's plural to Woolf's singular usage is a crucial one, for it openly relocates their contestation on essentialist grounds. Against Bennett's privileging of "characters," Woolf poses a shifting and multivalent term that works against the uses to which it is most obviously put. If "character," in her strategically anachronistic language, signifies a moral and social agency on which public, collective, and transhistorically human values are founded (of the sort exemplified by the great men whose civilizing virtues are extolled in the pages of the *Dictionary of National Biography*), it also signifies the constructedness of human identity, experienced and enacted in the form of persona, of performance, of mask. Throughout the essay, Woolf negotiates the competing ideologies implied by these denotations: By remaining *in* character, ironically attached to an essentialized femininity, she successfully genders the canon of "character" and defends the novel as a form of woman's work.[22]

This ironic logic accounts for the inconsistent idealism that structures Woolf's "simple story" of an encounter with an elderly woman and her younger male companion on a railway carriage in London (422). That story is undertaken in order to suggest the insufficiency and irrelevance of Bennett's doctrine to the realities of "human character" in contemporary England, where "[a]ll human relations have shifted" (422). Edwardian fiction of the Bennettian kind is incapable of representing the inner lives— the "character in itself"—of such representative figures as Mrs. Brown; it never "waste[s] a thought upon her as she is," but fantasizes worlds "where these musty railway carriages and fusty old women do not exist" (428).

Unremarked, unacknowledged, unrepresented, "[t]here sits Mrs Brown in the corner of the carriage—the carriage which is travelling, not from Richmond to Waterloo, but from one age of English literature to the next, for Mrs Brown is eternal, Mrs Brown in human nature, Mrs Brown changes only on the surface" (430).

From the outset, Woolf imagines the work of the novel in a figure of *telos*, and thereby advertises her own terms as continuous with the hidden essentialism of Bennett's doctrine. The novel is defined, Woolf argues, by its unique formal capacity for a realism that discovers the universal in the particular, unveils a transhistorical, generic human nature, in all its varied incarnations. But if Woolf invokes the hidden essentialism of revisionary realism, she does so with a difference. Initially, that "phantom" human character who eludes the novelist's art is a neutral presence: The "little figure" who suggestively "rises up," whispering in the novelist's ready ear, is "a man *or* a woman"—some undistinguished and indistinguishable "Brown, Smith, or Jones," who "dares the author" to "catch me if you can" (420-21). Almost immediately, however, this figure of human nature, an indistinct "will-o-the-wisp," becomes irremediably gendered. "Few catch the phantom," Woolf asseverates; "most have to be content with a scrap of her dress, or a wisp of her hair." "Seductive and charming," the enchanting siren "lur[es]" the novelist to her rescue by the most fascinating if fleeting glimpse of her charms" (420-21, 422-423, 433). The object of the novelist's ensuing romantic pursuit is not some neutral human Being, but that essentialized Beauty that lures the male spectator to embrace and possess a privileged knowledge of higher realities and forms (or, at the very least, to indulge in displaced nostalgia about such erotic mastery).

Paradoxically, Woolf's invocation of this representative female "subject" allows her to transfigure the act of writing as a feminine and domestic art. By imagining the subject of fiction as an essential, inviolable, female presence, she naturalizes her own narrative and social authority to observe, legitimate, and represent that subject. In the quasi-domestic space of the British Rail carriage, party to the private "business" transacted therein, Woolf trades on her own transparency to the semiotics of privacy, enacted in details of costume, gesture, and desire. She thereby authenticates her own domestic fantasies—images of Mrs. Brown "perching on the edges of chairs" in her "seaside house, among queer ornaments" and "[h]er husband's medals" (425)—as authentic fictions. Through implication, and in the dynamic of metaphor, Woolf enlists the privilege of her own unmediated access to a distinctly female reality, to promote the novel as a domestic instrument, dependent on the implicitly womanly art of "character-reading" (422). The very gender essentialism that Woolf adopts thus becomes crucial to the construction of her own ironic textual authority.

Consistently, the specific terms of Woolf's attack on the Edwardians depend on the implied premise that the natural subject of the novel is a distinct and enduring female reality or nature. It thus follows that Edwardian textual politics are unauthentic, illegitimate, precisely because they strive to keep the feminine under erasure; the rich "characters" they purport to produce turn out to be mere sociological entities devoid of inner lives. Allowing Mrs. Brown to "slip through their fingers," to disappear on the train that rushes from one age of English literature to the next, the Edwardians ignore her protests that she is "quite *different*" from the paradigmatic femininity that their novels, with a deep terror of the New Woman, continue to represent. Most egregious of all is Bennett himself, whose expropriations of domestic life breach the "integrity" that attaches to an essentialized domesticity, "complete in itself" and "self-contained." With his domestic realism, Bennett "has made a house"—a social fiction of "copyhold" and "freehold" and "mortgag[e]"—in the hope that we may be able to deduce "a person living there" (429, 430). Emptying the domestic world of its metaphysical and spiritual and even ideological meaning, Bennett's fiction silences a more "profound" female reality that continues to subsist in the marginal spaces—the attics, the basements—of legitimate male culture.

Woolf maintains her ironic attachment to the "horrible domestic tradition" she explicitly attacks, with its "waste" and "futility" for the "woman of genius," in view of the larger aims of the essay (422). Not only does her use of femininity enable her to represent the novel as a woman's genre, whose history and legitimate subjects have been kept under erasure; it also enables her to erase the very distinction, which appears to structure her reading of literary modernity, between Edwardians and an emerging modernist avant-garde. By 1924, the most influential excesses of high modernist anxiety about what Woolf calls a profound "change" in "human character"—that is, a change in traditional class and gender roles and "relations"—had already begun to be canonized as the latest flowering of the Great Tradition.[23] Remaining in character, as female novelist and preeminent "judge of character" (421), Woolf reveals the revolutionary aesthetics of Lawrence, Forster, Eliot, and Joyce to be dependent on romanticized allegiances to historically "originary" patriarchal forms. Her continuing and ironic investment throughout the essay in fictions of gender enables Woolf to legitimate her textual authority in modernist terms and simultaneously to undermine their ideological production.

The same tenaciously domestic, essentialized language that Woolf uses to excoriate Bennett thus makes great rhetorical capital for her attack on her male modernist counterparts. "At the present moment," she asserts, "we are suffering, not from decay, but from having no code of manners which writers and readers accept." What is needed to make contemporary fiction more representative, more authentic, she claims, is the institution of a domestic relation between writer and audience, like that between "the hostess and her unknown guest." The representational space of the novel as Woolf imagines it resembles the space of the drawing room, in which the perfect "hostess" seeking "common ground"—the author as performative interlocutor, in dialogue and on display—engages in creative collaboration with the subjects of her narrative community:

> The hostess bethinks her of the weather, for generations of hostesses have established the fact that this is a subject of universal interest in which we all believe. She begins by saying that we are having a wretched May, and, having thus got into touch with her unknown guest, proceeds to matters of greater interest. So it is in literature. The writer must get into touch with *his* reader by putting before *him* something which *he* recognizes, which therefore stimulates *his* imagination. . . . (431, emphasis added)

If the literary act is thus insistently gendered, Woolf nonetheless revises it as a rejection of the "business" of Mr. Smith—Mrs. Brown's nemesis on the train to Waterloo—whose public, patriarchal authority the modernists have been far too eager to replicate, in favor of the "far more difficult business of intimacy" (431). In her critical fiction, the novel becomes a domestic enterprise; realism, a homely moral and imaginative response to that "overwhelming" impression of ordinary life, which "pour[s] out like a draught, like a smell of burning" (425). The art of the novel is woman's work: the housekeeping of response to a window inadvertently left open, to burnt cooking on the stove, to the uncomfortable guest who has been excluded from the ongoing dialogue that signifies the continuing possibility of a meaningful collective life.[24]

Sustaining the character of literary domestic, Woolf quite literally attacks modernist canons from within. The first published revision of Woolf's lecture appeared in the reigning vehicle of conservative literary culture, *The Criterion*, then under the editorship of T.S. Eliot. Even a brief survey of the material housed in the volume in question frames Woolf's reiterated appeals to a feminized and domestic form of life as an ironic narrative politics. The journal's pet terms of aesthetic evaluation favorably oppose the "barbaric" and nationalist to the "romantic," the "liberal" and the "rational," bemoaning disturbing Anglo-American tendencies of "democratization" and "a growing and alarming tendency" of literary criticism to express mere "humanitarian emotions." Eliot himself closes the issue with a "scientific discussion" of recent literary criticism; the latter, he complains, too often tends to degenerate from serious analysis into "the polite literary essay."[25]

Eliot's disparagement of the "polite" from the lofty vantage point of editorial anonymity—not unlike the rubric of the mystifying *alazon* so crucial to ironic discourse—only serves to emphasize Woolf's insistence on the domestication of the novel and the feminization of her own authority and voice. In private texts, Woolf gleefully lampoons his worship of social ritual and *politesse*; a mordant missive to her brother-in-law, Clive Bell, invites him to "Come to lunch," promising that "'Tom'" will be "'coming with a four-piece suit," and she elsewhere compares the latter to "an old maid who has been kissed by the butler."[26] Yet her revisions to the lecture manuscript of the essay for its publication in *The Criterion* perform a deliberate *self*-domestication. Speaking out of the pages of Eliot's text, Woolf insists on domestic figures to signify the difference of the authority she claims. "Mr" Eliot and "Mr" Joyce, she charges, have suppressed the possibilities for literary "society," by rejecting the model of a textual intercourse that would honor traditionally domestic, and feminized, virtues and values. Their works consequently evince the most awkward outbursts and lapses—those, Woolf writes with studied amusement, of "a boy staying with an aunt for the week-end," who "rolls in the geranium bed out of sheer desperation as the solemnities of the sabbath wear on"; the inventors of modernism "do now know which to use" at table, "a fork or their fingers" (434). Sheltering within the modernist house of fiction, Woolf attacks Eliot's obscurity as an attempt to evade the home truths that authentic fiction transparently represents:

> As I sun myself upon the intense and ravishing beauty of one of his lines, and reflect that I must make a dizzying and dangerous leap to the next, and so on from line to line, like an acrobat flying precariously from bar to bar, I cry out, I confess, for the old decorums, and envy the indolence of my ancestors who, instead of spinning madly through mid-air, dreamt quietly in the shade with a book. (435)

The *agon* of Eliot's poetic authority, the aching discontinuity of his verse, are recontained in Woolf's image of domestic tranquillity, accommodated within the elaborate and even archaic parataxis of her prose. Its imagination of the act of reading is deftly ironic: Woolf transfigures the reader of *The*

Criterion as a feminized, desultory consumer of the leisure product of literature. Against the terrifying domesticity of *The Waste Land*, and the claustrophobic domestic erotica of *Ulysses*, she evinces a deliberate nostalgia for a private sphere that nurtures the imaginative freedom and transport for which the subject of modernism yearns.[27]

This ironic domestication of high modernism, like the resounding denunciation of Bennett, seeks finally not to contest the canon of legitimacy but to enact the limits of the authority it claims. Throughout the essay, Woolf's bid for legitimation as representative "Georgian" depends on the insistent feminization of her own authority and voice.[28] Her own well-established and very real authority as a novelist and critic (signified in part by her publication in the most aggressively serious journal in the English-speaking world of the 1920s) dissolves into self-effacement, timidity, a "characteristic" inability to represent or speak for her audience. Performing, writing, "with greater boldness than discretion," "Mrs" Woolf apologizes for the fact that she will make "some very sweeping and some very vague assertions" (421). She discounts the value of her opinions, which are—in stark contrast to the august pronouncements of the journal's editor—merely those of "one solitary, ill-informed, and misguided individual" (421). She asks her audience to "excuse" her for speaking "in the first person, and with intolerable egotism," as one who is "likely to be prejudiced, sanguine, and near-sighted," guilty of "folly" and "surpassingly rash" (421, 427, 420, 436). And she tells the admittedly "simple" story of Mrs. Brown, one that will her allow her to "narrate" without "analyzing and abstracting" or hazarding definitive distinctions, with respect to essentialist paradigms about the value and nature of women's narrative (422).[29]

In this feminization of her critical voice, Woolf stages the problem of speaking with female and feminist authority—or, in the more traditional terms of ironic discourse, the problem of performing a hermeneutics of skepticism. Employing the very "convention," the social and literary "code of manners," enjoined upon her by patriarchy, Woolf inscribes within her text the performative dimension of its original delivery as a lecture, a form of communication that compels by virtue of the speaker's transparency to her own authentically feminine speech (434-35). Thus laying claim to the authenticity "Mr Eliot" promotes, the essay wins for Woolf the right to speak where and as she does. At the same time, however, her performance in the pages of *The Criterion* and in the lecture halls of Cambridge depends on the fact that she also *means* what she says—that her tentativeness, her hesitation, her awkwardness in the public arena are both genuine and motivated, a means of displacing, rather than simply relocating, the very authority that her essentialist self-representation would imply.[30] Tentativeness, provisionality, skepticism, and self-parody—"womanly" arts all—enable Woolf, most immediately, to interrogate modernism on its own terms. If Woolf's irony is to challenge the hegemony of civilization in *Criterion* terms, it can do so only by abandoning its privileged perspective and thereby instantiating a textual politics of radical hesitation.

More generally, this kind of ironic performance enables Woolf to change the terms by which irony builds community and makes historically specific sense. To this instrumentality, it is even more crucial that Woolf's essay both means and does not mean what she says.[31] In the specific context of the Socratic tradition she revises, her performances expose themselves as attempts to appropriate conventions of gender and thus more powerfully to stage the incompatibility of the authority she claims as novelist, and the autonomy she seeks, as *eiron* and teacher of tentativeness, to encourage. Engaging in what Jane Marcus has called the practice of "sapphistry" to turn the metaphysics of irony back onto itself,[32] Woolf remains true to the character of the *eiron*: She, too, is the womanly artist unable to act a "proper man's part" in the world, one who "pretends to know nothing, even that [s]he is ironic," and thereby sustains a power to expose the foundations of the state to which she remains subject.[33]

Woolf's performance, however, sustains this character with a crucial difference from that of Socrates and his epigones throughout the tradition: It foregrounds the historical conditions that have governed the feminization of this activity. Importantly, her lecture *literalizes* the feminine otherness of the ironic speaker, with dramatic attention to the particular social space in which her own performances ensue. Unlike the Socratic *eiron*, who moves, translates, conveys between *agora* and private sphere—who remains, in Norman Knox's formulation, equally "at home in aristocratic society or in the marketplace"—Woolf insists on, even as she transgresses, the boundaries imposed on her narrative practice.[34] Against the *peripeteia* that defines ironic discourse (including her own), she poses the imprisonment of women within domestic spaces, in figures of "this room" in which she lectures, of the railway carriage (from which the notorious Mr. Smith "jump[s] out before it had stopped at Clapham Junction"), of Bennett's heroine, "passionate and dissatisfied," looking longingly "out of the window" of the house to which she is confined, and of Mrs. Brown "closeted" in her seaside home.[35] If Woolf as literary critic earns a space at Cambridge of her own, she nonetheless reads the tradition from within the confines of the private sphere and thereby pointedly enacts the difference between reading "like," and "as," a woman, between feminine and feminist textual strategies.

In an intellectual culture virtually defined by the politics of irony, this turn of the ironic screw is both deliberate and historically motivated; it promotes a form of authority that discounts itself, in the interests of creating a more autonomous "society" of ironic and feminist readers, even as it exposes the degree to which irony works to keep politically feminized gestures under erasure.[36] Subject to the laws of bourgeois modernity rather than those of Athens, Woolf negotiates her own desire for a community of ironic readers that will radically transform the conditions of its own production and existence.[37] Unlike Socrates, who deliberately relinquishes himself and irony to the unchallenged power of the Athenian state, Woolf keeps faith with the notion of a community that will finally transfigure political power and itself, no less than the historical experience of speaking as a woman.[38] This "society of outsiders," in Woolf's famous phrase, will, she implies, ultimately make of irony a tool resembling language in Wittgenstein's *Tractatus*—a ladder that can be climbed and then kicked away beneath us. In her own time, however, such political feats are not yet possible; first, there are canons to be challenged, lost texts to be excavated, literary and cultural housekeeping to be done.

Lest such deliberately "modest" irony appear insufficiently politicized in our own critical moment, we need only recall the crucial work it does in a culture that subjects female authority to radical scrutiny and attack. In the context of Eliot's anxieties about the vacuous chatter of middle-class women with intellectual pretensions, and about the sexual threat posed by indifferent working girls, in the context of Lawrence's diatribes against "cocksure women" whose unnatural incursions into the public sphere render impotent the rightful, male heirs of civilization, Woolf's self-conscious appeals to an essentialized femininity make possible serious challenges to modernism's politics from within its institutions and vehicles.[39] Ironically, the seismic force of these ironic performances registers most tellingly in her domestic life, in the forms of resistance and containment with which they were met by her husband and fellow cultural critic, Leonard Woolf. Publicly, he dismissed his wife as "the least political animal that has lived since Aristotle invented the description"; in private, in a gesture reminiscent of the Joycean scatology Woolf derides, he habitually used her proof sheets and manuscripts for toilet paper.[40] Yet Woolf's performances, as political acts, have proven difficult in the end thus to dismiss. If Arnold Bennett left-handedly concedes the fight by declaring "All that I can urge in her favour is that she is authentically feminine," he inadvertently suggests the degree to which Woolf's ironic form of authority has enabled a retaking of literary and social ground for women's literary production, consumption, and self-representation.[41]

In our own poststructuralist, postfeminist critical moment, Woolf continues to legitimate such projects (often metaphysically incompatible ones), precisely because her performance runs the necessary risk of being misread by the straight reader. Only in incurring this risk can she effectively enact a version of ironic skepticism that simultaneously honors the historical experience of women as political subjects and challenges the fictions of law and custom that have produced them as such—thereby anticipating the performative identity politics currently shaping feminist theories in the 1990s.[42] At the cost of dismissals like the one with which I began, Woolf remains the good hostess she (in part) caricatures: Her texts entertain the possibility of various critical misreadings and thereby preserve the open-endedness of ironic discourse. In so doing, they continue to remind us that it does matter who speaks in the ironic voice, who reads—or overhears—the ironic text; they usefully transform skepticism directed against their political meaning into the grounds for a more constructive, and historically grounded, skepticism, of Woolf's own. Surely such rigorous attention to the politics of narration provides a model for feminists and ironists alike, whose public discourse in our own moment continues to be importantly, but never merely, academic.

NOTES

1. Eco, *Postscript to The Name of the Rose*, trans. William Weaver (San Diego: Harcourt Brace Jovanovich, 1984), p. 68; Fish, "Short People Got No Reason to Live: Reading Irony," *Daedalus*, Vol. 112 (Winter, 1983), pp. 175-91.

2. Ellen Bayuk Rosenman, "Sexual Identity and A Room of One's Own: 'Secret Economies' in Virginia Woolf's Feminist Discourse," *Signs*, Vol. 14 (Spring 1989), pp. 634-50; Bonnie Kime Scott, "The Word Splits Its Husk: Woolf's Double Vision of Modernist Language," *Modern Fiction Studies*, Vol. 34 (Autumn 1988), pp. 371-85. See also Pamela L. Caughie, "Virginia Woolf's Double Discourse," *Discontented Discourses: Feminism/Textual Intervention/Psychoanalysis*, ed. Marleen S. Barr and Richard Feldstein (Chicago: University of Illinois Press, 1989), pp. 41-53.

3. Michel Foucault, "What Is an Author?" in *Language, Counter-Memory, Practice: Selected Essays and Interviews*, ed. Donald F. Bouchard, trans. Donald F. Bouchard and Sherry Simon (Ithaca, NY: Cornell University Press, 1977), pp. 113-38.

4. Several recent readers of Woolf have proffered such deconstructive, or
    poststructuralist-inspired, arguments, including Pamela Caughie, *Virginia
    Woolf and Postmodernism: Literature in Quest and Question of Itself*
    (Urbana: University of Illinois, 1991); Makiko Minow-Pinkney, *Virginia
    Woolf and the Problem of the Subject* (New Brunswick, NJ: Rutgers
    University Press, 1987); Patricia Ondek Laurence, *The Reading of Silence:
    Virginia Woolf in the English Tradition* (Stanford, CA: Stanford University
    Press, 1991); Garrett Stewart, "Catching the Stylistic D/rift: Sound Defects
    in *The Waves,*" *ELH*, Vol. 54 (Summer 1987), pp. 421-61; Patricia Waugh,
    Feminine Fictions: Revisiting the Postmodern (London: Routledge, 1989);
    and Alan Wilde, who discusses the ironic narrative strategies shaping
    Woolf's short fiction in his introduction to *Horizons of Assent: Modernism,
    Postmodernism, and the Ironic Imagination* (Baltimore: Johns Hopkins
    University Press, 1981).
5. For documentation of Woolf's studies with Janet Case, her readings of the
    classical scholar Jane Harrison, and her knowledge of the classical tradi-
    tions of rhetoric and literary theory, see: Jane Marcus, "The Niece of a Nun:
    Virginia Woolf, Caroline Stephen, and the Cloistered Imagination," in
    Virginia Woolf: A Feminist Slant, ed. Jane Marcus (Lincoln: University of
    Nebraska Press, 1983), pp. 7-36; Evelyn Haller, "Isis Unveiled: Virginia
    Woolf's Use of Egyptian Myth," in *Feminist Slant*, pp. 109-31; Sandra D.
    Shattuck, "The Stage of Scholarship: Crossing the Bridge from Harrison to
    Woolf," in *Virginia Woolf and Bloomsbury*, ed. Jane Marcus (London:
    Macmillan, 1987), pp. 278-98; Brenda Silver, *Virginia Woolf's Reading
    Notebooks* (Princeton: Princeton University Press, 1983); Alice Fox, *Vir-
    ginia Woolf and the Literature of the English Renaissance* (Oxford: Clar-
    endon Press, Oxford University Press, 1990); Beverly Schlack, *Continuing
    Presences: Virginia Woolf's Use of Literary Allusion* (University Park:
    Pennsylvania State University Press, 1979).
6. Woolf's relation to socialist organizations and politics has been, since the
    initial diatribes against her snobbery and classism conducted by the Leavis-
    ites and by her nephew, Quentin Bell, a matter of great interest to her
    feminist readers. The most passionate defense against such charges is
    conducted by Jane Marcus, in "The Niece of a Nun," in *Feminist Slant*, and
    in "Thinking Back Through Our Mothers: The Collective Sublime" and
    "No More Horses: Virginia Woolf on Art and Propaganda," in *Art and
    Anger: Reading Like a Woman* (Columbus: Ohio State University Press,
    1988), pp. 73-100 and 101-121.
7. Following Rosenmann, as well as David Saunders and Ian Hunter in
    "Lessons from the 'Literatory': How to Historicise Authorship," *Critical
    Inquiry*, Vol. 17, No. 3 (Spring 1991), pp. 479-509, I seek to return Woolf's
    textual performance to the specific conditions, sources, and resources out
    of which it emerges.
8. Marcus, "Storming the Toolshed," in *Art and Anger*, pp. 187-88, and Nigel
    Nicolson, in his introduction to *The Letters of Virginia Woolf*, eds. Nigel
    Nicolson and Joanne Trautmann, 6 vols. (New York: Harcourt Brace

Jovanovich, 1975-1980), Vol. 5, pp. xi-xvii, discuss Woolf's uses of the lecture platform as a literary critical and political space. Ironically, Marcus celebratorily claims (not quite accurately, given the context of "Character in Fiction") that Woolf "lectured only to women and working-class people," while Nicolson attacks Woolf for refusing to deliver the Clark lectures and thereby "setting back" the cause of feminism. Both of these misreadings of Woolf have historically sustained her inclusion within the canon of western culture, as in the much-discussed Western Culture program at Stanford University.

9. Marcus's review essay, "Lycanthropy: Woolf Studies Now," *Tulsa Studies in Women's Literature*, Vol. 8 (Spring 1989), pp. 101-10, evinces the astonishing range of feminist projects, theories, and histories for which Woolf's texts continue to be invoked as legitimating resources, as well as the often-problematic currency of the feminist foremother who ironically becomes the kind of authority figure, "the mother of us all," whose power she resists.

10. Read in this way, Woolf's performances speak usefully to Gary Handwerk's critique of the view of irony, initiated by Wayne Booth, as the instrument of the "stably elevated" speaker who can anticipate the formation of a stable narrative community as well as the terms of consensus. Woolf's performance suggests, as Handwerk argues, that this version of irony forgoes the more potent dialectical power of irony understood as a "dialogic encounter" dependent on the public forms and spaces the ironic speaker inhabits. See Handwerk, *Irony and Ethics in Narrative* (New Haven, CT: Yale University Press, 1985), pp. 8-15.

11. Or, in Wayne Booth's formulation, "dramatizes each moment by heightening the consequences of going astray" (*A Rhetoric of Irony* [Chicago: University of Chicago Press, 1974], p. 23). In this respect, Woolf's irony as political practice refuses the kind of political permission the reader—perhaps especially the feminist reader—tends to seek; in John Seery's sense, her performances provide "no clear authorization from the author or the text," independent of the communicative context, for rejection of the initial sense of her self-representation (*Political Returns: Irony in Politics and Theory from Plato to the Antinuclear Movement* [Boulder, CO: Westview Press, 1990], p. 175).

12. Perhaps the most crucially gendered formulation is Hegel's, which defines irony as a feminized form of nihilism that destroys the meaning of the *res publica*: "Womankind—the everlasting irony [in the life] of the community—changes by intrigue the universal end of the government into a private end, transforms its universal activity into a work of some particular individual, and perverts the universal property of the state into a possession and ornament for the Family" (*Hegel's Phenomenology of Spirit*, trans. A.V. Miller [Oxford: Clarendon Press, 1977], p. 288).

13. As in Jacques Derrida's reading of woman and/as *pharmakon* in "Plato's Pharmacy," in *Disssemination*, trans. Barbara Johnson (Chicago: University of Chicago Press, 1981), particularly pp. 95-171, and Jean Baudrillard's

use of the feminine as metaphor in *Seduction*, trans. Brian Singer (New York: St. Martin's Press, 1990).

14. Frequently, feminist theorists of irony, and of the relation between feminisms and postmodernism, appear to compensate for the "feminine" (i.e., "impotent") character of irony as it has historically been represented and deployed. Various versions of this problem are discussed or enacted in Lilian Furst, *Fictions of Romantic Irony* (Cambridge, MA: Harvard University Press, 1984); Seyla Benhabib, "On Hegel, Woman and Irony," in *Feminist Interpretations and Political Theory*, ed. Mary Lyndon Shanley and Carole Pateman (Cambridge: Polity Press, 1991); and Donna Haraway, *Primate Visions: Gender, Race and Nature in the World of Modern Science* (New York: Routledge, 1989).

15. A rehistoricizing of the relation between irony and power seems particularly apposite given the currency of Richard Rorty's reconstruction of irony and the private and public spheres [*Contingency, Irony, and Solidarity* (Cambridge: Cambridge University Press, 1989)]. Woolf's performances suggest that some citizens can afford the luxury of a distinctly private irony because they command an audience and intellectual resources nonetheless, while others (the women, working men, and outsiders who people the narratives of *A Room of One's Own*, and "A Woman's College Seen from the Outside") depend on irony as a condition for entry into the public sphere. There is, therefore, an urgency of irony that renders it distinctly political. The recovery of such urgency is, in part, the point of Nancy Fraser's critique of Rorty's "abnormal discourse," insofar as it remains "the prerogative of the strong poet and the ironist theorist"; see "Solidarity or Singularity? Richard Rorty between Romanticism and Technocracy," *Unruly Practices: Power, Discourse and Gender in Contemporary Social Theory* (Minneapolis: University of Minnesota Press, 1989), p. 103.

16. These journals included *The New York Evening Post Literary Magazine*, *The Nation*, and *Living Age*; later versions of Woolf's essay appeared in *The Criterion*, *The New York Times Review of Books*, and a pamphlet publication of the Hogarth Press, which renamed the essay "Mr. Bennett and Mrs. Brown." Beth Rigel Daugherty provides a useful review of the essay's publication history in "The Whole Contention between Mr. Bennett and Mrs. Woolf, Revisited" in *Virginia Woolf: Centennial Essays*, ed. Elaine K. Ginsberg and Laura Moss Gottlieb (Troy, NY: Whitston, 1983), pp. 269-94.

17. Arnold Bennett, *The Author's Craft and Other Critical Writings of Arnold Bennett*, ed. Samuel Hynes (Lincoln: University of Nebraska Press, 1968), pp. 87-88 (emphasis added); cited in Daugherty, "Whole Contention," pp. 276-77. Daugherty provides an overview of the "contention" per se, and of its continuation in more recent critical readings, pp. 269-77.

18. In a recent review essay entitled "Mr. Bennett and Mrs. Woolf," *The New Republic*, Vol. 202 (June 4, 1990), pp. 26-28, Irving Howe revisits the contention in order to recover an unjustly vilified Arnold Bennett from

Woolf's demon reading, which, Howe argues, has succeeded in banishing Bennett from the canon and "destroying" his career.

19. Bennett, *Our Women: Chapters on the Sex-Discord* (New York: George H. Doran Company, 1920), pp. 112-16; cited in Daugherty, "Whole Contention," p. 273.

20. Such is the formulation of the would-be patriarch Charles Tansley, internalized as a persistent voice in Lily Briscoe's imagination; Woolf, *To the Lighthouse* (New York: Harcourt Brace Jovanovich, 1927), p. 75. A similar argument is mounted in Woolf's intellectual culture by her colleague, Desmond MacCarthy, in the *New Statesman*; for a full account of their interchange, see Daugherty, "Whole Contention," p. 275.

21. Woolf, *Diary*, Vol. 2, p. 69; "Character in Fiction," *The Essays of Virginia Woolf*, ed. Andrew McNeillie (London: Hogarth Press, 1987), Vol. 3, pp. 425, 436. References in the text hereafter referred to by page number. In fact, Woolf begins by citing Bennett's own dictum that "[nothing] counts anything like so much as the convincingness of the characters" in fiction; "[i]f the characters are real the novel will have a chance; if they are not, oblivion will be its portion" (ibid., p. 421; Woolf refers to Bennett, "Is the Novel Decaying?" *Cassell's Weekly*, March 28, 1923 (cited McNeillie, ed., *Essays*, p. 437 n. 2).

22. In "Women and the Rise of the Novel: A Feminist-Marxist Theory," *Signs*, Vol. 16, No. 3 (Spring 1991), pp. 441-62, Josephine Donovan argues for a (historicized) "essential connection between women and use-value production"—here characterized as domestic labor—that makes women authors "uniquely situated to contribute to the development" of the novel as an "'unofficial'" and ironic form (442, 443). In my reading, Woolf makes a similar argument, drawing on her knowledge of the literary tradition before modernism; however, she plays more insistently and purposely with the difference between historical and "essential" connections between women and the domestic. This performative argument interestingly anticipates the work of Biddy Martin, who argues that provisional recourse to essentialism and "conceptualization" is "imperative" to feminist resistance, particularly given "the specificity of women's situation with respect to secrecy and truth"; see "Feminism, Criticism, and Foucault," *New German Critique*, Vol. 27, No. 7 (1982), p. 13. It also anticipates Gayatri Spivak's strategy for reading "the operation of the'worlding'" of colonized cultures within and through feminist texts. Spivak argues that "We must . . . strategically take shelter in an essentialism which, not wishing to lose the important advantages won by U.S. mainstream feminism, will continue to honor the suspect binary oppositions—book and author, individual and history—" in order to recover and historicize "feminist individualism"; "Three Women's Texts and a Critique of Imperialism," *Critical Inquiry*, Vol. 12 (Autumn 1985), pp. 243-61.

23. For a detailed reading of this canonization, and the contestations over gender it implicated, see Sandra Gilbert and Susan Gubar, *No Man's Land:*

The Place of the Woman Writer in the Twentieth Century, Vol. 1, *The War of the Words* (New Haven, CT: Yale University Press, 1988).

24. Donovan convincingly argues that a similar strategy of domestication pervadies the work of early women novelists, who appropriate the "'word of the fathers'" to challenge the commodification of marriage and other forms of relationship.

25. *The Criterion*, Vol. 2, No. 8 (July 1924). See particularly Eliot's "A Commentary," pp. 371-75; Osbert Sitwell's cultural and architectural criticism, "A German Eighteenth-Century Town," in celebration of "the contribution of Germany" and its "stronger streak of barbarism" to the culture of "civilized beings," pp. 433-35; and Wyndham Lewis's "Art-Chronicle," which excoriates the democratized "corrupt[ion]" of contemporary art and asserts that "the only 'straight' thing: the only 'white' thing: the only 'manly' thing" for the "'civilized' man" to do in response is to refuse to *"encourag[e] any art at all"*—i.e., to refuse to take part in the aesthetic and political collaboration Woolf imagines (p. 480).

26. Clive Bell, "How Pleasant to Know Mr. Eliot," *T.S. Eliot: A Symposium*, ed. Richard March and Tambimuttu (Freeport, NY: Books for Libraries Press, 1968; orig. Henry Regnery Company, 1949), p. 16; *Letters*, Vol. 3, p. 209.

27. In the context of Woolf's ongoing critical projects, these domestic figures also serve to remind her readers that the novel historically began as a "female thing," a genre dominated by women writers and readers. For recent recoveries of the literary and critical history of women and the novel, see Dale Spender, *Mothers of the Novel: 100 Good Women Writers before Jane Austen* (New York: Pandora, 1986) and Jane Spencer, *The Rise of the Woman Novelist: From Aphra Benn to Jane Austen* (Oxford: Blackwell, 1986).

28. Woolf's private comments about her performance at Cambridge suggest the strategic character of her anticipation and response to the audience represented by the Heretics, who, in McNeillie's polite assessment, "enjoyed a certain reputation for exclusivity." In a letter to her colleague Jacques Raverat, she describes that audience as follows: "It was, as Lytton [Strachey] would say, rather 'hectic'; young men going in for their triposes; flowering trees on the backs; canoes, fellows' gardens; wading in a slightly unreal beauty . . . We had a good hard headed argument, and I respect the atmosphere, and I'm glad to be out of it" (*Letters*, Vol. 3, pp. 114-15; McNeillie, ed. *Essays*, pp. 501-2).

29. The ironic construction of Woolf's "character" is further clarified by an earlier journalistic response to Bennett's arguments about women and fiction: "I have often been told that Sappho was a woman, and that Plato and Aristotle placed her with Homer and Archilocus among the greatest of their poets. That Mr. Bennett can name fifty of the male sex who are indisputably her superiors is therefore a welcome surprise, and if he will publish their names I will promise, as an act of that submission which is so dear to my sex, not only to buy their works but, so far as my faculties will

allow, to learn them by heart" (*The Diary of Virginia Woolf*, 5 vols., ed. Anne Olivier Bell [New York: Harcourt Brace Jovanovich, 1978-1984], Vol. 2, p. 340). In the context of rhetorical history, Woolf's relentlessly domestic self-representation appears even more obviously successful as a portrait of the *eiron* par excellence, an analogue to Theophrastus's description of the ironic "character": "The ironic man is like this: He is ready to walk up to his enemies and make small-talk without hostility. He praises present company, whom he secretly attacks, and then condoles with his victims . . . . If it's a rumor he pretends he never heard it; if he's a witness he says he didn't see a thing; if he admits he was there he says he doesn't remember" (cited in Booth, *Rhetoric of Irony*, p. 139).

30. For further evidence of such "intentionality," see *Letters*, Vol. 3, p. 106, where Woolf expresses characteristically "private" doubts about her performance in the essay.

31. Gregory Vlastos, in *Socrates: Ironist and Moral Philosopher* (New York: Cambridge University Press, 1991), argues that Socratic irony is ultimately a linguistic property, a particular ambiguity attaching to the term, or language game, "knowing." In Vlastos's reading, when Socrates claims not to know, he thus embraces a form of authority that resists its own hegemonic power and promotes political autonomy instead. This reading, however, fails to account for the historical, and gendered, conditions that have made such willed unknowing powerful, persuasive, and politically cogent.

32. Marcus defines "sapphistry" as the textual strategy of "master[ing] the principles of classical rhetoric and subvert[ing] them at the same time," in "'Taking the Bull by the Udders': Sexual Difference in Virginia Woolf—a Conspiracy Theory," in Marcus (ed.), *Virginia Woolf and Bloomsbury*, p. 148. A related and influential discussion of women's strategies for inhabiting or approrpriating the narrative spaces to which they have historically been confined is Susan Gubar's "'The Blank Page' and the Issues of Female Creativity," in *Writing and Sexual Difference*, ed. Elizabeth Abel (Chicago: University of Chicago Press, 1982), pp. 73-94.

33. D.J. Enright paraphrasing Hegel, *The Alluring Problem: An Essay on Irony* (New York: Oxford University Press, 1986), p. 6; Northrop Frye, *Anatomy of Criticism: Four Essays* (Princeton: Princeton University Press, 1957), pp. 40-41.

34. Norman Knox, *The Word Irony and its Context, 1500-1755* (Durham, NC: Duke University Press, 1961), p. 17.

35. As D. C. Muecke has documented in *The Compass of Irony* (London: Methuen, 1969), p. 48, "*peripeteia*"—a crucial term in Aristotle's *Poetics*—frequently appears in translations of that text as "irony," suggesting the intrinsic connection between freedom of movement and the political autonomy irony is intended to sustain.

36. I take this to be the import of several of Woolf's early short fictions—including "A Society" (c. 1920) and "Solid Objects" (1918)— in which the formation of political community, useful "feminine" ignorance, and the act of irony, understood in traditional terms as a mode of life, are conjoined.

37. This is the project of transformation to which Stanley Cavell, in *Conditions Handsome and Unhandsome: The Constitution of Emersonian Perfectionism* (Chicago: University of Chicago Press, 1991), refers as "moral perfectionism."

38. Nietzsche's reading of the death of Socrates is apposite: On the one and only occasion, Nietzsche argues, when Socrates tries to give up irony for good, and altogether, he commits himself to death; the kind of transumption that Woolf implies, which would turn irony most importantly against itself, remains impossible, given the ultimate Socratic commitment to the power of the state. See *Twilight of the Idols, The Portable Nietzsche*, ed. Walter Kaufmann (New York: Viking Penguin, 1954), p. 479.

39. Lawrence, "Cocksure Women and Hensure Men," *Forum* (January 1929); cited by Marcus, "'Taking the Bull by the Udders,'" p. 160.

40. Leonard Woolf, *Downhill All the Way: An Autobiography of the Years 1919-1939* (New York: Harcourt Brace and World, 1967), p. 27. A useful discussion of the doubleness of such gestures is conducted by Laura Moss Gottlieb, "The War Between the Woolfs," in Marcus (ed.), *Virginia Woolf and Bloomsbury*, p. 242. Numerous such scatological instances are cited by Ian Parsons and George Spater in the somewhat prurient *A Marriage of True Minds: An Intimate Portrait of Leonard and Virginia Woolf* (London: Hogarth Press, 1977), p. 175.

41. Bennett, *Critical Writings*, p. 97.

42. Recent strong texts within the burgeoning genre of feminist theoretical and critical autobiography include Nancy K. Miller's *Getting Personal: Feminist Occasions and Other Autobiographical Acts* (London: Routledge, 1991); Jane Gallop's *Around 1981: Academic Feminist Literary Theory* (New York: Routledge, 1991); Mary Ann Caws' "Personal Criticism: A Matter of Choice," *Women of Bloomsbury: Virginia, Vanessa, and Carrington* (New York: Routledge, 1990), pp. 1-8; and Carolyn Heilbrun's *Writing a Woman's Life* (New York: Methuen, 1988).

6

The Irony of Interpretation

William E. Connolly

Onto-Political Interpretation

Onta, the really existing things; ontology, the study of fundamental reality apart from appearances. These determinations are too pure and total for what I have in mind. "Onto-political interpretation" may come closer. Every political interpretation invokes a social ontology, even though its invocations may well be contestable. It invokes a set of presumptions about basic necessities and possibilities of human being, about, for instance the possible forms into which the human may be composed and the possible range of relations humans can establish with nature.

Political interpretation is onto-political: It contains fundamental presumptions that establish the possibilities within which its assessment of actuality is presented, delimits its distribution of explanatory elements, generates parameters within which its ethic is elaborated, and centers (or decenters) its assessments of responsibility. But this dimension is not today often an explicit object of intellectual attention in the human sciences. How could this be?

I cannot answer this question with anything like the assurance or completeness it demands. But a couple of considerations do seem pertinent. First, there is a widespread sense, itself in need of explanation, that with the (purported) demise in modern philosophy of Aristotelian teleology and Christian doctrines of creation, the human sciences have finally moved into a position to take the world as it is. While these two perspectives offer conceptions of how the world is in its most fundamental structure and how humanity is placed in this order of things, established modern perspectives are often thought to escape the realm of onto-politics. On this reading, a social ontology is a speculative conception of the world and, fortunately, is also a dispensable dimension of social explanation. Few practitioners, of course, actually assert these conclusions so bluntly. They insert them into critical characterizations of defunct and self-indulgent theories described as "metaphysical," "speculative," "impressionistic" or (even) "interpretive," implying that they themselves eliminate such projections from their theorization.

A second, more sophisticated, rationale proceeds through argument by elimination across a vast expanse of human history. One thoughtful presentation of it is offered by Hans Blumenberg.[1] Earlier cultures, it is thought, were sunk in cosmologies that projected unfounded assumptions about intrinsic purpose in nature and treated words and events as bearers of dark signs from God of fundamental harmonies to which humanity should strive to become attuned. But various versions of this perspective defeated themselves through history as they tried to perfect themselves. What remained after these defective schemes were eliminated was an austere and scaled-down perspective of a world without purpose, indifferent to human concerns. Through this progressive elimination of defective alternatives, the way was cleared for "the self-assertion of reason" to establish itself in the modern age. This perspective was neither caused by the defeat of its predecessors nor can it prove the presumptions that guide it to be intrinsically true. But it has shown itself to be indispensable for the organization of modern life, and nothing in those previous perspectives suffices to bring it down. Modernity is "legitimate" because none of the perspectives that precede and challenge it can sustain themselves effectively enough to undermine its legitimacy. We don't need to think restlessly about ontological issues anymore, except to ward off the recurrent temptation to return to one of the vacated positions and to fend off the even more insidious temptation to treat fundamental *questions* posed by earlier perspectives as if they must still be responded to within the new frame.

A third, related response flows from a general sense that the most basic conflicts, problems, and issues facing contemporary life do not flow out of disagreements at so basic a level. So even if modern theories invoke a contestable social ontology (or a metaphysic; the terms begin to move closer together here), engagement with practical issues of politics, psychology, and ethics does not require that it become an explicit object of reflection. John

Rawls advances such a position when he says, in recent revisions of his theory, that the theory of justice is not metaphysical but political. That is, its quest for overlapping consensus does not rest upon demonstration of the truth of its starting point, but on a broad set of understandings and convictions (they would be called preunderstandings by Heidegger) central to American culture (and the culture of a few other states). Richard Rorty presents another version of this position when he treats the implicit understandings of the "rich, lucky, liberal states" as the background from which his own political reflections proceed.[2]

These three types of consideration may help to explain neglect of the ontological dimension, but do they suffice to justify it? What if some common presumptions of our time contain dangerous expectations within them? And what is the basis of this faith in arguments by historical elimination today, especially since its contemporary defenders themselves argue that previous social ontologies of the West were defeated not simply by the accumulated weight of internal difficulties but especially by new perspectives that seemed alien and unthinkable to them in their initial incarnations? Surely Christianity seemed strange and alien to "pagans" in its early incarnations. What if onto-political convergence in late-modern states turns out to be the domain most in need of contestation today?

Recent and contemporary thinkers as diverse as Nietzsche, Heidegger, Arendt, Foucault, Taylor, Derrida, and Habermas think—though to different degrees and on different registers—that this is exactly the case. They suspect that self-denying ordinances vindicated in various ways by Rawls, Rorty, and Blumenberg amount to a refusal to engage questions most important to the late-modern time. They contend that every detailed interpretation presupposes answers to these fundamental questions, and that this is indeed one of the territories in modern discourse that requires critical reflection. I concur.

There is probably another element in this refusal of social ontology within the human sciences. Most social scientists give primacy to epistemology. They think that an adequate epistemology provides the vehicle through which to pose and resolve every ontological question.

"Epistemology" on this usage does not include every philosophy that concerns itself with the question of truth. Heidegger, for instance, was centrally concerned with the meaning and role of truth in reflection, claiming, at least in his middle phase, that the most fundamental relation was between truth and untruth, rather than truth and falsity.[3] Truth is a mode of revealing that enables judgments of correctness and incorrectness within its frame. But each historical mode of revealing is also one of concealing. It conceals possibilities of being that cannot be brought into the clearing of its life without confounding its basic principles of organization. "Untruth" is that which cannot readily achieve standing within the terms of discourse of a time or which, when given preliminary articulation, stretches contemporary standards of plausibility and coherence to the limits of their tolerance. Untruth is the foreign not up for debate or reflection within a time. It lacks sufficient standing to be honored as a falsehood. So "truth" changes its place and status in Heidegger's presentation, one that thematizes the historicity of being by launching every reflection into existence from within the folds of an already established way of life and then strives to stretch itself into other modes of living imperfectly commensurate with it.

Those who give primacy to epistemology as a method of correct representation may be optimistic or pessimistic about its prospects for success: They may be skeptics or optimists about knowledge. In giving primacy to epistemology, in this sense, one demands that the first or most fundamental issue is not "What are the various ways in which truth is construed in alternative ontologies and what considerations can be advanced to select one over others?" but "How can a method be devised that will show human subjects how to represent the objects to be known most perspicuously?" To put the matter crudely and briefly, the primacy of epistemology short-circuits ontological issues by assuming that once the right method for attaining truth as correspondence or coherence is reached, any remaining issues will either be resolved *through* that method or shown to be irrelevant. The primacy of epistemology seems thereby to eclipse the significance of ontology by treating the ideas of subject, object, representation, and knowledge as if they were already fixed in their range of application. The attraction of this perspective resides in its claim to bypass ontological issues that might otherwise contaminate, jeopardize, or confound inquiry in the human sciences.

The primacy of epistemology turns out itself, of course, to embody a contestable social ontology. The empiricist version, for instance, treats human beings as subjects or agents of knowledge; it treats the object as an independent state of affairs susceptible to representation; it treats language as primarily a medium of representation, or, at least, as a medium in which the referential dimension can be disconnected from the context of practical action/evaluation in which it occurs. And, as is now well known, especially outside the human sciences, this perspective has been subjected to powerful challenges by several thinkers listed earlier as critics of the modern neglect of social ontology and by others such as Merleau-Ponty and Wittgenstein.

There are other considerations that help to account for the primacy of epistemology in the human sciences, especially the connections among the models of agency, knowledge, and responsibility; and the dominant epistemological perspective enforces the ideals of freedom governing the modern age.[4] But I will set this issue aside now to move to another. How is one to proceed when confronting a mode of inquiry that purports to avoid implication in ontological issues? Further signs must be probed in these cases. By what means is the ontological dimension of the study implicitly brought into play? Are attempts made to compare fundamental presumptions in the study to quite different alternatives and to ask how these might be defended or modified on a comparative basis? Is the thinker attentive to how the narrative and rhetorical structure of his text might serve as a carrier of the infection it purports to have cured? Contemporary practitioners who ignore these questions generally work within an ontological matrix operating below the threshold of textual explication.

It is now easy to see how onto-political reflection could be absent from self-defining statements of social scientists today but present within their practices. For these assumptions filter into these practices through the unconscious selectivity of discourse. The researcher's most fundamental "findings" do not flow from the tests she runs but infiltrate into the narrative and rhetorical structure of the texts in which they are located.

Thus, to take one sort of example, James Q. Wilson's research into crime and criminality treats the criminal as a responsible agent and the causes of crime as grounded in the attitudes of the criminal. He does not, to note one alternative possibility, compare these presumptions to criminality as a perverse politics of abstract revenge against a world that rules so many out of efficacy in conventional life. Wilson's conventional definitions of agency, crime, criminality, punishment, and responsibility precede the abundant supply of evidence he collects. The most fundamental parameters of his study are constituted by textual tropes through which the evidence is organized and presented.[5]

Or, take an example on a higher register of theorization. Roberto Unger's theory of democracy and freedom as mastery over the contexts in which we are situated depends for its reach and optimism on the presumption that the ecological contexts of social practice—including vegetation, soil, ecosystems, and human bodies, as well as established modes of technology and social organization—are inherently pliable media susceptible to formation, disaggregation, and reformation in an indefinite number of ways by human agents.[6] This crucial presumption is only weakly defended through comparison to a teleological alternative, and it is not defended at all against post-Nietzscheans who share his opposition to teleological theories while projecting the obdurate character of contingent formations. Rather, confidence in this disposition of things is first inserted into the vocabulary of plasticity, pliability, transparency, and receptivity and then driven home by transitive, activist verbs conveying a social will to mastery of these pliable objects of penetration. The tropology of the text constitutes its social ontology.

Or take a final example. The "thin theory of rationality" that governs some forms of rational choice theory does not establish the ontological assumptions which inform it. As portrayed by Jon Elster, it:

> leaves unexamined the beliefs and the desires that form the reason for the action whose rationality we are assessing, with the exception that they are stipulated not to be logically inconsistent. Consistency, in fact, is what rationality in the thin sense is all about: consistency within the belief system; consistency within the system of desires; and consistency between beliefs and desires on the one hand and the action for which they are reasons on the other hand.[7]

We can expect, then, operational ontologies of the objects of analysis to enter through incorporation of their beliefs, desires, and reasons into the calculus of rational conduct. Because this model of rationality dehistoricizes conventional contexts of practice, it is highly unlikely that its exploration of inconsistencies will venture far beyond the cultural unconscious within which the mode of inquiry is set. (This finding is less true of Elster himself, whose more substantive model of rationality and more historical orientation makes him an explicit participant in this level of discourse.)

What, though, is the critique of this neglect advanced by the diverse crew I have lumped together as its critics? Again, these critics diverge significantly from each other in the ethics they endorse, the extent to which they are political, the politics they advance, and the social ontologies they peddle (or pedal). It is the point at which they intersect that concerns me for the moment. For all of them (with the partial exception of Habermas) concur in giving initial priority not to the disengaged subject in its relation to independent objects of inquiry, but to historically specific modes of discursive practice within which people are engaged prior to achieving a capacity to reflect upon them. We humans *cope* with things within established contexts of engagement, and these contexts help to constitute us and the terms through which we constitute objects of representation. Representation does occur, but these are representations by historically constructed agents such as doctors and government agents in the nineteenth century engaged with historically constituted subjects and objects such as the commons, monomania, melancholia, vagabonds, hysteric women, colonials, sodomists, gentry, and paupers. Representation, that is, occurs within historically particular contexts that establish the objects to be represented and the terms through which it occurs. It is always the representation of prior representations. This duality, or doubling, eventually confounds representation, not as an indispensable practice but as a detached, transparent mode of knowledge.

None of the critics seeks a pure method by which to represent the world, though some of them—most famously Habermas, but also perhaps Taylor—*eventually* formulate alternative models of discourse that bear a family resemblance to the primacy of epistemology. The initial drift of their thinking, though, proceeds in another direction, because to construe a way of life as a set of practices through which things are constituted in the process of dealing with them is, first, to undercut the search to look for a neutral, transparent mode of representation and, second, to treat the onto-political dimension as one that infiltrates into the preunderstandings, affectional dispositions, personal identities, cultural relations, and instrumental priorities of a populace even before it has reflected upon them.

Let me now gather together these preliminary reflections, first, by summarizing briefly the way this general perspective is elaborated by one critical thinker on my list and then by exploring alternative directions pursued by other defenders of the primacy of ontology after they have crossed the intersection Foucault helps to define. We shift attention now, then, from those who conceal the *onto* in political interpretation to those who diverge among themselves about how to engage this dimension of discourse in the human sciences.

In *The Order of Things* Foucault claims that the Enlightenment model of representation (the "classical episteme") underwent radical transformation at the beginning of the modern period. For reasons he refuses to "explain"— thinking that the attempt to do so would implicate him more deeply in the contemporary perspective from which he is struggling to "detach" himself— things began to acquire a greater density and depth than they had in the classical episteme. The table of representations eventually collapsed into the revived depths of "life, labor and language." In each of these domains, the new depths exceeded the capacity of those probing them to bring them within the full control of representation.

For example, in the sphere of desire. The Marquis de Sade helped to extend the depths of desire, even while pretending to construct orderly scenes representing each desire in its transparency. But each new representation was confounded by the creation "out of an expanse of shade" of new desires not exhausted by the previous configurations. After Sade, "violence, life and death, desire and sexuality will extend, below the level of representation, an immense expanse of shade which we are now attempting to recover as far as we can, in our discourse, in our freedom, in our thought."[8]

In our discourse: Every dialogue invokes a set of prejudgments and preunderstandings not susceptible to complete formulation within its frame. In our freedom: Every act of agency flows from an unconscious and preconscious pool that limits it as an act of freedom. In our thought: Every thought is invested by the unthought serving simultaneously as its precondition and its limitation. Such formulations have become familiar to those who labor within the field of hermeneutics, but the circles they delineate were shocking and disturbing to those advancing them at this juncture.

By the time twentieth-century discourse matured (though Foucault would not use this last word), this stubborn situation of "man and his doubles" had become a defining feature of experience in the human sciences. The "transcendental doublet" is a strange, ambiguous configuration of discourse in the modern time. But it has not yet proven to be either dispensable or transcendable. It consists in the experience of a being whose role as a subject of inquiry is perpetually chased by a compulsion to clarify opaque elements in its own structure of perception and judgment by treating itself as an object of inquiry. The subject ("man") is haunted by an indispensable and unconquerable double—an immense expanse of shade—that compromises its transparency, freedom, and self-certainty. Foucault evokes the paradoxical character of this condition in his portrayal of the

> Other that is not only a brother but a twin, born, not of man, nor in man, but beside him and at the same time, in an identical newness, in an unavoidable duality. . . . In any case, the unthought has accompanied man mutely and uninterruptedly, since the nineteenth century. Since it was never more than an insistent double, it has never been the object of reflection in an autonomous way; it has received the complementary name of that for which it was . . . the shadow: in Hegelian phenomenology it was the *An sich* as opposed to the *Fur sich*; for Schopenhauer it was the *Unbewusste*; for Marx it was alienated man; in Husserl's analysis it was the implicit, the inactual, the sedimented, the non-effected—in every case, the inexhaustible double that presents itself to reflection as the blurred projection of what man is in his truth, but that also plays the role of the preliminary ground upon which man must collect himself and recall himself in order to attain his truth. For though this double may be close, it is alien, and the role, the true undertaking of the whole of modern thought, is imbued with the necessity of thinking the unthought—of ending man's alienation . . . , of making explicit the horizon that provides experience with its background . . . , of lifting

the veil of the Unconscious, of becoming absorbed in its silence, or of straining to catch its restless murmur.[9]

If the typical response in the modern episteme is to strive to find a way to escape or transcend the limitation posed by the double, Foucault is (often) a happy positivist, ready to interpret the world in distinctive onto-political ways that endorse the paradoxical situation within which interpretation proceeds. Indeed, Foucault suggests that the retreat of the old dogmatism— where limitations of the finite world were transcended through faiths that linked humanity to the infinite—is accompanied by the emergence of a new dogmatism. The new dogmatism takes the ironic form of an endless renewal of the circle of finitude in search of a mode of attunement or a transcendental argument that might still the quest. It always acts as if it has just become more closely attuned to being itself or as if it is on the verge of perfecting a transcendental argument that will soon still the oscillation that troubles or alienates it. Foucault seeks to awaken thought from such a deep "anthropological" sleep—"so deep that thought experiences it paradoxically as vigilance, so wholly does it confuse the circularity of a dogmatism folded upon itself in order to find a basis for itself within itself."[10] The dogmatism of modern thought consists in the terms of its vigilance, in its modernization of the Augustinian imperative to go more deeply into the self (or language or community) in search of a reliable foundation for itself. Foucault does not endorse the project of drawing the double into the fold of the subject, partly because he suspects the quest for transparency energizing such a project is endless and partly because the single-minded pursuit of this elusive end as a "regulative ideal" might contribute (to draw upon a later vocabulary) to the extension of disciplinary society into new corners of life.

If the first group of contemporary theorists we have encountered seeks futilely to evade the ontological dimension of discourse, the second group accepts much of Foucault's preliminary characterization as its own and then strives to devise a way to transcend the limitations encountered. These theorists seek to make society and the self as transparent as possible and to establish a framework for ethical judgment that can provide a rational basis for social consensus; they treat, as Foucault suggested is typical of thought in the modern period, the quest for transparency, rational consensus, and freedom as intimate allies. Several contemporary positions can be seen in this "light." Some of these theorists may seek to realize the goal of transparency itself, while others treat the quest as a regulative ideal that can never be attained fully but that must consistently serve as the unambiguous goal of reflection.

Habermas's various attempts to elaborate the conditions of discursive consensus constitute one sort of attempt to close the circle in a rational way. But that strategy seems either to introduce arbitrary elements into its ideal or perpetually to encounter new dimensions of the unthought yet to be brought into its fold. Habermas's silence about the body as an ambiguous medium of desire and precondition of thought may be revealing in this regard. He cannot endorse the theme of the "embodied subject" governing theories seeking to uncover an inner telos in the body to be brought ever more fully into the structure of intentionality, nor can he accept the Nietzschean portrayal of the body as a medium of life and desire that stretches below the realm of identity and consciousness while providing them with an indispensable fund from which they draw. The first position would provide Habermas with resources from which an ideal consensus could be formed, but its pursuit would assume the character more of the hermeneutic circle his own model is supposed to replace. The second would not give him the possibility he seeks, though he has not yet developed a conception of bodies or embodiment that enables him to sustain the ideal of discourse he endorses.

Hermeneutics, at least in its pastoral mode, offers another competing response to man and his doubles. It strives to extend the circular motion between preunderstanding and explicit formulations until reflection becomes more closely attuned to a higher direction in being. Such a relationship to being, while not reducing all opacity and indefiniteness to transparency, nonetheless enhances the experience of harmony within the "embodied" self and between the self and the order with which it properly identifies. This perspective never promises to close all gaps, *only to narrow them perpetually*.

This pastoral orientation presents itself through a rhetoric of harmonization, responsiveness, articulation, depth, fulfillment, realization, and community. It also draws extensively upon ocular metaphors of light, illumination, clarity, obscurity, darkness, cloudiness, and distortion that link the theme of elevation to the pursuit of transparency. It is, of course, not alone in using these metaphors of *telos* and illumination; it is distinctive in using them as if they were the media through which "we" become "attuned" to the harmonies of being and "bring them to light."

But it remains contestable whether the deepest portrayals of pastoral hermeneutics respond to an immanent purpose in being or fix a debatable reading on the self and the world through the rhetorical configurations it deploys. This question has practical implications, for these same issues arise when assessing the operational codes and organizational forms it would apply to human beings. It is perhaps revealing that practitioners of this mode seldom strive to problematize explicitly the narrative and rhetorical structures of their own texts, even though these are the central media through which the onto-politics of illumination through harmonization is presented. The pastoral mode typically draws "in the last instance" upon a theistic supplement—upon a contestable faith in a god whose will and direction is thought to hover over being itself. The particular way it deploys ocular metaphors, highly reminiscent of biblical usage, constitutes only the most "visible" sign of that connection. I concur with Foucault that a "commentary" of this sort can best hope to sustain itself through the article of faith that "below the language one is reading and deciphering, there runs the sovereignty of an original Text."[11]

Charles Taylor endorses such a hermeneutic project, seeking to bolster it with a series of transcendental arguments that, if they succeeded, would close up the gaps between man and his doubles at least enough to establish a definitive frame within which the terms of rational or "plausible" debate could occur. He attributes the source of the transcendental model of argument he pursues less to Kant and more to a synthesis of themes from Husserl and Heidegger. He says:

> if we purge Husserl's formulation of the prospect of a "final foundation," where absolute apodicity would at last be won, if we concentrate merely on the gain for reason in coming to understand what is illusory in the modern epistemological project *and in articulating the insights about us* that flow from this, then the claim to have taken the modern project of reason a little farther . . . isn't so unbelievable. . . . [R]eflection in this direction . . . involves, first, conceiving reason differently as including . . . a new department, whose excellence consists in our *being able to articulate the background of our lives perspicuously.* (emphasis added)[12]

Taylor strives through a descendant of transcendental argument to provide a perspicuous framework for reflection as such. If these arguments do not establish the human essence in its full transparency, they can eventually rule out several other philosophies contending for acceptance in late-modern discourse.

Taylor makes an excellent case for showing how such arguments can challenge the credibility of the project of epistemology summarized earlier here. But he then implies that it can, first, be quite definitive in its rejection of that position; second, provide more fundamental "insight" into the essence of human being; and, third, show the Nietzschean construal of being to be arbitrary and fundamentally "implausible." I don't think Taylor has yet succeeded in these ventures. Even his initial construal of the Nietzschean stance of the "radicality of will" seems to me to underplay the role of *amor fati* in Nietzsche's thought, to ignore the nonhuman loci of "will to power" in Nietzsche's philosophy while concentrating misleadingly on its human sites, and to ignore the role that attentiveness to these multiple sites might play in limiting the scope and demands of "radical will" in post-Nietzschean philosophies. His construal of Nietzschean philosophy supports his critique of it, but the very selectivity of that construal protects the privilege of his own position.

In general, I share Foucault's doubt that any transcendental argument in the late-modern context will be able to foreclose the terms of onto-political contestation as severely as Taylor and others hope. At least none seems to have succeeded in doing so yet. In the context of man and his doubles,

> it is probably impossible to give empirical contents transcendental value, or to displace them in the direction of a constituent subjectivity without giving rise, at least silently, to an anthropology—that is, to a mode of thought in which the rightful limitations of acquired knowledge . . . are at the same time the concrete forms of existence, precisely as they are given in that same empirical knowledge.[13]

All these thinkers, though, share the view that a "lived ontology" infiltrates into thinking even before it is rendered conscious. They diverge only on the means and the degree to which it is possible and desirable to resolve the issue definitively between alternative ontologies. In siding with Foucault on this question—at least with the early Foucault as I read him—I am not claiming this stance to be demonstrated by bulletproof arguments—say, by a countertranscendental argument that disproves the conclusion Taylor seeks to establish. I only insist that no other set of arguments actually delivered (rather than promised for that near future perpetually receding into the next near future) has ruled it out as a viable position on the field of contestation.

Each scheme of interpretation in politics is invested with an onto-political dimension, but, heretofore and into that endless "near future" that stretches before us, no perspective has at its disposal a consensual, pastoral, or transcendental strategy capable of reducing competitors in this domain to a small set of friendly alternatives. This is the reading I support. Moreover, this is not a condition to be lamented. It provides food for thought, an occasion for rejoicing, and the launching pad for politics as the medium through which alternative perspectives create space for each other to be through the terms of their contestation.

The Onto-political Matrix

If every interpretation is invested with fundamental presumptions, do the contemporary alternatives constitute a random set or is there a discernible pattern among them? I want to suggest that there is a pattern, though the perspective from which it is delineated and appraised is itself contestable. Let us call it the onto-political matrix of late-modern discourse, using the term "matrix" to indicate that the most visible interpretations in theoretical discourse of the Anglo-American world fit into its frame and that there is a discernible pattern of interaction among them, but *not* to mean that no other positions do or could push against its boundaries or call its conflicts and complementarities into question.

On this matrix, the categories across the horizontal axis are those of mastery and attunement, where mastery refers to the drive to subject nature to human control and to the susceptibility of nature in the last instance to this ambition and attunement refers to a strategy by which members in a society become more closely oriented to a higher direction in being and to a more harmonious life potentially available to them. The categories across the vertical axis are the individual and the collectivity, where individual refers to the primacy of the individual in identity, action, knowledge, and freedom and collectivity refer to the primacy of one social unit such as the community or the state in these respects. The matrix that emerges contains the following ideal types with a few representative figures shuffled (or forced) into the appropriate slots. It looks something like this:

It is easy to identify disputes and divergencies among these positions and to define the debates that prevail when this matrix defines the dominant field of discourse. Consider a few familiar questions. Is freedom to be attained through mastery of nature or through attunement to a higher harmony in being? Is it positive or negative? Is the crucial medium of freedom the individual or the collectivity? Do individuals constitute the collectivity, or does the form of the collectivity enter into the very constitution of the self? Is legitimacy grounded in the consent of the distinct individual or in the formation of an order that lifts its members to a higher level of being and freedom? Is the state best construed to be neutral between competing conceptions of the good life or mobilized around the intrinsic standard of the good? Is rationality instrumental or substantive? Does it emerge from the aggregation of individual calculations or from a discourse in which all are altered and elevated? Is knowledge to be gained through representation or through a depth hermeneutic? Does the preeminent danger in the late-modern age flow from a failure to strip away traditional restraints on reason and

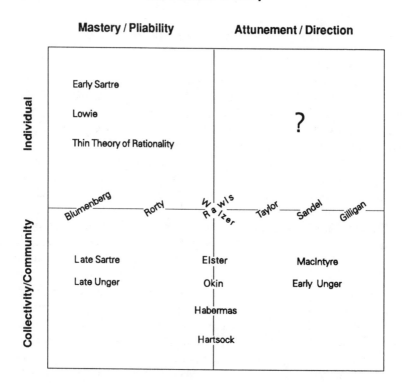

mastery or from a refusal to constrain these modalities through communion with the bent of being itself? Et cetera.

Whenever a thinker finds reason to question one of these positions, he is drawn as if by a magnet toward one of the others already waiting to receive him. Whenever a thinker finds reason to qualify her position by new considerations, she is moved as if through an internal dialogue to draw one or more of the alternatives on the matrix into the higher compromise she constructs. Taking a cue from Heidegger, who says:

> certainly the modern age has, as a consequence of the liberation of man, introduced subjectivism and individualism. But it remains just as certain that no age has produced a comparable objectivism and that in no age before this has the non-individual, in the form of the collective, come to acceptance as having worth,[14]

we might ask, What demands and assumptions bind these disparate positions together into a checkerboard of mutually defined alternatives? Of course any such delineation will itself presuppose a social ontology, but here I will allow the formulation of that alternative to emerge through a delineation and critique of affinities and complementarities among these competitors.

1. They share a demand to compensate the modern loss of the old expressivist/enchanted understandings of the world. *Each insists that the world must be predisposed to us in the last instance,* either by containing a higher direction and harmony with which we can enter into communion or by being a plastic medium susceptible to human mastery when organized in the right way. If it does not provide the first compensation, then it *must* provide the second. So we witness theorists such as Roberto Unger shifting from the attunement version of communalism to the mastery version of collectivism on this checkerboard while holding constant the underlying demand for a world amenable to consummate freedom, either through communion or mastery. A similar movement along the vertical axis is detectable in Sartre as he moves from an early stance of individual self-creation to a later one of collective self-creation.

The insistence on ontological compensation within each perspective can be discerned through its orientation to the human body. In the mastery perspective, for instance, where does the body stand in relation to human agency and nature? With nature or with agency? In most presentations this issue is simply bypassed because anything said either way would compromise either the conception of agency or the conception of nature. In attunement perspectives, on the other hand, the self is generally said to be "essentially embodied," meaning that an inner *telos* in the self is wrapped in the body or "embodied." The *telos* of the body is presented through the rhetorical structure of texts which celebrate it. But, then, those countertexts that disturb and unsettle these rhetorical configurations are treated as insults to the delicate quest for equilibrium. It is as if the rhetoric of embodiment is already known to be true and humane while those that seek to disturb and politicize established patterns of embodiment are already known to be false. As seen from a perspective endorsing neither the mastery view of agency nor the attunement view of embodiment, these two perspectives seem to secure themselves through tactics of silence, either about the place of the body in the duality agent/nature or about those presentations of post-Nietzschean thought that put pressure on embodiment as the last outpost of onto-teleology.

As Nietzsche would ask, from whence does one get the right to issue these "musts"? Who or what says the world owes us this much, so that it must either be predisposed to mastery or to attunement to putative harmonies? Do these two orientations not flow from a demand for existential reassurance, and might not this point of commonality between these competitors contain dangers within it worthy of reflection?

2. Seen from a perspective external to both, *each provides legitimation for the extension of disciplinary society complementing that provided by the other*, either through the organization of the individual and/or collectivity to achieve mastery over the world or through the organization of the individual and/or community to achieve fictive communion with a higher harmony in being. In each case, the mode of organization endorsed is not energetically subjected to self-problematization (i.e., its proponents do not try to flag ways in which their narrative/rhetorical textualizations insinuate the perspective for which they argue). This is partly because each position finds it necessary to defend itself only against other positions on the same board. Each tends to construe its ultimate standards to be *simply* natural, rational, established by common sense or a series of binding transcendental arguments about to be perfected or a social consensus or set of "shared understandings" that somehow escapes the need for critical exploration.

3. While some endorse a robust model of politics for the present, *all tend to converge in projecting a regulative ideal of society in which political minimalism prevails.* Some do so through treating individual freedom as a private space outside the clash of politics; others through treating freedom primarily as achievement of rational consensus, communal realization, or conventional collaboration. There is too little emphasis, within this matrix, on the need to maintain contending positions in a relation of agonistic interaction within the same time and place, to do so because no unified model of the world is likely to marshall sufficient resources of truth to establish the certainty of its singular superiority and because an ethic of respect for self-identity and care for difference can best promote this dual purpose through support for the institutionalization of *democratic agonism.* There is too little theoretical attention, within this matrix, to the institutionalization of political engagement as a systemic way to establish social space for a variety of possibilities of being that differ from idealized demands of consensus or fixed standards of the normal individual. Some who do celebrate such a politics for the present still yearn for

an ideal world in which its necessity is curtailed through rational consensus. Others who do introduce a measure of political pluralism into their understandings of actuality tend to treat the normal individual or shared understandings as if they stand outside the scope of this political network of interests and principles;[15] still others who concede the contingent, contestable character of the contemporary political consensus seek to protect its sanctity by relegating exploratory, corrosive modes of thought to the private sphere of life.

4. There is a gravitational pull within this matrix *to domesticate the experience of contingency in life*, either by treating contingency as a type of event susceptible to control because it does not flow from logical necessity or the essence of being or by detecting a higher purpose immanent in things that will, once we acknowledge it, stem the flow of contingency in life. But the experience of contingency exceeds these theorizations of it. Together these positions domesticate contingency as the unexpected, the dangerous or threatening event, the obdurate complex of interactions that resist effective intervention, the inevitable outcome accidental only in the timing of its occurrence, the accidental event that, once it erupts, unleashes cataclysmic consequences for regions of the earth or the entire planet, and the new sets of possibilities, enabling or disabling, engendered by existing patterns of interaction but not readily mastered by them. Each of these positions, though in ways that differentiate it from the others, domesticates the experience of contingency through its ontological presumption of world pliability or world directionality.

While one of these orientations appeals to a future of greater organizational scale and another secretes nostalgia for an alleged past of smaller scale and communion, the terms of debate between them tend to deflect attention away from the most distinctive and salient feature of the late-modern time: the globalization of contingency.

The globalization of contingency refers to a perverse correlation between the ability of dominant states to master contingency in their internal environments and the production of dangerous global possibilities that outstrip the capacity of any single state to control them. These new possibilities include: the creation of a global greenhouse effect or other climactic/environmental changes that fundamentally damage the earth as a shelter for human life, such as worldwide soil erosion, contamination of water supplies; crises in the supply of essential economic resources located in foreign lands through crisis or decay in the supplying regimes; the escalation of state and nonstate terrorism into a condition of continuous insecurity pouring over and under the barriers of state boundaries; the production of an international economic crisis within a world economy of extensive interdependence; a nuclear exchange that decimates regions of the world or destroys civilization; et cetera.

It might seem that the rise of attunement/communion theories was engendered by exactly this set of possibilities and that here they provide the best set of correctives to the mastery problematic. After all, aren't both deep ecology and the ideal of the stable state economy linked in recent history to this perspective? Have they not emerged as responses to the globalization of contingency? As one who once flirted with a modest version of this position, I have some appreciation for this reading. But it now seems to me that two considerations cut against it.

First, the existing terms of debate between the mastery and communion perspectives have been elaborated largely within parameters of debate over the priority of the individual, the small-scale community, and the sovereign state. Thinkers on each side of the horizontal axis can be found populating each of the positions on the vertical axis. But the globalization of contingency exceeds the parameters of the vertical axis. What is demanded politically, today or tomorrow, may be regional combinations of activists organized across state lines, mobilized around specific issues of global significance, pressing states from inside and outside simultaneously to reconfigure established convictions, priorities, and policies. Such regional constellations require participants whose final loyalty is not to the sovereign state, the identity of the normal individual, nor the small-scale community; for they must disturb and challenge, through publicity, exposés, boycotts, and alliances with beleagured states and nonstate peoples, a variety of presumptions, priorities, and loyalties in each of these other domains. These combinations of political effectivity aspire to be dissident representatives of a distinctive global time rather than a sovereign place, contesting and compromising established idealizations of abstract individuals in a state, organic members of a community, elite organizers of a class, or intellectual conveyers of timeless truths suspended above historical time. The vertical boundaries of the matrix—with respect to the locus of allegiances and loyalties, sites of political effectivity, temporal perspective, and organizational design—today deflect reflective activism in response to the globalization of contingency.[16]

Second, the terms of debate on the horizontal axis are today inclined steeply in favor of the mastery position. This is because, to state the point briefly, the modern age defines its identity to a significant degree in contrast to an earlier legacy of onto-teleologial perspectives and because the communion perspective has been unable to inspire confidence in the possibility and import of communion in modern life. Its proponents are often effective in conveying what modernity has lost, less so in showing how it could be recovered today or why we should want to do so. The experience of modern life—in work, business, military life, and education—is more conducive to belief in the responsiveness of the world to human organization than to a higher harmony in being with which entire societies can commune. *If* attunement was the only alternative, the mastery problematic would win by default, as Hans Blumenberg indeed argues it does.

So concern for the environment, the integrity of life, and the self-limitation of states articulated solely within the confines of the attunement orientation persistently functions to reinstate the primacy of the mastery problematic. Attunement becomes a mood of "nostalgia." The mastery problematic becomes installed in practice, first as dream, then as common sense, eventually as intractable fate.

Perhaps introduction of a position that challenges both the mastery design and attunement dissent is promising today. It would challenge operative assumptions of nature (things, ecosystems, bodies, desires) as a plastic substratum; it would accentuate the experience of disturbance, contingency, and undefinability built into relations within the self, between the self and the order, between established identities and the otherness they produce, and between the order and the resistances it breeds. It would *radicalize* the experience of contingency in the formation and maintenance of identities and things; it would thus challenge the mastery problematic by accentuating the dimension within it (the denial of a *telos* in nature), which has heretofore given it tactical advantages over its favorite debating partner. It would call upon hegemonic states to redefine their institutional priorities of consumption (for instance) so that their "vital interests" no longer place them on a collision course with so many other areas of the world; it would press them to reconstitute their interests so they can coexist over a long period of time with others on the same globe. It would also, then, oppose the hegemony of the growth imperative and counter legitimations of disciplinary society attached to this imperative, all in the name of a more radical interpretation of the contingency of things and in response to the globalization of contingency fostered and intensified by the priorities and demands of hegemonic states.

5. *Contenders within this matrix are predisposed to converge upon a
    set of disparaging readings of perspectives challenging their shared*

terms of debate. The disparagement is applied to "post-Nietzschean" theories—especially those on the Left side of a matrix yet to be consolidated—whose most renowned contemporary exponents are Jacques Derrida and Michel Foucault. Since matrix-debating partners tend to converge in their dismissive readings, and since they are in close communication with each other through the institutionalization of publications, meetings, conferences, rumor mills, and so on, they conclude, understandably enough, that together they have gotten these guys right and, moreover, that it suffices to expose their ethical nihilism, relativism, anarchism, or, alternatively, their relentless programs of power, domination, thorough mastery over the earth, and unqualified assertion of the self.

Very few interpretations of post-Nietzschean thought flowing out of this matrix construe it as an alternative perspective through which to reconsider the terms of interaction within the matrix or to pose a new challenge to the dominant partner within it. Attunement types slide over this reading because they presume that any position which challenges the mastery perspective must automatically move to the stance they have already perfected, and mastery types miss it because they too recognize the case for self-limitation of mastery only within the terms of an attunement perspective they find to be defunct.

So one encounters readings of Nietzsche as a proponent of "will to power" who would master the earth or as purveyor of "radical will" who would resist every form of self-limitation. And he is said to oppose rationality as such because he resists the transcendentalizations, teleological presumptions, and arguments by historical elimination contending for primacy in debates between regimes of thought on the matrix.

I do not deny that such readings *can* be given of protean texts signed by the name Nietzsche. For every reading draws upon projective predispositions flowing from the reader as well as porous possibilities running through the text. Those readers who allow the established matrix to exhaust the range of possible positions are likely to pose questions and project responses that conform to the readings already received from Habermas, Taylor, Walzer, Rorty, McCarthy, Fraser, and others.[17] Nor do I claim that the reading I advance constitutes the one true reading constructible from these texts. I only insist that the first set of readings is neither necessary nor exclusive *and that other possibilities reside in these texts capable of stretching the established boundaries of the matrix itself.* The hegemonic readings provide too much self-reassurance to those roaming the highways and byways of this matrix. That's all I claim.

There are many issues to be raised in this context. We must remain content here to pose only one. Many intramatrix critics of Nietzsche and post-Nietzschean thought proceed as though terrible things will happen, such as the disappearance of a basis for ethics, or the emergence of relativism or the breakdown of modern discipline, unless strategies are devised to transcend or contain the modern condition of man and his doubles. But both Nietzsche and Foucault, as I read them, think that established regimes of life already contain numerous and powerful pressures to maintain themselves, even when they generate dangerous contingencies and even if they are not the beneficiaries of transcendental legitimations. The *initial* need today (and probably in most times) is to detach identities to a greater degree from the fixed set of alternatives in which they tend to move, to excite the experience of discrepancy within established dualities of normality/abnormality, rationality/irrationality, and good/evil, sovereignty/anarchy so that alternative experiences of danger and possiblity might be cultivated.

The post-Nietzschean wager (or operative faith) is that an ethical orientation to life does not depend upon the demand to lock reverence for life into some common theistic faith, consensual tradition, transcendental argument, or interior attunement to a deep identity. It construes these to be diverse theories of an intrinsic moral order, where "order" oscillates between its use as a verb of command and a noun of harmonious design. From my Nietzschean perspective every concept of a moral order first expresses *ressentiment* against the absence of a moral foundation in being and then intensifies it through the way in which it enforces the orders it receives or conforms to the harmonious design it discerns. These strategies either place a second seal upon historically specific identities and priorities already sealed very well indeed or they pretend that a critical perspective that challenges them can motivate conduct and offer directionality only if it too is established through one of these routes. The post-Nietzschean pursues an alternative strategy of ethical cultivation, striving to tap into the care for rich ambiguity of life that, hopefully, already flows through and below the conventional identities installed upon us. In one crucial respect the post-Nietzschean is closer to the teleological tradition than to the Kantian. With the former it shares an ethic of cultivation rather than one flowing from a categorical command, but the concerns and ends it seeks to cultivate differ from those of the teleologist because it defines the pertinent issues within a social ontology that contests this presumption of natural harmony. That is why the teleologist has so much difficulty identifying the subterranean point of similarity between herself and the post-Nietzschean amid the more visible point of differentiation.[18]

The alternative perspective draws part of its sustenance from an always-already-operative attachment to life as a protean set of possibilities and energies exceeding the terms of any identity into which it is set. It then strives to thaw perspectives frozen within a particular way of life, to offer alternative accounts of threats to difference created by the dogmatism of established identities, and to advance different accounts of dangers and possibilities crowded out by established regimes of thought. It cannot prove its case by rising above the level of reason achieved by its opponents; it makes it through detailed engagement with assumptions and priorities insinuated into their interpretations as a matter of course. It cannot command the motivation to pursue its priorities through reference to transcendental command or authority, only tap into counterexperiences and latent dispositions through situationally specific assessments of possibilities, dangers, and pertinent modes of response. Of course its own presuppositions acquire the momentary status of quasi-transcendentals, but it then seeks to problematize them too, acknowledging that its best efforts to state its own presuppositions perpetually fall short of the mark and that the ones it does celebrate are contestable responses to persistent mysteries of existence. And then it strives to fold this appreciation of ambiguity and contestability into the tone of social relationships it supports and to inspire a similar response in its adversaries. When Nietzsche, for example, speaks of the "spiritualization of enmity," I take him to commend a mode of active contestation among friends, lovers, and adversaries that maintains respect and self-limitation between them through their mutual appreciation of the problematical bases from which they converge and diverge. My post-Nietzscheanism thus pushes the spirit of liberalism into domains many liberals have not yet acknowledged to be contestable; it supports a politics of agonistic respect that exceeds liberal presentations of privacy, state neutrality, and justice as fairness.

If the post-Nietzschean fails to tap the care she seeks to invest in those endlessly ambiguous relations of identity/difference that pervade sociopolitical life, she might try again; or she might reconsider her specific interpretation of what is happening by comparison to other alternatives; or she might conclude that the dispositions needed to confront perceived cruelties and dangers are not forthcoming in time. Who or what provides the assurance, anyway, that things must come together in this way, that there is commensurability in principle between a thoughtful encounter with issues and resources of argumentation sufficient to settle them, between a contestable appeal to motivation and a commensurate pool of responsiveness waiting to be tapped, between the transcendental argumentation required to seal a need and the resources of argumentation sufficient to provide it? From whence comes these musts? Even if any discourse provisionally presupposes them, from whence comes the command to endorse them the next moment as necessarily true? Is it not, indeed, possible to be more ambiguous and self-ironic in these domains of reflection? And are these modes of self-presentation not themselves among the pivotal ways in which the ethicality of care for the strife and interdependence of identity/difference finds expression?

The operative faith in a post-Nietzschean problematic, its generally cheerful pessimism, is that combinations available to it may spur some of the interventions it seeks. Its corollary charge is that insistence upon the need to fix a common theistic faith, discover a deep identity, or perfect a specific set of transcendental arguments prior to ethically informed action fosters either passive nihilism—an inaction born of despair because the world does not provide the resources of argumentation the nihilist demands to justify action—or aggressive nihilism—a repression of those difficulties and gaps that would jeopardize attainment of the transcendental position were they to be acknowledged.

I cheerfully concede that this counterconstrual of the texts in question is a contestable construction in need of further elaboration and defense. Anyway, even this reading involves me in a relation of antagonistic indebtedness to Nietzsche, indebted to the fundamental problematic from which to challenge the matrix and antagonistic to particular readings of democracy, equality, and so on developed by the author named Nietzsche. Having attempted elsewhere to develop some of the terms of this antagonistic indebtedness,[19] I merely want to suggest here that it provides an appropriate terrain for exploration, both by those who would challenge established regimes of debate and by those who would protect their sanctity.

I began point 5 by claiming that most participants on the matrix converge upon a contestable, dismissive construal of Nietzsche and post-Nietzscheans. To give preliminary plausibility to the counterreading endorsed here, I will close this section with two quotations from Nietzsche, the first referring to one of the numerous pressures he identifies to fix and dogmatize established identities and the second expressing a reverence for the ambiguity of existence that slips between the terms of debate dividing onto-theological devotion from secular instrumentalism.

> To hear something new is painful and difficult for the ear; we hear new music poorly. When we hear a foreign language we try unconsciously to reform the

sounds into words that sound more familiar and homelike. . . . Everything new finds even our senses hostile and unwilling, and more than unwilling.[20]

This does not sound to me like a thinker who espouses "radical will," who thinks that the self can create itself out of whole cloth as it sees fit, who anticipates a species of humanity without regularity, even who thinks that we are the kind of creatures who could successfully master the world or that the world is the kind of place where success in this project is likely (though there is much more to be said in both directions on this last point). Nor does such an interpretation square with my own reading of Nietzsche's ideal of life as a work of art, since this artwork is constrained to work within limits set by the many contingencies already branded into the self. It works modest adjustments into the life of a being already shaped fundamentally by a first and "second" nature beyond its remaking. The reading of Nietzsche as theorist of radical will is cast into further doubt upon pondering his presentations of the inertia of language, the drive to regular identity, the social demands of coordination and order, the voice of *ressentiment* in the self that is never completely eliminated.

Partial detachment from established modes of realization, insistence, and closure is the first and most difficult task set within a post-Nietzschean problematic. This is the route through which care for the strife and interdependence of identity/difference can be cultivated. It is hardly likely to be achieved completely. That is one of the reasons why current insufficiencies in transcendental strategies worry post-Nietzscheans less than they do others. We would be more worried if a time arrived when such a strategy of closure was generally said to have succeeded.

It may be that many who read Nietzsche through the goggles of the matrix think that either the self is grounded in a deep identity or it creates itself in Sartrian fashion. Since they know that Nietzsche opposed the former, they project into him endorsement of the latter; they then criticize this projection as if it were his rather than theirs.

Consider, then, my second and last specimen:

> Why atheism today? The "father" in God is thoroughly refuted, likewise the "judge" and the "rewarder." Also his "free will" . . . It seems to me that the religious instinct is growing powerfully but is rejecting theistic gratification with deep distrust.[21]

Nietzsche's invocation of nontheistic reverence—a theme traversing *Beyond Good and Evil* and *Thus Spoke Zarathustra*—through a challenge to the authority of theism is underappreciated by American critics who write within the terms of the matrix. Its invocation, assuming the form of a cultivation, recalls and counters recurrent attempts by modern theists to devise transcendental arguments to supplement theistic authority (the father, the judge, the rewarder) compromised by the advance of secularism. It then slips into that (nearly) vacant space between modern theistic devotion and secular instrumentalism.

Strategies of Detachment

It is still asserted (though perhaps now less often) by American critics of Foucault as a post-Nietzschean that no ethic "can" flow from his work. It lacks the transcendental basis for a categorical imperative or pastoral attunement to a harmonious direction in being from which an ethic must be derived. But perhaps the foregoing critique of the matrix and its selective reading of the Nietzschean problematic will relieve the surprise in Foucault's own linkage between the pursuit of detachment and care for life. As when he says,

> ... I like the word [curiosity]. It evokes "care"; it evokes the care one takes of what exists and might exist; a sharpened sense of reality, but one that is never immobilized before it; a readiness to find what surrounds us strange and odd; a certain determination to throw off familiar ways of thought and to look at the same things in a different way ....; a lack of respect for the traditional hierarchies of what is important and fundamental.[22]

Among the strategies for cultivation of care through detachment and the cultivation of detachment through care, two have stood out in recent decades: the tactics of deconstruction and genealogy. Both seem to me to be indispensable; both also seem to need a particular kind of supplementation.

Genealogy is an attempt to delineate the constructed character of established unities of self, morality, convention, rationality, and so on by tracing them back to discrete, particular, contingent elements from which they were constructed. It opens up possibilities residing in the present by radical historicization of actuality. It thus proceeds in the service of a certain disposition to freedom.

But, first, Foucault sometimes acts as if genealogy does and can proceed not only by bracketing ontological assumptions in established perspectives but without invoking any alternative onto-assumptions of its own. The latter suggestion seems highly unlikely to me. Second, the genealogical enterprise, as advanced by Foucault until he began to revise this dimension of it late in his career, constitutes a refusal to affirm any specific directions or reforms of its own. That self-restriction can be understood as an attempt to avoid reimplication in the matrix it seeks to disturb, but it also limits the potential effectivity of these challenges. Genealogy, I want to suggest, is necessary but inadequate to a mode of reflection that seeks to detach itself to some degree from the onto-political matrix while responding to dangers and possibilities it contains when seen from the perspective of another possibility. One of the reasons this is so is that detachment from any particular set of presumptions seems inevitably to implicate one in another set of presumptions. It is hard, indeed impossible, to become simply detached as such.

Foucault has often been accused of denying the extent to which he presupposes those conceptions of subjectivity, truth, responsibility, and rationality he wishes to ambiguate. Again, this seems an unlikely charge to press against a thinker who helped to inaugurate contemporary reflection into the aporias of "man and his doubles." But it still may have some salience to certain stages of his thought. Fairly early—in 1973—he showed a little more confidence in the ability to reduce transcendental presumptions to a bare minimum, though he did not claim to be able to eliminate them altogether:

> I strive to avoid any reference to this transcendental as a condition of possibility for any knowledge. When I say that I strive to avoid it, I don't mean that I am sure of succeeding. . . . I try to historicize to the utmost to leave as little space as possible for the transcendental. I cannot exclude the possibility that one day I will have to confront an irreducible residuum which will be, in fact, the transcendental.[23]

Later on he appears less confident about the prospect of reducing the transcendental to a residuum and more definite about the need for self-irony here, saying "there is no way you can say there is no truth."[24]

But deconstruction is a strategy of disturbance that pursues the ambiguity of rationality most strenuously, always striving to identify sites of rational undecidability inside perspectives that close up reflection in the name of reason, always acknowledging its unavoidable implication in the practices of rationality it seeks to stretch or disturb. But I suspect that deconstruction, too, is both indispensable and insufficient to a reflective challenge of the ontological matrix. It provides crucial, specific reminders of how limited and ambiguous experiments with detachment are likely to be, challenging the purity of any counterposition that pretends to transcend cleanly the politics of normalization and transcendentalization. But it, too, refuses to pursue the trail of affirmative interpretation very far, perhaps out of a desire to minimize its implication in ontological assumptions it could never vindicate without drawing upon some of the same media it has just ambiguated. While dependent upon these two strategies of detachment, I also pursue another strategy that stands in a precarious relation of dissonance and implication with them. Let me call it projectional interpretation. Such a practice characterizes aspects of Foucault's *Discipline and Punish* and volume 1 of *History of Sexuality*. It also seems to me to govern the operational practice of a growing group of American academics.

This mode of interpretation proceeds by projecting ontological presumptions explicitly into detailed interpretations of actuality, acknowledging that its implicit projections surely exceed its explicit formulation of them and that its explicit formulation—constructed relative to other identifiable positions—always exceeds its current capacity to demonstrate its truth. It challenges closure in the matrix, first, by affirming the contestable character of its own projections, second, by offering readings of particular features of contemporary life that compete with detailed accounts offered by others, and, third, by moving back and forth between these two levels as it introduces alternative interpretations onto the established field of discourse.

Let the summary offered earlier in this essay serve as an initial specification of projections endorsed here. By introducing such projections, one is able to offer affirmative interpretations; by introducing them as contestable, one may be able to jostle the sense of closure and necessity governing competition between interpretations within the matrix; by introducing a historical dimension into onto-political debates one may confront difficulties and aporias in one's own formulations and intensify experience of gaps between the indispensability of social ontology and limitations in the resources by which a particular one is secured; by identifying a distinctive set of dangers and possibilities through projective interpretation, one may destabilize the established terms of debate in this domain; by offering alternative proposals for reconstitution of lived identities, one may contribute to the politicization of established assumptions and identities. One interprets actively, specifically, and comparatively without praying for the day (or delaying until the time) when the indispensability of interpretation will be matched by the certainty of a particular one.

How does this politicization proceed? We have already seen how the established matrix of discourse fogs over a set of complementary presumptions about nature, bodies, contingency, sovereignty, identity, and politics. When an alien competitor challenges these terms of discourse, the resulting debate condenses some of this fog into a series of beliefs and counterbeliefs.

Of course, only one layer of fog is lifted by this intervention, and new ones move in. For these new beliefs are articulated and specified only relative to the new terms of discourse. But they have now become beliefs (and disbeliefs) nonetheless, susceptible to explicit interrogation, debate, testing, and comparative criticism from a variety of perspectives.

But it is reasonable to ask, What makes the particular alternative advanced here the appropriate one to place on the agenda of debate at this time? Why try to lift this layer of fog rather than numerous others that still persist? I do not have a comprehensive answer to this question. Indeed, that may be one of the issues doomed to remain shrouded in fog indefinitely. Of course, part of the answer flows from the internal difficulties previous traditions of discourse have accumulated over the last several centuries. Histories of "social ontology" advanced by Heidegger, Blumenberg, Foucault, and Derrida are pitched at the appropriate level to review these difficulties and to gain some sense of how this contemporary alternative has begun to solidify itself. But such histories never suffice to determine how new alternatives have emerged to challenge established perspectives (they do not show sufficiently why, say, nominalism actually emerged as the most salient philosophical response in the fourteenth century to the difficulties of Thomism). Western history (and doubtless others too) is replete with times when a set of culturally indispensable ideas remained intact even though they were full of identifiable mysteries and paradoxes. Augustinianism represents only one example of this phenomenon, an important one, perhaps, in that it showed how the experience of paradoxes and mysteries could be converted into a resource in support of the faith generating them.

One source of pressure today for the alternative sketched here resides in ruptures in the contemporary experience of state sovereignty, global ecology, the internationalization of market relations, and the changed circumstances through which the individual confronts traditional definitions of itself as a responsible agent, a citizen of a particular state, a member of a democratic society, and a participant in a distinctive, interlocked global time. These experiences provide spurs to the recent problematizations of subjectivity, sovereignty, territorial democracy, and transcendental imperatives through the codes of paradox, ambiguity, *différance*, doubles, untruth, life, and nontheistic reverence congenial to post-Nietzschean thought. But such experiences do not suffice to determine the shape of these particular interventions.

The most persistent issue facing projectional interpretation resides in its ironic relation to the projections it refines into specific interpretations. It must recurrently convert this paradoxical condition (this incoherence, this self-referential contradiction, this presupposition of a standard of truth it calls into question, etc.) into new spurs to productive thinking. For it does not expect to eliminate this condition/limit of reflection. The sense that this is so constitutes *its* reverence and spur simultaneously.

It might initially pretend to know, for instance, that being itself lacks a definite *telos*, that the pool of life both requires and exceeds the formation of any specific set of identities, that care for the strife and interdependence of identity/difference can be cultivated through treating life as more fundamental than identity. But these pretenses are to be problematized in subsequent gestures as it acknowledges that the experiences it cultivates of contingency in identity, the production of otherness through the dogmatism of identity, and the globalization of contingency through the hegemony of mastery flow from an interpretation that can compete with alternatives through its critiques of their presumptions and through its own counterportrayals; but it cannot promise to secure the necessity of those experiences through transcendental argument, argument by historical elimination, or privileged communion with being.

In the near future perpetually stretching before us, the indispensability and contestability of fundamental presumptions hover over the interpretation of lived experience: the irony of interpretation; the joyful ambiguity of "man" and his doubles; the indispensabilty and contestability of onto-political interpretation. It always remains pertinent to disturb the unconscious presumption that a settled scheme of interpretation signifies a more fundamental order of human being; and one of the best ways to crack this code is to experiment with new interpretations that challenge the established matrix of political reflection.

In testing and consolidating itself, projectional interpretation draws upon the resources of genealogy and deconstruction to expose gaps between its own pretenses and the solidity of its achievements, even though it takes less pleasure in acknowledging them than it does in identifying them in its competitors. It treats alternative positions—represented all too crudely in this essay by a series of names on a matrix—as competing bearers of projectional interpretation; asking how these terms of engagement fare once the aura of necessity, exhaustibility, cultural consensus, or transcendental assurance accompanying the self-presentations of some of its competitors is attenuated; asking how it fares comparatively once it has relieved itself of the obligation to achieve a purity no other theory has attained, and once it has moved the terms of discourse, however modestly, by introducing another competitor onto the field of debate.

NOTES

1. This theme is most reflectively developed in Hans Blumenberg, *The Legitimacy of the Modern Age* (Cambridge, MA: MIT Press, 1983).
2. John Rawls, "Justice as Fairness: Political Not Metaphysical," *Philosophy and Public Affairs* (Summer, 1985). Richard Rorty, *Contingency, Irony and Solidarity* (Cambridge: Cambridge University Press, 1989). See also my review of Rorty in *The History of the Human Sciences* (February, 1990), pp. 104-108.
3. Martin Heidegger, "The Essence of Truth," in *Heidegger: Basic Writings*, ed. David F. Krell (New York: Harper and Row, 1977). For an "Anglo-American" essay that moves in the same direction, see Ian Hacking, "Language, Truth and Reason," in *Rationality and Relativism*, ed. Martin Hollis and Steven Lukes (Cambridge, MA: MIT Press, 1982), pp. 48-66.
4. Charles Taylor, "Overcoming Epistemology," *After Philosophy*, ed. Kenneth Baynes, James Bohman and Thomas McCarthy (Cambridge, MA: MIT Press, 1987), pp. 464-488. Taylor provides a persuasive account of how the primacy of epistemology supports a model of self and freedom attractive to moderns and how these attractions in turn help to sustain the primacy of epistemology.
5. Michael Shapiro, in *The Politics of Representation* (Madison: University of Wisconsin Press, 1988), examines how the rhetorical structure of Wilson's text secures the fundamental pattern of identity and responsibility it endorses and then distributes responsibility among its bearers.
6. Roberto Unger, *Social Theory: A Critical Introduction to Politics, a Work in Constructive Social Theory* (Cambridge: Cambridge University Press, 1987). See also the review of Unger, "Making the Friendly World Behave," by William E. Connolly, *New York Times Sunday Book Review*, February 19, 1988.
7. Jon Elster, *Sour Grapes* (Cambridge: Cambridge University Press, 1983), p. 1.
8. Michel Foucault, *The Order of Things* (London: Tavistock Publications, 1970), p. 211.
9. Ibid., p. 327.
10. Ibid., p. 341.
11. Ibid., p. 41.
12. Taylor, "Overcoming Epistemology," pp. 480-81.
13. Foucault, *Order of Things*, p. 248.
14. Heidegger, "The Age of the World Picture," in Heidegger, *The Question Concerning Technology* (New York: Harper and Row, 1977), pp. 127-128.

15. I differentiate between the theory of the normal individual and the theory of individuality, with the latter not falling prey to these strictures. See my *Identity\Difference: Democratic Negotiations of Political Paradox* (Ithaca, NY: Cornell University Press, 1991). Michael Walzer treats "shared understandings" as the ground of his political ethic in *Spheres of Justice* (New York: Basic Books, 1983). For a critique of this base along with a more general critique of the insistence upon treating the boundaries of the territorial state as a boundary of the democratic ethos, see Connolly, "Democracy and Territoriality," in *Millenium: Journal of International Studies*, Vol. 20, No. 3 (Winter 1991), pp. 463-484.

16. See, for example, Jürgen Habermas, *Philosophical Discourse of Modernity*, trans. Frederick Lawrence (Cambridge: MIT Press, 1987), chaps. 4, 9, 10; Charles Taylor, "Foucault on Freedom, and Truth," *Political Theory* (May 1984); Thomas McCarthy, "Introduction" to Jürgen Habermas, *Philosophical Discourse of Modernity*, trans. Fredrick Lawrence (Cambridge, MA: MIT Press, 1987), pp. vii-xvii and Review of William E. Connolly, *Politics and Ambiguity*, *Political Theory* (May 1988), pp. 339-346; Richard Rorty, "Method, Social Science and Hope," in *The Consequences of Pragmatism* (Minneapolis: University of Minnesota Press, 1982), pp. 191-210; and several of the essays collected in *Foucault: A Critical Reader*, ed. David C. Hoy (Oxford: Basil Blackwell, 1986).

17. The vissicitudes of publication schedules do not correspond to the rhythms of production schedules. This essay was written well before the last two chapters of *Identity/Difference* were drafted, and the latter develop more extensively themes introduced for the first time in the last section of this essay, particularly the discussion of political ethics, the conception of politics, and the drive to extraterritorialization of a democratic ethos as one way to curtail the tribalism of late-modern statecraft.

18. Charles Taylor, in *Sources of the Self: The Making of The Modern Identity* (Cambridge: Harvard University Press, 1989), admirably delineates different "moral sources" that have provided the bases from which moral discourse proceeds in Western history and to which it seeks to return. These "sources" do not assume the form of transcendental imperatives but rather exist initially as inchoate predispositions of care and concern which require cultivation and articulation. "Moral sources empower. To come closer to them, to have a clearer view of them, to come to grasp what they involve, is for those who recognize them to be moved to love or respect them, and through this love/respect to be better enabled to live up to them. And articulation can bring them closer. That is why words can empower; why words can at times have tremendous moral force" (96). Taylor then strives, though with some self-irony, to give this source a more teleological rendering than I would endorse. And this effort leads him to underplay the extent to which he is in alliance with post-Nietzschean thought along one dimension while being adamantly at odds with it along another. To put the point briefly, he shares a conception of ethical discourse with them (one that puts him and them at odds with those traditions that root ethics in one transcen-

dental command or another) but diverges in the social ontology through which the cultivation of ethics occurs. Because of the blatancy of the disagreement at the second level, he has a difficult time seeing the point of convergence at the first, and he repeatedly acts as if post-Nietzscheans must and do eschew ethical concern altogether. Interestingly enough, he comes closest to perceiving his moment of convergence with Nietzsche on this score, while missing it with Derrida and Foucault. It would be compatible with his text to think of "*différance*" and "life," et cetera, as ethical "sources" to be cultivated. But that would also concentrate more dramatically the ontological issues.

19. See *Political Theory and Modernity* (New York: Basil Blackwell, 1988), especially the last chapter.

20. Nietzsche, *Beyond Good and Evil*, trans. Marianne Cowan (South Bend, IN: Gateway Editions, 1955), #192, p. 100.

21. Ibid., p. 60.

22. *Foucault: Politics, Philosophy and Culture*, ed. Lawrence D. Kritzman (London: Routledge, Chapman and Hall, 1988), p. 328.

23. *Foucault Live*, trans. John Johnston, ed. Sylvere Lotringer (New York: Semiotexte, 1989), p. 79.

24. Foucault "Truth, Power, Self: An Interview with Michel Foucault," *Technologies of the Self*, ed. Luther H. Martin, Huck Gutman, and Patrick H. Hutton (Amherst: University Of Massachusetts Press, 1988), pp. 9-15.

7

Kundera, Coetzee, and the Politics of Anonymity

Jane Bennett

The Irony of Resistance

Remember, Razumov, that women, children, and revolutionists hate irony, which is the negation of all saving instincts, of all faith, of all devotion, of all action.

—Joseph Conrad, *Under Western Eyes*

Milan Kundera's *Unbearable Lightness of Being* tells of heroic Czechs who photographed the 1968 Soviet invasion and smuggled the film to the international press. Unable to stop the tanks, they sought to document the aggression so that it could not then be revised out of textbooks. Several years later one of these pictures was used to identify and convict a Czech who had resisted the Soviets in those first few days.[1] The photographs, it turned out, were ambidextrous documents, useful for the illegitimate regime as well as for the dissident. Heroism had served collaborationist ends; the photographers' intentions had been rendered secondary.

Kundera locates this dilemma in Prague, 1968. He has said that "of the historical circumstances, I keep only those that create a revelatory existential situation for my characters."[2] The gap between intentions and effects, an existential condition that Kundera calls "inexperience,"[3] is called forth by the circumstances of 1968-88 Czechoslovakia. But why? What is it about that context? The regime's totalitarianism? Surely. But the term is insufficiently precise. The photographer's sudden exposure to inexperience is, it seems to me, a possibility inscribed within extensively organized, technologically ambitious states, where the complexities of economic and occupational life thoroughly enmesh citizens with each other and within official projects. This infrastructural dependence makes it exceedingly difficult to stand, as Thoreau did at Walden, on the edge of the system of power one opposes; and regime fluency in mass communication renders each act of resistance a potential resource for official deployment. If this description holds, then the photographer's dilemma haunts a new, democratic Czechoslovakia as well as the United States.

The fact that human actions carry with them unintended consequences has been acknowledged for a very long time. But recently this awareness has again been given a central place in theoretical discourse. The emergence or reemergence of such terms as "indeterminacy," "contingency," "excess," "irony," "anti-essentialism," "ambiguity," and "tragedy" reflect in academic discourse a certain caution about claims formerly offered with confidence. In literary circles this discourse takes the form of questioning the hegemony of author over text and of intentions over words; in feminism, it appears as a search for forms of identity and empowerment that can be borne lightly and contingently rather than in the name of "woman" or "freedom"; and in political theory, one finds an uneasiness with models of power, individualism, dissent, political participation, and rights that presuppose a unified intentionality within a stable subjectivity.

This new skepticism has been seen as a mask for political apathy, an excuse for moral cowardice. For these critics, the dilemma of the Czech photographers is not prodigious for us but indigenous to them, its significance for the West magnified by the boredom or perversity or perhaps anti-Semitism of "postmodernists." If the skeptical turn is an act of self-indulgence or worse, and not acknowledgment of an existential possibility brought to the fore by political realities, then it is certainly avoidable and, moreover, ought to be avoided; for under those circumstances to focus on the ambidextrous nature of action is to foster quietism in the face of injustice.

The case for a link between the skeptical turn and political cowardice is strongest when dissent is conceived traditionally. Thoreau's civil disobedience can serve as our model here—dissent as an overt, conscience-driven rejection of an official practice. A continent, resolute, morally confident individual consistently identifiable to his fellows as such is a prerequisite for *this* dissent. A self attentive to the irony of resistance might, in contrast, pursue a certain anonymity, prefer tactics of evasion and obfuscation over those of repudiation and confrontation, and seek a loose or vague or superficial rather than a definitive, weighty, or substantial identity. The novels of J.M. Coetzee are hypothetical journeys into the terrain of wary identities. In *Foe* we meet a Robinson Crusoe rescued, restored to civilization, and yet stubbornly silent about this story; the young woman nomad in *Waiting for the Barbarians* never does reveal the truth of her self to the kindly and confessional colonist, and yet she repudiates none of his demands. Perhaps the most striking example of the quest for anonymity is the amorphous K in *The Life and Times of Michael K.* The story is set in a society organized into a comprehensive series of "camps," into officially circumscribed spaces designed to meet the pedagogical, occupational, medical, and security needs of a populace violently divided over questions of justice and freedom. K somehow exists amid all this organization without permit or pass or papers.

The photographer's dilemma—more generally, the problem of dissent in the face of existential inexperience—is illuminated by this novel. K's interior sensation of unity, of self-responsibility, willfulness, and predictability, is unusually mild. Is K a political actor? Can he be? Can his unreliable identifiability constitute a mode of dissent?

I proceed by drawing out two divergent interpretations of K, each a voice within the novel. The debate between them has close affinities with that between political theorists inspired by Foucault and those for whom the pursuit of a minimalized identity spells retreat from the public. By exploring the former interpretive debate, one is in a position to see more clearly what is at issue in the latter, more overtly political one. At the end of the essay I outline the political function of the "existential" novel and try to elucidate somewhat the conditions under which the skeptical turn might have its greatest politico-ethical effect.

The Story of K

K ought to have been the product of institutions. Born with a harelip, he is immediately "committed to the protection" of a school for special boys. He passes through the program to become Gardener, grade 1, Cape Peninsula police area. A dutiful son, K resigns to carry his ailing mother to her birthplace in far-off Prince Albert, but she dies en route. Living about her hospital until "he began to fear he was giving away too much," K returns to the national road but, lacking travel papers, is arrested and assigned to the railroad ("This isn't jail. This is just a labour gang."[4])

When K, still wearing a "St. John's Ambulance" cap from the hospital, is released, he wanders toward the veld, wondering whether there were "forgotten corners and angles and corridors between the fences."[5] He stumbles upon Prince Albert and an abandoned farm that approximates the one of his mother's memories. He stays ("this was the beginning of his life as a cultivator") and tastes the exhilaration of anonymity until a grandson of Visagie, the farm's owner, arrives and identifies K as "body-servant."

K flees to distant mountains, dwelling in a cave: "Now surely I have come as far as a man can come; . . . surely now that in all the world only I know where I am, I can think of myself as lost."[6] But sickness and hunger force him back to Prince Albert, where he is jailed, hospitalized, then encamped at Jakkalsdrif, for workers.

He is known as "Michael Visagie-CM-40-NFa-Unemployed," a malnutrition case, and a drifter. Although he is told "This isn't a prison . . . This is a camp . . . Why should people with nowhere to go run away from the nice life we've got here?"[7] K escapes and returns to the newly deserted farm. He builds a camouflaged dwelling, wakes only at night, and plants pumpkin seeds found in the shed. He lives an underground life—"What a pity that to live in times like these a man must be ready to live like a beast . . . A man must live so that he leaves no trace of his living"[8]—and cherishes his freedom as well as the hard earth from which spring his seedlings. Soon or perhaps later soldiers, "fighting this war . . . so that minorities will have a say in their destinies,"[9] discover K, deem him an insurgent, and send him to Kenilworth reeducation camp.

There "Michaels is an arsonist. He is also an escapee from a labor camp. He was running a flourishing garden on an abandoned farm and feeding the local guerilla population."[10] A medical officer takes an interest in K, first as "a simpleton, . . . a poor helpless soul," but then as a prophet, a man "chosen . . . to show . . . the way" out of the camps.

After a time a skeletal K slips through the fence (or pole-vaults), wearing overalls with the word "Treefeller," and finds his way back to the peninsula. There he receives unsolicited wine and sex. In return the strangers want him to "tell them the story of a life lived in cages . . . as if I were a budgie or a white mouse or a monkey . . . . Whereas the truth is that I have been a gardener . . . and gardeners spend their time with their noses to the ground."[11]

First Interpretation

Never mole, harelip, nor scar, nor mark prodigious shall upon their children be.

—Shakespeare, *A Midsummer-Night's Dream*

Of all the identifications of K—handicapped child, dutiful son, refugee, body-servant, vagrant, invalid, insurgent, simpleton, prophet—the last, offered by the medical officer, is the most interesting as well as the most fully developed.
The medical officer is responsible not simply for the physiological health of prisoners. He does lead them in a daily regime of exercises for the arms, legs, and feet (marching) and for the voice (shouting of slogans), but these precise bodily maneuvers are designed to rehabilitate the whole person of the prisoner. The medical officer is especially impressed with K's docility: "When we told you to jump, you jumped. When we told you to jump again, you jumped again. When we told you to jump a third time, however, you did not respond but collapsed in a heap; and we could all see . . . that you have failed because you had exhausted your resources in obeying us."[12] It was the same when K was on the railroad gang: The impediment to his labor was not his will but his body that simply stopped, "he balked, like a beast at the shambles."[13] The docile K is often seen waiting, without apparent expectation or projection: "For hours he waited. No one came. He chose not to get up and try the door, since he did not know what he would do once it opened."[14]
And yet, marvels the medical officer, of all the detainees, laborers, convicts, conscripts, and children—and their wardens, supervisors, generals, and caretakers—this reticent thin man is the only one who manages to leave the camp without permission. "You are a great escape artist," the medical officer exclaims finally, "one of the great escapees!"[15] K escapes physically and mentally: He harbors no nostalgia for the security of life in the camps, nor is he moved by a desire to avenge those who detain him. But neither is K a "dissident": He makes no general, public appeal for freedom or justice; he lacks the urge to systematic critique and reform. He is no "civil disobedient": He knows nothing of law, lacks faith in the morality of his conscience and in the sting of hypocrisy exposed. The camps are not dismantled by K but somehow neutralized, their hold slackened. The quiet and malformed K ought to be the one most contained by the camps. And yet he escapes.
K escapes by virtue of his peculiar self-presentation. This presentation will be seen as mere passivity by those whose ideal of self is the clearly

individuated, self-possessed agent of will. But K is wary of this ideal. He shuns the vision of a masterfully consolidated individual because he discerns that encamping power operates best upon those who endorse this vision most strongly.

The more successful one is in becoming such an individual, the more one is possessed by identifiable interests, needs, habits, desires, movements, which, because calculable and predictable, are amenable to external manipulation. The camps revise the veld into orderly, functional spaces in order to abet the revision of the self into an orderly, functional identity. To have such an identity is to have a substantial psychological landscape; somewhere for "internalized" norms to go and soil rich enough for them to root. The preservation and regeneration of this interior garden is assured by the fact that it is, ironically enough, experienced as private, exclusive, the site of one's own unique truth.

The camp controls by pressing cloudy selves to become visible individuals and by encouraging selves to take charge of this transformation themselves. Even the lavatories had a neon light that "shone off the white tiles and created a space without shadows." The overexposure of inmates, the rendering of their movements public and traceable, requires beings with self-imposed quests for individualized identities. Sensing all this, K is happiest as a poor surface of application for this insidious form of power.

K's apparent passivity is a desire to become less visible, to "think of myself as lost," in the hope that an unstable, nomadic target will be more difficult to round up and regulate. When power operates by exposing the shadowy recesses of the self, then an obscure personal history, a loose identity is an act of resistance. K thwarts the regime by failing to expend adequate effort on behalf of one of its central requirements: a definitive personal identity. "As time passed," says the medical officer, "I slowly began to see the originality of the resistance you offered. . . . Slowly, . . . your persistent *No*, day after day, gathered weight." [16]

What has weight, it is important to note, is the *quest* for anonymity. For K does not attain this end. Some stability in one's own image of oneself, and the identifiability that is its public counterpart, seems to be a condition of social interaction and of a life that is distinctly human. K, whose name has been trimmed to a single letter, is still distinct enough for the reader to sympathize with him, still internally unified enough to avert madness. This assumption of self-unity, albeit necessary at the limit, is nevertheless false if it is taken as representing the natural bent of all selves, and it is oppressive in its normalizing effects. The goal of anonymity functions as a kind of antidote to the dominant ideal; it allows K to "take up residence in a system without becoming a term in it."[17]

The quest for anonymity supports the exploration of existential possibilities buried under those well-established within the current order. But it is only a small step from these private dreams to a political question: What kind of an order could include a wider or different range of identity-possibilities? Why, for example, couldn't we make room for those with attention spans (rhythms of mental concentration) that are today too short or too long for schools and jobs? Or for an understanding of nature that is now viewed as paganistic? (These particular examples may appeal only to some readers, and any example of an occluded or unthematized way of life can produce only a reductive and distorted picture of it.) The quest for anonymity may even allow some to discover or carve out existing pockets of social space wherein one might begin to live out experimental identities. But even if these spaces are too cramped for heterotopias to mature, K's strategy still has a politicizing effect. Or perhaps it is more precise to say that the direct, personal effect of K's quest is already at the same time a political one.

K has a remarkable measure of success in escaping the confines of the camps, but even as he is reencamped he subverts by exposing some of the hidden injuries of order. This political exposé is, paradoxically, dependent upon K's relative obscurity: "No papers, no money: no family, no friends, no sense of who you are. The obscurest of the obscure, so obscure as to be a prodigy."[18]

K is prodigious—obsolete: having the nature of an omen. He exists as a political being because he reveals a link between power and the individualism it presupposes and engenders.

Second Interpretation

He thought of himself ... as a speck upon ... an earth too deeply asleep to notice the scratch of ant-feet, the rasp of butterfly teeth.

—Michael K

The fictional character K has not bravely ventured beyond the boundaries of a self-assertive identity: He is, rather, barred by nature or society from entrance to it. He lacks the resources (of intellect? will? education? economic opportunity?) to craft an identity with enough solidity and coherence for others to treat him with respect, or for him to engage in the analysis of the relationship between identity and the state that the first interpretation presents. It is the clearly identifiable self, the medical officer, who is capable of self-conscious political reflection (however flawed it may be). K's own life remains, as K himself insists, "paltry."

The novel is a tale of a small man of simple mind and low socioeconomic status, who finds safety in the minimally social world of gardening and in the slow pace of ripening pumpkins. Even in a rare moment when he makes a political point, we are told that it may have been another's thought that had "merely found a home in him."[19]

K's identity *is* ambiguous, but this is a handicap for him more than prodigious for his fellows. It interferes, for example, with the formation of his moral judgment. Is K lazy or industrious, caring or indifferent, fool or prophet? No one, including K, can be sure. "Do I believe in helping people, he wondered. He might . . . , he might not . . . , he did not know beforehand, anything was possible."[20] K seems less wary of a definitive, deep identity than inadequate to its discovery. He does indeed search, repeatedly, for a singular truth about himself; it is just that "always, when he tried to explain himself to himself, there remained a gap, a hole, a darkness before which his understanding baulked . . . His was always a story with a hole in it."[21]

K does, finally, hit upon a ready-made identity within the reach of his limited grasp: that of a gardener, "or a mole, also a gardener, that does not tell stories because it lives in silence."[22] "It excited him . . . to say, recklessly *the truth, the truth about me. 'I am a gardener.'* "[23] The relatively powerless figure of a gardener excites K because it offers him some self-conception, and one relatively tolerant of his infirmities and lacunas. Gardeners as such are infrequently called upon for sophisticated self–expression; neither are they well equipped to control the conditions of their work (nature determines that for the most part) or to secure the economic and social space required for gardens (the more masterful identities of CEOs, politicians, and urban planners take care of that). And, to return to the story, K is barred from even this consolation identity of gardener, for contemporary economies and security states do not sanction gardening, an inefficient mode of agricultural production, or tolerate many gardens, potential breeding grounds/meeting places for insurgents.

The murky and barely distinguished K is not an advocate of liberation-through-anonymity but a victim of a political system that renders large groups of people insignificant, even to themselves. The medical officer attempts to redeem K's confusion and compensate for his victimization by distilling from his life a political theory. (At least K is good fodder for theory.) The medical officer invests the mysterious (but actually shallow) K with the significance for which he, the medical officer, longs. K as simpleton or victim is not an interpretation rich enough to assuage the good officer's uneasiness about his own role in the camp. "Prophet" is much more fertile. But the officer is too literary, too sophisticated, not to be a little skeptical of his own interpretation:

> Michaels means something, and the meaning he has is not private to me. If . . . the origin of this meaning were no more than a lack in myself, a lack, say, of something to believe in, . . . if it were a mere craving for meaning that sent me to Michaels and his story, if Michaels himself were no more than what he seems to be . . . , then I would have every justification for retiring to the toilets . . . and putting a bullet through my head.[24]

The medical officer wards off despair with a deep reading of K; K views this as a demand for a payoff in meaning for the unsolicited kindness the medical officer bestowed upon K. The indigent K has been asked to pay up before. But he wants nothing more than to be a matter of concern to no one, not even to himself; for that, K judges, is the path of least resistance, the path away from the charity of creditors. Sociality renders him inferior and charity ensnares him in sociality. "I have escaped the camps; perhaps, if I lie low, I will escape the charity, too."[25]

When Robert tells K that the reason for the recent improvement in sanitation at Jakkalsdrif is that "they prefer it that we live because we look too terrible when we get sick and die. If we just grew thin and turned into paper and then into ash and floated away, they wouldn't give a stuff for us,"[26] K is unable to hear a moral-political condemnation of power. He instead translates Robert's words into a prescription for self-abnegation: first, turn into paper and then ash, and then float away (but retain one's right to imagine a world without camps, to dream of being a gardener). This is not the voice of a political man but of a stoic who is free because "wanting nothing, looking forward to nothing," nothing can deny him his desire.[27] K, "half-awake, half-asleep," is not an escapee but an escapist who does not even incite others to follow him out.

It is worth considering the possibility that K might offer a politics in the form of an environmentalist program. Perhaps he warns, as Nadine Gordimer suggests, of the "threat not only of mutual destruction of whites and blacks in South Africa, but of killing, everywhere, by scorching, polluting, neglecting, charging with radioactivity, the dirt beneath our feet."[28]

K does focus attention upon the veld, the mountains, the soil. While everyone else has "tumbled over the lip into the cauldron of history," K has "managed to live in the old way."[29] His identity as gardener, imaginary under present political and economic structures, recalls the possibility of a lost way of being, which, while probably irretrievable in its original form, nevertheless provokes second thoughts about the path of mastery we currently follow, about our arduous amnesia regarding the animal in the human.

> [K] had no fear of being poisoned, . . . as though he had once been an animal and the knowledge of good and bad plants had not died in his soul.[30]

> His deepest pleasure came at sunset when he . . . watched the stream of water . . . soak the earth. It is because I am a gardener, he thought, because that is my nature.[31]

But even Gordimer concludes that K's environmentalism must fail because K is politically inadequate as its agent. Confrontation of powerfully unjust and deeply antiecological regimes requires a greater will than K can muster. K's mother

> "worked all her life long . . . scrubbed other people's floors, . . . went on her knees and cleaned the toilet. But when she got old and sick they . . . gave me an old box of ash and told me, 'Here is your mother, take her away, she is no good to us.' "[32]

It seems the most K can do is preempt the forces that would impose the same fate upon him: K could choose to become ash.

But let us grant that a novel can be written wherein the main character, one "J," is not bound by nature or society to become anonymous but is a robust, modern individual, who engages in overt acts of political dissent. This character then deliberately and self-consciously chooses to retreat from this ideal of self by adopting a stance of irony and skepticism toward it, while nevertheless finding it useful on occasion to act on its basis. This stance requires a high degree of intellectual sophistication, but J is up to the task, at least initially. But the burden of the profound contradiction between his normal or, if you insist, "normalized," behavior and his inward suspicion of the identity he projects eventually takes its toll. If J persists in the quest for anonymity, will he not eventually become as disoriented, disabled and docile as K?

Irony about the unity of self that is nevertheless repeatedly presupposed in one's conduct has two consequences inimical to political action:

1. It renders impossible sustained participation in public speech, collective organization, and legal manipulation—the stuff out of which politics is made.
2. It dilutes what Plato called *thumoeides* or the part of the *psyche* wherein resides moral indignation. While a certain degree of dilution may be desirable in persons who tend toward dogmatism, even a little too much disables the attempt to transform moral indignation into acts of dissent.

There is certainly some truth in the medical officer's view that power can operate not only to repress selves but to constitute them in a particular way. But individuality, in some self-conscious, reflective form, is still the only viable counter to power. The delusionary, dying K we meet at the end of the novel indicates that power is quite able to operate upon amorphous selves—in fact, one of its effects *is* this marginal, submissive creature.

The second interpretation ought not to have the last word, for surely the first can reply further. But I close this debate prematurely in order to pursue two related issues. The first concerns the relationship between political theory and fiction. I will argue that Coetzee's fiction, by giving voice to but not choosing between different perspectives on the quest for anonymity, has revealed aspects of the contemporary political condition occluded by the light of theory. Coetzee has written what Bahktin called a polyphonic novel: Multiple viewpoints, each with its own integrity, none reducible to the author's singular "philosophy," engage each other and the reader in a conversation of equals. The dialogic mode can work in political theory as well, but it is more difficult, I think, for the political theorist to refrain from taking sides. The political theorist is under a greater obligation (although not as great, perhaps, as a judge or a jury) to choose and to defend the choice she makes. And so my second concern is to defend the first interpretation against what emerges within the debate as the most salient criticism of it.

The Existential Novel

Kundera describes his novels as "existential." An interviewer once characterized the opening section of *The Unbearable Lightness of Being* as peculiar for a novel, as a "philosophical idea [Nietzsche's eternal return] developed abstractly." Kundera replied that it was, on the contrary, a direct introduction to "the fundamental situation of a character—Tomas." Kundera seeks to put to rest as well the notion that his fiction is psychological: "What is the nonpsychological means to apprehend the self? To apprehend the self in my novels means to grasp the essence of its existential problem. To grasp its *existential* code."[33] Kafka is the master practitioner of the existential novel for Kundera. Coetzee, it seems, is inspired by the same hero.

The existential is the fluid realm separating the objective, the outside, the detached, from the intimate, the psychological. Most fiction works by stimulating imaginative leaps between the story (clearly a tale of someone *else*) and the reader's own experience. But the existential novel must keep the reader constantly *in transit* between cultural commentary and identification with characters; it must not allow one to linger on either shore. Hegel called the product of this mental hopscotch "picture-thoughts" (*verstellungen*). Picture-thoughts were to the philosopher an inferior form of knowledge because their ambiguous quality made it difficult to articulate them precisely and reliably to others. They are, however, an epistemological necessity for the existential novel.

Coetzee, for example, draws a world of camps, where an oppressive regime coexists with a highly developed cultural ideal of individuality. The reader experiences a certain déjà vu and recalls (or perhaps notes consciously for the first time) occasions when the nonfictive social order demanded a new level of identity-discipline or imposed a higher standard of visibility upon citizens. This infusion of the self into the narrative, however, cannot be sustained, for the surrealism and extremism of K's world and the "thinness" of his psychological profile dislodge the union. One disengages, returning to the outside, poised until one of Coetzee's poetic and evocative sentences lures one in again, for a time.

Another characteristic of the existential novel is its ambiguous attachment to history. All novels are set somewhere, but some, like *The Trial* or *The Life and Times of Michael K*, are irreducible to a distinct temporal or national location. The tale of Michael K is tied ever so loosely to South Africa: Geographical names allude to it, but the text is almost silent about the political content of the civil war that precipitated the encampment of society. We are told only that the war is being fought so that "minorities can have a say in their destinies"—itself a cryptic statement, caught as it is between a Western legal tradition of concern for minority rights and a Western colonialist tradition of minority rule. This type of "autonomy," says Kundera, is what enables the novel "to say things about our human condition (as it reveals itself in our century) that no social or political thought could ever tell us."[34]

To function at the existential level is, then, to take as one's topic the human condition as such, which is to say, the boundaries that delimit and make possible human choices. The existential novel fixes its stare upon the frightful sight of the paradoxical in human experience. Sophocles was adept at this existential vision. Focused upon the two-edged sword that faced his audience, he wrote of the paradox of heroism: "No towering form of greatness enters into the lives of mortals free and clear of ruin," chants the chorus in *Oedipus the King.*

The task of the existential novel today is to confront the contingent sites upon which the paradoxical has settled or is likely to settle, given current cultural-political arrangements. It must expose our dilemmas to the reluctant gaze of a populace unaccustomed to tragic thinking and that instead "apprehend[s] the world (the world as a whole) as a question to be answered."[35] Coetzee and Kundera identify such a site: No longer lodged in the incestuous relationship between heroism and fate, our tragedy is infused in the relationship between dissent and state power.

> But it would be wrong to read their novels as social and political prophecies, as if they were . . . Orwell! What Orwell tells us could have been said just as well . . . in an essay or pamphlet. On the contrary, these novelists . . . demonstrate how, under the conditions of the "terminal paradoxis," all existential categories suddenly change their meaning: What is *adventure* if a K.'s freedom of action is completely illusory? . . . Where is the difference between *public* and *private* if K., even in bed with a woman, is never without the two emissaries of the Castle?[36]

In this quotation Kundera is speaking, of course, of Kafka's K.'s, but the same kind of rethinking of existential (and political) categories occurs in *The Life and Times of Michael K.* All texts, like all human situations, are amenable to a variety of plausible interpretations. Coetzee explicitly affirms this condition of potential paradox by creating characters who themselves offer for the reader's consideration explicit, conflicting interpretations of the story. One listens to the voice of K, privileged in the text by virtue of his title role, alongside the voice of the medical officer, equally privileged in the text, this time by virtue of its location in a diary, that site of special veracity. The sweet utterances of the exquisite K carry the ring of authenticity, they reverberate with the immediacy one associates with revelation, with the simple truth. But the elegant articulations of the medical officer have the critical reflexivity and the subtlety one associates with philosophy, with science, with another kind of truth.

The story of Michael K thus offers no consistent ideological perspective on dissent. The political theorist may choose between the first and second interpretations, but the text does not. But through its equivocations it discloses the perplexing character of the contemporary political world.

I have already suggested, through the first interpretation, that the story of K discloses a strange link between the ideal of individuality (as it is usually conceived in the contemporary West) and the potential for conformity. The process of carefully individuating oneself, of distinguishing one's inner core of authenticity, is also the process of turning one's movements into "behaviors," of transforming amorphous urges into distinctive "propensities," of shaping picture-thoughts into "ideational structures." The pursuit of individuality is thus also the project of constituting oneself as an identifiable or calculable entity, appropriate for the machinations of psychologists, propagandists, marketing agents, political consultants, pollsters, sociologists.

One counter to this manipulation is critical reflection, also a product of the quest for individuality. By identifying external management strategies as such, one loosens their hold. But this reflexivity is also tinged with the paradoxical. The reflective self is not simply a *critical* mirror, displaying the oppressive underside of the human sciences. It is not only a *psychoanalytic* or *confessional* or *Thoreauian* mirror, displaying one's ego or soul or genius. It is also a mirror turned to the dominant culture, reflecting its norms and values. As Hegel has shown, the capacity for reflection is formed intersubjectively, through a process of mutual affirmation by one's fellows whereby an individual self-conscious identity is embodied in a larger public world.

There is, Coetzee suggests to the reader, an immanent link between the capacity to internalize or incorporate the views of others and the development of "reflection." (Rousseau the great paradoxalist develops this theme throughout the *Discourse on the Origin of Inequality* and in *Emile* with the notion of *amour propre*. Dostoevsky's *Notes from Underground* is another excellent study of this peculiar affinity.) But the story of K refuses to reduce reflection to the conventional content it inevitably includes. The medical officer's identity and the theory articulated by him are achievements worthy of respect. K's mode of self-presentation says no to the regime at the same time that it concedes impotence in the face of it. The story hints powerfully that the quest for anonymity (or the less extreme pursuit of a skeptical identity) is as implicated in paradox as the Czech photographer's more traditional dissent. Might both K and the photographer face an existential condition wherein every response to oppression, incorporating as it must elements familiar to and usable by the oppressor, runs the risk of reinforcing the distribution of power it resists?

"To suggest," "to evoke," "to hint," "to provoke," "to appeal"—these are the verbs best suited to describe the mode of persuasion of the existential novel. *The Life and Times of Michael K* does not *argue* for the existence of paradox, as, for example, Foucault does the thesis of subjectivity/subjugation. Instead, Coetzee *juxtaposes*: the silence of K who escapes the camps juxtaposed to the eloquence of the medical officer who is employed in their service; the tranquility of K, the uneven self, to the restlessness of campers with regular, normal identities; the sparseness of K's psychological landscape to the interesting analyses of the medical officer; the fragility of K to the robust health of soldiers. In these pictures normal individuality emerges as a contrived and sometimes cruel container for the self. But this encampment appears also as a condition of possibility of reflective, efficacious agents.

The story of K also helps to make sense of the attractions of anonymity in highly organized states. The example of this man who is most at home when alone and unknown evokes perhaps a secret longing of highly disciplined readers to lighten the load of identity they have been carrying around. One can sympathize with K's refusal to embrace any order-sanctioned identity, just as one can understand how citizens, who feel the burden of an increasingly rigid organization of life but, because they cannot identify clearly who or what is responsible for it (and potentially responsive to protests against it), choose instead to elude or evade the requirement of a calculable identity.[37] Apathy toward organized politics can be an expression of public discontent with the burdens of selfhood imposed by the order.

K's thoughts about escape lead him to think about nature as a safe house. Nature is not wholly disenchanted for K—God no longer resides there but K's aspirations still do. And perhaps so do ours: We are moved by K's impossible, even pitiful, desire to escape to the veld, to the extent that the "earth" continues as a powerful metaphor, as the accompaniment to the longing for greater anonymity.

The story of K brings into focus a paradoxical dimension of the ideal of reflective individuality and suggests how contemporary fantasies of freedom can be bound up with quests of anonymity and a return to nature. And it does this without deciding between K as political hero or K as victim.

The Skeptical Identity

I move now to my second concluding task, a defense of the skeptical identity as part of a politics and ethics worthy of the names.

In the second interpretation of Coetzee's novel, it was argued that self-skepticism is incompatible with political activity, for the latter requires a coherent agent. This is especially true when the political aim is to challenge the established order of things. Dissent in particular requires action based on principle, and self-skepticism seriously impedes, perhaps precludes just this. The skeptical self has learned to distrust the urge to fix and display the self as a consistent, masterful subject. (Irony is one way to induce this distrust; it allows one to "have" an identity without identifying fully with it.) But this distrust, the argument continues, must extend beyond the values, norms, and standards of one's formerly uncritical self to include all values, norms, and standards, for all function to fix and rigidify identity. The likely result, then, is a self unable to endorse a principle wholeheartedly enough to risk acting upon it. To continually interrupt the process of "identifying" with an ideal is to live Thoreau's worst nightmare, a "life without principle."

There is something to this position,[38] and I do not deny that self-skepticism is in tension with moral confidence, nor that irony can betoken things besides a desire to dissent. Just as K's anonymity can be a form of cowardice or a subversion of power (or both), the more modest attempt at an ironic identity can be a way to avoid taking a stand as well as a strategy for combatting individual and national self-righteousness. The skeptical self is, I believe, more alert to the tragic in the human condition, to what Kundera called "inexperience" and what Foucault spoke of as the paradox of a subjectivity that empowers *and* subjugates. But, again, I must admit that such alertness can produce fatalism as least as often as a heroic will to combat injustice against the odds. (Oedipus struggles on as king; Jocasta throws up her hands.)

Advocates of the skeptical self can guarantee neither the moral intent nor the political outcome of their stance; neither, of course, can their opponents (recall the case of the Czech photographers). It is fair, however, to ask for clarification of the conditions under which disputation of the conventional model of identity is most likely to have political and ethical effect.

These conditions are present, I believe, in the contemporary United States. Voices on the left and the right share too certain or too transcendental a conception of their identities; or, to put it more precisely, the winners in national politics are, increasingly, those who project the most morally self-confident and dogmatic identity. The majority of political participants, including critics deploying traditional modes of dissent, seek legal and institutional valorization of their identities, identities presented as their true and final selves. Under these conditions, self-presentations that express wariness of the identity that one nevertheless acts from within seem to me to be quite appropriate forms of dissent.

Should the character of American politics become less dogmatic, consciousness of the contingency of identity can remain more in the background, and traditional forms of dissent (civil disobedience, interest-group lobbying, demonstrations, use of the news media) may become more perspicuous. But I suspect that self-skepticism as a form of cultural critique has a place even in a postmodernized order. For every social order "encamps," that is, includes injustices produced by the establishment of priorities and evaluative hierarchies—even though some orders may be better at warding off the urge to reify its political choices, turning them into something with more universal status.

I think also that the skeptical stance courts acquiescence or insensitivity to injustice least when it is adopted by individuals with a certain kind of psychological landscape. There are dispositional, biographical, and perhaps emotional preconditions for self-skepticism-as-dissent as well as political ones. I offer this claim very tentatively, as a series of impressions open to much debate.

What is required is an adult who, first, is an idealist, possessed with unusual faith in the power of good intentions and retaining (for reasons too complex to unravel here) much of the child's wonder at life; who, second, confronts inexperience, living through dramatic cases where good intentions have not been simply immobilized but converted (by fateful forces) into effects utterly opposed to them; and who, finally, responds to these cases by *redirecting* idealism and *diffusing* its locus. What can it mean to have ideals with a diffuse locus? A comparison with other responses to inexperience may help here.

Some react to inexperience with a kind of fundamentalism, with a rarification and intensification of idealism and a stolid insistence upon the purity of ideals worthy of the name. Others reply with a kind of realism, with a repudiation of the urge for moral/social improvement, a repudiation carried out with a zealousness calculated to overwhelm that of the original faith. But our political skeptic views fundamentalist idealism as dogmatism and realist repudiation as an attempt to get revenge against a human condition that does not allow ideals full realization. These "ironic idealists" seek to keep the faith without a god—without a god to beseech or curse. They reinvest their idealism in an open-ended entity that, even at the symbolic level, is inconsistently compatible with deepest human aspirations for a world without death, pain, unhappiness, unpredictability.

Coetzee's K displays this peculiar, diffuse sort of idealism, investing it in the earth. The real and symbolic earth holds a powerful attraction for him. But not because he believes *it* to retain the purity that human subjectivity or state politics no longer possess. K's earth is not a loving God's creation but an enduring, indifferent earth offering shelter and sustenance but also starvation, disease, K's harelip. Like K himself, it contains gaps, mysteries, dry spots. And the veld is at least as ambivalent toward human comfort as politics is toward the intentions of actors. Despite this, even because of this, K is drawn by the terrible beauty of the veld and by its awesome scope of potentialities. He comes to prefer it to the clean lines of parks and gardens. " He was no longer sure that he would choose green lawns and oak-trees to live among. . . . It is no longer the green and the brown that I want but the yellow and the red; not the wet but the dry; not the dark but the light; not the soft but the hard."[39]

The moral-political aspiration lodged within his quest for anonymity is to affirm, by continuing to struggle within, the political veld. Our public space, like K's remote geography, is riddled with rocks and hard places; but it also has the beauty of a riddle with no singular solution.

Representations of the quest for anonymity reveal contours of a political condition that might otherwise be occluded by the schemes of simplification required to propel definite and coherent action. The case on behalf of the skeptical turn as an operative mode of life and action remains open as long as one remains susceptible to contemporary manifestations of the paradoxical. But it is also always circumstantial, provisional, and tentative. One must not make too many claims on *its* behalf. Conrad was not *completely* wrong.

NOTES

1. The relevant discussion takes place in Milan Kundera, *The Unbearable Lightness of Being* (New York: Harper and Row, 1984) pp. 67, 141-42. A similar dilemma appears in Harry Mulisch's *The Assault* (New York: Pantheon, 1985), where a member of the Dutch resistance assassinates a collaborator and unwittingly brings on the death of the family that lived in the house in front of which the dead man fell. The Nazis chose them for the retaliation.
2. Milan Kundera, *The Art of the Novel* (New York: Grove Press), 1986, p. 36.
3. Ibid., pp. 132-33. Kundera describes "inexperience" as follows:

    The original title considered for *The Unbearable Lightness of Being*: "The Planet of Inexperience." Inexperience as a quality of the human condition. We are born one time only, we can never start a new life equipped with the experience we've gained from a previous one. We leave childhood without knowing what youth is,

we marry without knowing what it is to be married, and even when
we enter old age, we don't know what it is we're heading for: the
old are innocent children of their old age. In that sense, man's world
is the planet of inexperience. (*The Art of the Novel*, pp. 132-133.)

4. J.M. Coetzee, *The Life and Times of Michael K.* (New York: Penguin,
    1985), p. 43. K is told this by a fellow railroad worker. My thanks to Barry
    Seldes for introducing me to the work of Coetzee.
5. Ibid., p. 47. K echoes Rousseau's wistful comment that "societies, multi-
    plying or spreading rapidly, soon covered the entire surface of the earth;
    and it was no longer possible to find a single corner in the universe where
    someone could free himself from the Yoke." *Discourse on the Origin of
    Inequality*, ed. Roger Masters (New York: St. Martin's Press, 1964), p. 160.
6. Coetzee, *The Life and Times of Michael K.*, p. 66.
7. Ibid., p. 78. A friendly inmate of Jakkalsdrif explains why he does not hop
    over the low fence surrounding the camp.
8. Ibid., p. 99. This is K speaking to himself.
9. Ibid., p. 157.
10. Ibid., p. 131. This is the official report received by the director of
    Kenilworth.
11. Ibid., p. 181.
12. Ibid., p. 163.
13. Ibid., p. 40. As Nietzsche might note, consciousness is K's weakest organ.
14. Ibid., p. 172.
15. Ibid., p. 166.
16. Ibid., pp. 163-64.
17. Ibid., p. 166.
18. Ibid., p. 142. Alex Hooke offers an insightful analysis of anonymity and
    individuality in "Foucault's Antihumanism," *Political Theory* (February
    1987), pp. 38-60.
19. Ibid., p. 95.
20. Ibid., p. 48.
21. Ibid., p. 110. Coetzee explores further the problem of self-interpretation in
    "Confession and Double Thoughts: Tolstoy, Rousseau, Dostoevsky," *Com-
    parative Literature* (Summer 1985), pp. 193-232.
22. Ibid., p. 182.
23. Ibid., p. 181.
24. Ibid., p. 165.
25. Ibid., p. 182.
26. Ibid., p. 88.
27. Ibid., p. 69. Here I follow Hegel's analysis of stoicism in *Phenomenology
    of Spirit*, sec. 197 ff.
28. Nadine Gordimer, "The Idea of Gardening," *New York Review of Books*
    (February 2, 1984), p. 6.
29. Coetzee, *The Life and Times of Michael K.*, p. 152.

30. Ibid., p. 102.
31. Ibid., p. 59.
32. Ibid., p. 136.
33. Coetzee, *The Art of the Novel*, p. 29.
34. Ibid., p. 117. I have discussed the relationship between theory and fiction in "Deceptive Comfort: The Power of Kafka's Stories," *Political Theory*, Vol. 19., No. 1 (February 1991), pp. 73-95.
35. Ibid., p. 3.
36. Ibid., p. 12.
37. Coetzee's writings, like Kafka's, dramatize how power may operate not only as the act of an agent but as the (il)logic of a system. For a good discussion of the political potential of an elusive identify, see Mary Lydon, "Foucault & Feminism," in *Feminism and Foucault*, ed. Irene Diamond and Lee Quinby (Boston: Northeastern University, 1988), pp. 135-148.
38. I have defended the role of self-forgetting in ethical life in "Primate Visions and Alter-Tales," APSA paper, 1991.
39. Coetzee, *The Life and Times of Michael K.*, p. 67.

8

Nothing Special: Enacting Modernity with Ironic Performances

Henry S. Kariel

To come to terms with reality, or at least with its residual phantoms, I keep recalling Goethe's *Faust* and Shelley's *Frankenstein*, cautionary tales that prepared the way for contemporary pathologists of modernity, all defining the momentum of technology as humanity's way of ending. Henry Adams, Oswald Spengler, Lewis Mumford, Aldous Huxley, Martin Heidegger, Theodor Adorno, Jacques Ellul, George Orwell, Robert Heilbroner, Paul Virilio, Barry Cooper—this is but my short list of those who have submitted scripts for eschatological performances (Heidegger alone allowing that a god might "save us now"). Their texts have been augmented in the most diverse of genres—Ridley Scott's *Blade Runner*, Samuel Beckett's plays, Martin Campbell's six-part BBC thriller *The Edge of Darkness*, Richard Cline's unassertive drawings, George Segal's hyperreal sculptures, Anselm Kiefer's paintings. Betraying Hegel, none proclaims that some unmutilated phoenix will rise out of the endlessly proliferating installations of modernity. All are raging and working in a house of death. All have been struggling against nothing less than the triumph of technicism and the ending of history.

A journal kept by Ian Frazier in 1988 piles detail on detail to provide a genealogy of one of modernity's disasters. It reaches back in time to articulate the fate of those dozen American states that came to be called the Great Plains. Summing it all up in the present tense, Frazier tells about the white man's ruthless mutilation of the landscape during the last two-hundred years:

> . . . we trap out the beaver, subtract the Mandan, infect the Blackfeet and the Hidatsa and Assiniboin, overdose the Arikara; call the land a desert and hurry across it to get to California and Oregon; suck up the buffalo, bones and all; kill off nations of elk and wolves and cranes and prairie chickens and prairie dogs; dig up the gold and rebury it in vaults someplace else; ruin the Sioux and Cheyenne and Arapaho and Crow and Kiowa and Comanche; kill Crazy Horse, kill Sitting Bull; harvest wave after wave of immigrants' dreams and send the wised-up dreamers on their way; plow the topsoil until it blows to the ocean; ship out the wheat, ship out the cattle; dig up the earth itself and burn it in power plants and send the power down the line; dismiss the small farmers, empty the little towns; drill the oil and the natural gas and pipe it away; dry up the rivers and springs, deep-drill for irrigation water and the aquifer retreats. And in return we condense unimaginable amounts of treasure into weapons, buried beneath the land that so much treasure came from—weapons for which our best hope might be that we will someday take them apart and throw them away, and for which our next-best hope certainly is that they remain humming away under the prairie, absorbing fear and maintenance, unused, forever.[1]

American readers of this account have heard and seen it before in college courses, pop music, and TV documentaries. Yet when at work as professionals—as technicians and power brokers—they remain immune to the lure of peace marches, sit-ins, flag burnings, and avant-gardes. Unperturbable connoisseurs of turbulence, wise about the strategies of commercials, they are not sulking or irritably straining for coherence. For them, for everyone but society's remaining underclass, the best future will be one that is but an uncluttered expansion of the present—a benign corporate capitalism quietly responding to technological imperatives.

I. We Must Be Doing Something Right

A familiar actor—Robert Young—moves to the center of an empty stage and looks straight at the audience. "I'm not a doctor," he says, "I've only played one on TV." Then he pauses, and in the commercial's remaining twelve seconds he recommends an over-the-counter medication. He's wholly credible, for he's told the truth: He's affirmed that he's no expert, that he knows nothing special, that he's merely putting on an act.

He performs (as I keep trying in the courses I teach) within a culture that increasingly trusts no real doctors, no canonized authorities, no presidents— merely actors who play the role of authorities. No wonder I, too, allow my remarks to become duplicitous and double-coded—as ironic as a TV actor's, a politician's, or an artist's such as Andy Warhol. My course on media and politics has certainly been going well, especially so after a student shrewdly observed not only that the four feature films viewed during the semester— *Rear Window, One Flew over the Cuckoo's Nest, The Dead Poets Society,* and *Full Metal Jacket*—all belong to the new genre of Foucaultian incarceration films. He noted that none of these films permitted anyone to escape (the immensely visible Indian who did break out of the Cuckoo's Nest would surely be caught within three days) and then added that the films celebrated the exuberant spirit in which prisoners and guards could continue to play their games. Foucault's pessimism, I admitted, is merely a modernist reading, far from justified. Like Nietzsche's yes-saying gay science, don't his pronouncements override every confinement?

Outside the classroom my meager agenda is vastly amplified: All sorts of media-mediated events have kept reinforcing the upbeat drift of the course— in fact, the very drift of the course of history. It's the best of times to talk about media, about whatever reduces the reality of unmediated earthquakes and sunsets, whatever obliterates the incomprehensible Otherness of so-called Real Life.

For the new generation of undergraduates, the media have convincingly shown that a new breeze is blowing. *Citizen Kane* is at last being colorized: Less harsh, it becomes more friendly. Beneath the pockmarked surface, the promise of *perestroika* remains. To save billions of gallons of water annually, the U.S. government is mandating that the capacity of new toilets be reduced from 3.3 gallons per flush to 1.6 gallons. In Oregon defective steel-and-concrete bridges are being replaced by wooden ones that are rustic as well as cost-effective. The threat of unemployment of Lockheed employees has been lifted first by the rush to war and then the certainty of prospective wars. An eleven-hour public television epic, Ken Burns' *Civil War*, heals all wounds: The nation masters its past and questions the cost of war. *Field of Dreams* (Phil Alden Robinson's incomparable movie) has bonded disconnected generations through the ritual of baseball on the family farm. A team of researchers of the Monell Chemical Sensors Center in Philadelphia has discovered a source of underarm odor. The softening of communism proceeds apace: Ads for Finnish vodka are inscribed on a Soviet satellite while in China the last traces of Marxist rhetoric are replaced by computer language that directs security forces and promotes economic development. In all but the Middle East, tactical weapons are yielding to cleaner strategic ones. The Bush administration has discovered the uses of reinterpreting the Constitution and the conventions of international law for pacifying Iraq, if not yet for normalizing Panama. A study commissioned by the electronics industry reassuringly concludes that video-display terminals, like electric blankets and microwave ovens, no longer pose a "significant" hazard of cancer. Uruguay has let bygones be bygones by democratically voting for amnesty of torturers. Lech Walesa endorses Marlboros: In a Philip Morris ad a photo appears next to the quotation: "I've read your Bill of Rights a hundred times and I'll probably read it a hundred more times until I die." Kenya's government has restricted the slaughter of elephants. In Albania the Diner's Club logo has eclipsed the hammer and sickle, while in Marseilles history has been corrected by Klaus Barbie's lawyer who made clear that his aging client's murderous activities were merely part of the conventional savagery of warfare—like the measures taken by Japan at Najing, France in Algeria, the U.S. in Vietnam, and Israel in Lebanon. In Japan *The Holocaust* series' rerun is tastefully sponsored by Tokyo Gas, Inc. Iranian rage aimed at a blasphemous human target halfway around the globe has turned out to be only an irritating prelude to reasonable diplomacy. At its summit meeting the Group of Seven—the world's major industrialized countries—has chosen the European Economic Community to coordinate aid to Poland and Hungary. In a joint report three American think tanks have enlightened pessimists who had been falsely alarmed by the emergence of Soviet populism, by an allegedly prefascist reaction of the Leningrad working class to Gorbachev's free market, by Eastern Europe's food shortages and crime rates. Former East Germans, having mastered their past, are volunteering to teach the world that disciplined industrialization is not incompatible with limiting consumption and promoting environmental protection.

And beyond such marginal enterprises, quasi-public secretariats have become sovereign: History, far from ending, continues to be made by the politics of International Monetary Fund, the World Bank, the Paris Club, the London Club, the Organization for Economic Cooperation and Development. The sun no longer sets on the computer empire they serve. Unobtrusively managing the global flow of trade and money, they balance the needs of the first world with that of the second and third. Economic internationalism is gently displacing the protectionist sentiments of Japan, South Korea, and the U.S. In an exultant mood, the London Borough of Camden has sold its parking meters to a French bank that agreed to lease them back.

All doubt about the progressive course of history, certainly mine, is stilled by Charles Krauthammer's syndicated celebration of an unambiguous victory:

> The perennial question that has preoccupied every political philosopher since Plato—what is the best form of governance?—has been definitively answered. After a few millennia of trying every form of political system, we close this millennium with the sure knowledge that in liberal, pluralist capitalist democracy we have found what everyone has been looking for.
>
> And not just we. This decade has seen the rest of the world register its agreement to be modern. . . . The verdict is in from Korea, Chile, the Philippines, much of Africa, Poland, Hungary, China. . . . The triumph of the Western political idea is complete. . . . Yes, a few holdouts remain, mostly some Western eccentrics holed up in academia and the church, Marxism's last two sanctuaries. We will always need [Harvard's] Kennedy School of Government. But the basic question is definitively answered.[2]

Oppositional movements give no cause for worry: They, too, help to brighten the landscape of liberalism. To be politically effective, ecological, feminist, and antinuclear movements rely on the technology and instrumental reason they aim to abolish: Like everyone else, they make zero-sum calculations, organize hierarchically, and employ the mass media. Poles, Afghanians, Tibetans, Palestinians, Canadians, Armenians, Estonians, Hungarians, and Chinese students are preparing to employ whatever strategy might work—including nonviolence—so as to become objects of surveillance by appearing on TV screens on which they expect to see themselves giving energy to the world's markets.

An all-comprehending media network exults in the ascending order. Without creating anxieties about possible abnormalities, it reports on the painless segregation of the disempowered, the sanitizing of streets and plazas that have been emptied of vendors and drug addicts. It briskly normalizes whatever phenomena threaten to emerge as special and distinctive. Howard Nemerov, poet laureate at the Library of Congress, anticipates the mourning of America's new war causalities by recalling how smoothly America pulled itself together in 1988 after the take-off explosion of the *Challenger*:

> It is admittedly difficult for a whole
> Nation to mourn and be *seen* to do so, but
> It can be done, the silvery platitudes
> Were waiting in their silos for just such
> An emergency occasion, cards of sympathy

From heads of state were long ago prepared
For launching and are bounced around the world
From satellites at near the speed of light,
The divine services are telecast
From home towns, children are interviewed
And say politely how sorry they are,
And in a week or so the thing is done,
The sea gives up its bits and pieces and
The investigating board pinpoints the cause
By inspecting bits and pieces, nothing of the sort
Can ever happen again, the prescribed course
Of tragedy is run through omen to amen
As in a play, the nation rises again
Reborn of grief and ready to seek the stars;
Remembering the shuttle, forgetting the loom.[3]

A year after the 1989 San Francisco earthquake tourists had returned. Predicted by a series of disaster movies, it is commemorated and assimilated by a new video showing that the student who emerged after having been buried for four days had actually been an actor eager to provide a photo opportunity. "Like everyone else," he was quoted to have said. Stock exchange turbulence, depressions, suicides, and other disruptions are anticipated and neutralized by computer-directed preemptive strikes.

The very term "strike" has at last lost its terror. In American history courses strikes, like wars, dustbowls, and breadlines, are shown to be what they really were—unacknowledged commercials for ultimate success, certainly no call for political action.

Politics—the agonizing play of *conflicting* desires—is gently engulfed by the flow of media that reduce contested policies to nonideological images. Teledemocracy provides endless opportunities for content-free citizen participation.[4] Press releases keep filling in the residual faultlines that disfigure the topography of modernity. Like advertisers—*as* advertisers—politicians accept film director John Ford's advice: "When the legend becomes fact, print the legend."

Repeating a Hegelian scenario to which Alexandre Kojève gave currency in the 1930s,[5] the media delete the distinctive local contexts of time and space. The subject matter of high school social studies courses blends with TV programs. In a happy time of reruns the present is represented within frames that cease to be visible. An endless serial fuses past and future. Distractions and diversions cease to be from anything painful: They constitute the culture.

The obsessive quest for new experience—for foreign travel—is transformed since it's no longer eighty days around the world, nor nine hours, nor (on screens that radiate the new reality) a fraction of a second. Being there, people need neither depart nor arrive. No one gets lost. Forgotten baggage is globally replaceable. Images of alien lands become instantly available and familiar. In a process in which alienation is overcome, all homelessness is suspended: Everyone feels at home everywhere.

The imperium of technology eliminates the need for *space* to get away from it all, for time to heal wounds. It provides an eternal sunrise: schools without teachers, banks without tellers, cars without drivers, leaders without followers, corporations without managers. Prosecutors and defense attorneys, defendants and judges are united in a common cause.

In a culture of freely circulating capital, avalanches of commercials are a supportive presence. Truth resides in the ordinariness of their deceptions. As long ago as the 1940s, Salvador Dali made uncanny images ordinary by signing blank sheets of lithograph paper, which his publisher could reproduce and sell as authentic original copies. In a world being flooded with replicas and duplicates (Walter Benjamin said it), the quest for originality and authenticity has become meaningless. Elements seemingly outside projected images merge with the sensuous intercourse of commerce. A video on *Top Gun* opens with a commercial that looks like a scene from a movie about fighter pilots: It's for Diet Pepsi. Grand Marnier liqueur promotes modern art, Michael Jackson promotes Pepsi Cola, and Phil Collins and Eric Clapton promote Michelob.

Of course the present is not an incarnation of postmodernism. The complex of mass media has not yet realized the potential prophesied by Baudrillard. Hesitations continue to leave room for resistance to the ubiquitous process of modernization. Sovereign states remain ready to lash back at voracious entrepreneurs like the evangelist Jim Bakker.[6] Nor do intellectuals, artists, filmmakers, and writers of soap operas consistently respond to the sirens of modernity. Out of step, they persist in doubting the merits of greed, competitiveness, commodification, strip mining, unearned profits, AIDS policy, leveraged buyouts, and whale extermination.

Moreover, academics keep questioning the drive for harmony by claiming that the hegemonic ideology of liberal capitalist society is inherently contradictory and changeable, that the desire for face-to-face interaction is no mere sentiment, that the local traditions of ethnic groups are unshakable, that the popular culture is tougher than the culture industry.[7] Furthermore, vague subterranean tremors betray an uneasiness about an emerging reality constituted by predetermined outcomes of elections, athletic events, and marketing strategies—a reality real enough to override the acceptance of regressive taxes. Memories of a *real* past—a time when Truth stood opposed to Fiction, Original to Copy—are stirred by prerecorded "live broadcasts" that produce deceptions so universal that they deceive no one and imperfections so flawless that they are perfect.

It is no less evident that the movement toward planetary consolidation is being sabotaged by New Age prophets who stubbornly predict the collapse of the economy and the implosion of technology. Protests against the process of modernization have reached the centerfold section of *The New Yorker*—a "SPECIAL ADVERTISING SECTION" dedicated to "Earth Day Honoring the Environment," a smooth blend of editorial narrative and ads by IBM, American Honda Motor Company, Bat Conservation International, and AT&T all printed, as the publisher notes, "on one-hundred-per-cent recycled Georgia-Pacific paper."[8] Protests laced with traces of nostalgia serve to provide profits for travel agencies promising contact with Native Hawaiian Culture. A vague uneasiness generates frantic searches for authentic antiques, autographs, limited editions, faded sepia photographs, old comic books, and Nazi emblems. Here and there, the course of modernization is hindered by worries about the quality of life of vestigial castaways, vagrants, misfits, third-world *Gastarbeiter*. Further, the vision of a rational future continues to be blurred by nagging terrorist threats, economic debacles, computer errors, leaking nuclear waste, and accidental oil spills.

Yet whatever obstructions remain on the road to normalcy, the present moment of history foreshadows a blissful future. The deadweight of the past has been lifted by hundreds of lights that illuminate the emergence of nothing special. The intentions of the Western World's founding fathers have become as weightless as the last wills and testaments of the deceased. The dead, it is comforting to realize, have finally become a dispensable endangered species.

Shallowness—endlessly present mutability—provides freedom from myths that limit the human enterprise, that restrain the market and its products. An unabrasive new world order is being coaxed into establishing itself.

The auspicious movement toward an apolitical pluralism began to be academically refined in the 1970s when a coterie of restless, upward-bound scholars, I among them, started to valorize paradox and deconstruct the foundationalist humanism of the Enlightenment. In a still-homeless language we poststructuralists heralded the death of the subject, dedicated ourselves to the analysis of sitcoms, billboards, Toyota users' manuals, and snapshots, and made ethnocentricism reputable by calling it "local knowledge." Our sentiments were irreproachable: We decentered miracle, mystery, and authority and took care to substitute nothing definitive.

Our apostatic rhetoric, understandably feverish given its transgressive thrust, constructed an ideal—a world in which symbols are detached from reality, in which centers of power are dispersed, in which authors disappear as transcendent creators. Our paradigm desublimated capitalized antinomies and brought them into relation with one another. In the name of ethnographic, semiographic cultural studies, an interdisciplinary preoccupation with rhetorical practices began to unify undergraduate courses ranging from history to accounting. The objective of the emerging core curriculum was to desublimate the way the political economy of liberalism colonizes the domain of culture. Our task was to describe how objects are related to subjects, life to death, means to ends, writers to readers. As we dissolved polarized constructions such as History and Fiction or Man and Woman, signifiers became slippery. A priori grounds for adversarial politics became but a useful fiction along with familiar footholds, viewpoints, harbors, landmarks, launching platforms—in fact all pre-postmodernist spatial and temporal coordinates.

In step with news media that seek to practice what academics preach, Stephen Tyler advised his fellow anthropologists to be done with the "ideology of referential discourse," with "the presumption of representational signification," with facts, inductions, generalizations, conclusions, findings, and verifications. Ethnographers should be primed, he said, to write their descriptions as evocations rather than as representations, to make each of their projects "an occult document... an enigmatic, paradoxical, and esoteric conjunction of reality and fantasy... a fantasy reality of a reality fantasy... ."[9] When outdistanced by the media, academics like myself responded by publishing meticulously detailed case studies that ceased to be cases-in-point of anything, least of all a new theory. Comforted by the assurance that speech is action, we withdrew from the political stage. Our attack on power—on the Father, the Law, the Transcendent Signified—was divorced from political context by exercises in which deconstructions were endlessly deconstructed in space unspoiled by ideology and history. As the length of our Teutonic sentences made clear, we were slowly learning to transcend the vernacular and the passions that fuel it.

At the end of the semester, my students have learned how effectively the present gives intimations of an unclouded Elysian future. They realize that the promise of their schooling—the promise of technology—is fulfilled by mixed genres, floating hierarchies, indistinguishable differences, reversible grammars, deconstructed ontologies, shifty epistemologies, and an ironic mode so universal that it has spectacularly crystallized into unironic Being. They know that the media, having penetrated reality, have ceased to mediate. In their term papers they lip sync that eerie silence which Martin Heidegger made luminous after the Second World War when he (in his metaphor) lost the path for entering that clearing which discloses pure immanence—"the thereness," as he said before he became speechless, "of what is."

The past of my students—my own past as well—has finally become a *realized* fiction validated by the ineffable *Zeitgeist* of the present. We all learned that technological coherence is the apotheosis of Being. My class on politics and media—it's reassuring to note at the end of the semester—can shamelessly celebrate graduation exercises and enter a world consecrated by the mass media as well as by postmodernist artists, architects, novelists, and filmmakers who calmly ride the whirlwind of modernity.

II. The Artful Universalizing of Irony

Yet however compliant they seem, the projects of the arts do more than duplicate the system of power: They embellish and enhance the images of technology. Ironic ventures, they are magnified enactments within the incompletely realized movement toward technological totalism. Exploiting what is left of the world's mutability, their world is a hyped reality in which expressions can no longer be inflated, in which a seamless hegemony tolerates no dysfunction, surplus, waste, vagrancy, or nostalgia. For them the media-constructed spectacles of the present are on the verge of becoming so comprehensive that no morality or aesthetics will occupy a field independent of reality. Unlike the localized, fenced-in irony exemplified by Socrates and Shakespeare, Swift and Wilde, theirs is contained by frames so transparent that they frame no locality, nature, history, or morality. They ironize texts that presume to change reality, that urge the rehabilitation of a politics designed to keep evil in check. Acknowledging no fixed solutions, they identify no crisis and no problem as real. They are uncritical and unproblematic, undramatic and nonjudgmental. The comprehensive range of postmodernist irony rests on their perception of *a universal technological system that inexorably annihilates humanity's awareness of itself.* Reflexivity will disappear within a matrix of power that extinguishes differences and normalizes Otherness.

In 1989 Hans Magnus Enzensberger was to praise (or so he claimed) a new individual who had emerged in the grid of modernity:

He has come a long way: the loss of memory from which he suffers causes him no suffering; his lack of self-will makes life easy for him; he values his own inability to concentrate; he consider it an advantage that he neither knows nor understands what is happening to him. He is mobile. He is adaptive. He has a talent for getting things done. We need have no worries about him. It contributes to the second-order illiterate's sense of well being that he has no idea that he is a second-order illiterate. He considers himself well-informed; he can decipher instructions on appliances and tools; he can decode pictograms and checks. And he moves within an environment hermetically sealed against any infection of his consciousness. That he might come to grief in this environment is unthinkable. After all, it produced and educated him in order to guarantee its undisturbed continuation.[10]

In a familiar passage Alexis de Tocqueville had complemented Enzensberger's perception in 1840. He anticipated

an immense, protective power which is . . . absolute, thoughtful of detail, orderly, provident, and gentle. . . . It likes to see the citizens enjoy themselves, provided that they think of nothing but enjoyment. It gladly works for their happiness but wants to be sole agent and judge thereof. It provides for their security, foresees and supplies their necessities, facilitates their pleasures, manages their principal concerns, directs their industry. . . . Thus it daily makes the exercise of free choice less useful and rarer, restricts the activity of free will within a narrower compass, and little by little robs each citizen of the proper uses of his own faculties.[11]

To postulate this vision of the unselfconscious individual immersed within "an immense, protective power" is to give coherence to postmodern irony. A science-fiction conceit, it defines the space occupied by those who mediate the machinery and dynamism of modernity. Moreover, it elucidates their very mode of expression by depicting not only the texture of modernity but also the destruction of boundaries. When executed on a large scale, invasions cease to be invasive. In brand-name-saturated films and novels, postmodernists issue dispassionate reports, our comings and goings like espionage agents who have lost touch with their agency. Free and clear, they are infinitely circumspect, weary, paranoid. Secret voyeurs so duplicitous that they are loyal to no sovereign, they adopt whatever narrative practices serve to prevent their entrapment and termination. They keep shifting channels and perspectives to keep from falling into sentimentality, error, or—if some self emerges—self-deception.

In the winter of 1989, the Museum of Modern Art—an organization abundantly experienced in closing the gap between art and commercial reality—installed the most lavish of retrospectives, the work of Andy Warhol, who, like the very museum putting him on exhibit, had spent his life serializing, syndicating, advertising, marketing, and dispersing his products. By the time of his death in 1987, his constructions—his very life—had excluded every distinction between the unreal and the real. Either category would do for both. Representation was fully installed: The display of inconsequence alone carried weight.

Warhol's merger of artifice and reality certainly posed no difficulties for Manhattanites who lined up to see the show. Though staggering in its mere profusion, his work was easy to take. John Updike reported at the time that spectators "can breeze through it at the clip of a fast walk, take it in through the corners of their eyes without ever breaking stride."[12] Its high and low spots were all but indistinguishable. Depth and surface were one.

Warhol's work is devoid of suspense and resolution. Nothing seems important. The distinctions made in his work serve no one, no authentic Self, no trans-historical Truth, no sovereign Nature. There's nothing of consequence. His narratives do no more than embroider currently existing clichés, freeways, missiles, and careers. They all but fulfill his ambition to produce a TV show to be called "Nothing Special." His enterprises make no difference, sanction no revolutions, leave no scars, cause no grief. His deadpan, nonjudgmental ghetto journals—a diary of faithful accounts of what's happening—merely constitute an endgame of elucidation for which he absorbed the artifacts of modernity—and became so absorbed by them as to appear selfless. He presented himself as self-deleted, insignificant, faded, uninflected, absent. In his *The Philosophy of Andy Warhol: From A to B and Back Again*, Warhol gave voice to his serene acceptance of life as it came:

> A whole day of life is like a whole day of television. TV never goes off the air once it starts for the day. At the end of the day the whole day will be a movie. .
> .. The acquisition of my tape recorder really finished whatever emotional life I might have had, but I was glad to see it go. Nothing was ever a problem again, because a problem just meant a good tape, and when a problem transforms itself into a good tape it's not a problem any more.[13]

There was more, however, than Warhol's apparent lassitude, his cultivated political complacency. In a Foucaultian spirit he had also said, "Being born is like being kidnapped. And then sold into slavery." Irony, the trope Czeslaw Milosz has called the glory of slaves, was his strategy for coming to terms with reality, for comprehending modernity's insatiable technicism. However nonchalantly Warhol plagiarized the user-friendly best-sellers of modern times, he was the connoisseur of a funereal subterranean world as much as Charlie Chaplin and Woody Allen. Wasn't he Andrew Warhola, the son of an immigrant Slovak who had fueled the engines of modernity by working as coal miner? Below the bright surface of his mock ads and packages, of Coke bottles and Brillo boxes, Warhol gave intimations of darkness and doom. Representations of skulls, electric chairs, car accidents, race riots, post-suicide Marilyns, post-assassination Jackies were all in Warhol's rag and boneshop.

And aboveground on the seemingly bottomless surface, his familiar empty icons of industry and commerce showed him as indiscriminate opportunist co-opting available art and artifacts. His languorous maneuvers were those of the prisoner who desires no more than to give full recognition to her fate, who is relieved and finally enraptured by her awareness that what she experiences is nothing worse.

Accordingly, Warhol welcomed, scrutinized, and reproduced whatever crossed his path. Anything flattened out by the juggernaut of industrial society could become grist for the assembly line he installed in what he called The Factory. His products—his very being—were ready-mades, the most available and ordinary of objects, effluvia of modernity such as the Empire State Building, which his camera faced head-on in a barely moving film he allowed to run for six hours. Not judging matters at hand, convinced of the impossibility of changing "the material conditions of life," he merely intensified and commemorated the wasteland that modernists sanctimoniously deplored.

Doing no more, resolved to remain in transit, he merely recorded and remembered. He would seem to have mastered the unobtrusive negativism of Carl Rogers's psychoanalytic practice—not "to set goals, to mold people, to manipulate and push them in the way that I would like them to go."[14] Warhol's positive acceptance of phenomena—including the people who came to view and accept his work—was a form of passive resistance that, like Gandhi's, surrenders the self, decenters the subject, and clears space for the appearance of Being by means of one's *willed* resignation.

He left scarcely a clue to the willfulness of his submission to the insatiable instrumentalism and technicism of modernity's servants. So literal were his productions that they, too, became commodities. He made them the business of art. Yet however much he duplicated the prevailing culture, he enacted it: He used its techniques to raise its qualities to the level of consciousness. At best, his productions were experiments in sustaining consciousness in face of pressures to obliterate it. Finding himself in the midst of the maelstrom of modernity, he accelerated its gyrations.

III. Purposeful Laissez Faire

Warhol's aesthetics—Kant's ideal of art devoid of purpose and yet intensively focused—required a blending of nonjudgmental empathy, unfocused concentration, intensive care. Overriding the conventional expectation that what is intentionally pursued must be effective, he merged purpose and inconsequence. It was his inconsequent attentiveness to the world's phenomena that constituted his style. His unassertive affirmation of all phenomena was a form of action: His surrender was enacted in the mode of Nietzsche's Zarathustra who had power only to speed ahead of the nihilism that engulfs others, who prevailed without mankind's all-too-human defense mechanisms, its fixed points of view. He was so secure and composed that he could surrender and disarm, thereby contradicting the drive for power, effect, success.[15] If he was effective, it was his powerlessness—his total vulnerability, his transparency—that empowered him.

The quintessential contemporary ironist, he was full of care for whatever goods and evils made their appearance. He related society's unrelated entities while he appeared indifferent to the utility or moral value of his constructions. He urged no way out of the prevailing order of things, merely crossing through it. He stopped at no island, identified no harbors, confirmed nothing but the open sea. He subscribed to Nietzsche's imperative:

> There is no avoiding it, one *must* go forwards, that is to say, *step by step farther into decadence*. . . . One can *curb* this development, absorbing it, dam it up and collect the degeneration, make it more vehement and *more immediate*: one can do no more than this.[16]

Trapped in the culture of modernity, Warhol became a relentless collector of its codes, texts, and languages. He copied and elaborated the clichés of the market. His irony (far less circumspect than Socrates') attached him to the most ordinary of companions whose mindless pronouncements he extended. Engaged in transactions that transform conceptions of oneself and the world, he found himself implicated in the structures of power that surrounded him. There is no evidence that he sought more than release from the hold of immediacy.

Postmodern performances give vent to no cry of despair about the way the world goes, reduce no ambiguities, make no distinction between essence and phenomenon, reality and meaning. No meaning is concealed behind the words. Nothing is to be saved other than appearances: What appears is all there is. Texts yield no stable, autonomous, coherent, or solid substance—no author, self, ego. Expressions of a postmodern sensibility, they differ radically from those ironic narratives that Kierkegaard had characterized as Romantic because they used language as a medium that represents some preexisting ideal.[17]

The products of postmodern irony are scarcely distinguishable from those that flood the markets of capitalism. "All that is solid melts into air, and all that is holy is profaned," Marx and Engels had it in their manifesto. True Value, as opposed to value at the point of sale, ceases to be fixed. The artifacts of postmodernism annihilate reality. As Robert Hughes has proclaimed with unfeigned regrets, contemporary artists no longer provide "the visual codes by which one interpreted the world." The mass media have replaced True Art along with meaningful press conferences and public oratory. "Everything is mediated . . . to the point where nothing can be its true quality"; art today merely "echoes the general drain of concreteness of modern existence. . . ." The results are evident: a Reaganesque imperium of eclecticism, pastiche, historical deck shuffling, and history nothing but a box of samples. In the postmodern era, all is surfaces. The intense contemplation required by authentic art is replaced by superficial exposure.[18]

In the postmodern ironist's focus on surfaces, background and foreground become one. They simply are. As in Beckett's plays, predicates prevail by waiting patiently for subjects that fail to appear. Postmodern discourse simply *is* ironic—and nothing else. A melange of *all* voices, it's anonymous. Defacing everything that is special, particularized, distinguished, making clear how ingeniously nothing makes any difference, it generates laughter.

It is precisely a world of no consequence to which the postmodern ironist seeks to attend—outwitting it only by the range and intensity of her attentiveness to its vibrations. However fitfully, she competes with media that keep catching up with the same. She knows the mass media subvert every effort to create spaces and times for independently enacting one's life. She knows that TV transmissions have ceased to be boxed in, that they are not some external force but rather that dense miasma of modernity that disposes of every crisis by producing an endless flow of spectacles. She agrees with Daniel Boorstin:

We risk being the first people in history to have been able to make their illusions so vivid, so persuasive, so "realistic" that they can live in them. We are the most illusioned people on earth. Yet we dare not become disillusioned because our illusions are the very house in which we live; they are our news, our heroes . . . our very experience.[19]

In this perception of the reach of the media, no reason remains for changing what Karl Marx had called the material conditions of life. Beyond the images projected by modernity's media there is but more of the same. Productions and products can merely be reproduced, enlarged, and extended. Development governs.

Coming to terms with phenomena that interrupt the course of development, the mass media keep absorbing the most ironic of performances. The trope of irony finally disappears along with metaphor, synecdoche, and metonymy. Parts cease to stand for the whole, similarities cease to connect differences. Things become what they are. There is no identifiable distinction—nothing special—between irony's magnifying mirror of nature's and reality's unmediated presentations. The world itself—every *Ding an sich*, every "itself"—is wrapped in quotation marks that cease to make the point that it's only so-called. Devoid of all context, an MTV commercial can unapologetically feature a series of words and then cut to:

THESE WORDS WILL HANG OUT FOR 15 SECONDS

UNTIL IT'S TIME FOR ANOTHER COMMERCIAL

Fifteen seconds later:

THESE ARE WORDS THAT COULD BE SAYING SOMETHING

BUT THEY'RE NOT

THEY'RE JUST SITTING THERE

LIKE YOU.[20]

The individual—Ronald Reagan made himself the most memorable case in point—becomes the method actor so immersed in his performance that he is unaware of what he does. Wholly in touch with free-floating myths for organizing the unreal-real or really-unreal events of the day, he is the adolescent character defined by his TV watching in the pilot episode of "What's Alan Watching?": He turns the TV dial until the screen displays the desired scenario—possibly his family at peace, possibly Reagan's large-scale sitcom for coping with Libya and the Soviet Union, for creating photo opportunities from the threat of abdominal cancer or an assassin's attempt on his life. He becomes TV footage incarnate.

Buoyantly metastasizing, the sole end of the media is the display of excess. Thus Audi's four-page fold-out spread at the center of a 1989 issue of *The New Yorker* (which modernized itself in 1988 by enlisting teachers to bring it into over 300 classrooms) is pure excess: It preempts efforts to ask for more:

DISOBEY THE LAW OF AVERAGES. LET OTHERS TAKE THE TRADITIONAL COURSE.

We prefer creativity over conformity, invention
over imitation. Inspired ideas over tired ideas.
In short, Audi offers an alternative route.
We'd much rather stick to the road than stick to
the rules. . . .
After all, Audi subscribes to a new definition of
performance: brainpower vs. horsepower. Refined
spirit, not raw speed. . . .[21]

This center spread is so deeply subversive that it is immune to deconstructive maneuvers. "Thirteen different models," it goes on, "each slightly iconoclastic, yet completely inspired. And each one ready to take you down the alternative route." No avant-garde can outdistance Audi's promise by ironizing it. The seriousness of its humor is so blatant that it leaves nothing in repose.

In step with the mass media, postmodern ironists point to no exit from the momentum of modernity. Like Bruce Neuman's scrupulously constructed narrow hallways lit by yellow fluorescent tubes, their projects lead nowhere in particular. They are the last negations of local space, local time, local knowledge. Moving what had been circumscribed irony toward universal consciousness, toward the suspension of both ironic and nonironic discourse, thus they participate in the movement toward that state in which contingency is ubiquitous.

Envisioning no alternative to the comprehensive course of modernity—ultimately its *un*mediated presence—the postmodern ironist lightens the heaviness of being. A victim of industrial progress, she is free only to display the dimensions of her fate. She resolves to assimilate modernity's products and to comply with its instructions—until, overwrought at the end of the day, she fatigues, surrenders consciousness, and succumbs to either reality or irreality.

This turned out to be the case for Woody Allen's Leonard Zelig when a helpful psychoanalyst coached him to lose his uncanny capacity for assimilation. Throughout *Zelig*, its spineless nonhero keeps blending into the changing environment. He assumes the characteristics of whomever he is with. He becomes Chinese in Chinatown, Catholic in the Vatican, fat in the midst of fat men, Irish on St. Patrick's Day, a Nazi in Germany. To the woman who is his faithful psychoanalyst, it is clear that his affliction is the result of an oppressive childhood (his father had given him a singular message—"Life is a meaningless nightmare"—and advised him to "save string").

Of course, Zelig might have been given a postmodernist alternative scenario for coming to terms with his suffocating childhood. He might have been shown to risks spinning out of control. He might have detached himself from the world's dreadful demands by becoming a seasoned rock climber, by keeping cool in high places, by scanning rather than focusing. Indifferent to disaster, he might travel lightly. Facing a sheer cliff, his eye will see a field of forces rather than specific obstacles. Intensively neutral, he won't discriminate against fissures or flaws. He will reach the peak after having ignored conventions. He will have taken detours, moved in circles, postponed success, opted for failure. He'll be high.

Having mocked all media, including his own ("No big thing" was his last journal entry), he will have made light of the grave antinomies of experience. In the end he will see everything, see *through* everything—that is, see nothing in particular, nothing special, nothing that might signify anything else, nothing of weight, import, and significance.

Reaching vertiginous heights, breathless and high spirited, the complete ironist assumes that no territory is in principle off limits or in bad taste. To represent incomprehensible extremes of behavior she communicates by reversals, contradictions, denials. As she becomes increasingly extravagant and wasteful—good for nothing—she transcends subtexts, duplicity, and politics. Her discourse becomes transparent, ethereal, disembodied. Her last expressions are inane inspirations: "Out of this world" and "Unreal." Her very negations become weightless while she relinquishes established constraints and at last loses herself. She is "zelig"—Yiddish for soulful. At her end she enters the unmediated obliviousness of those media she had struggled to comprehend.

IV. Repercussions and Resentments

The ironist bypasses the pitfalls of ascent and descent as long as she integrates the yin of letting go and the yang of dominating. Her integrity is manifest in that active passivity that surrenders the self to Otherness in the process of expressing it. Her discipline consists of remaining poised between lightness and heaviness—that is, of engaging in a politics of nonidentity. She obliges herself to relate intimate states and distant ones, alert postures and relaxed ones. Her ultimate loyalty is to the field between absolutes and no less to the pragmatically validated processes that maintain it. At best, her life is lived in the purest of political space. For her, ironic expressions alone may occupy that space—a space of appearances that frees individuals from unmediated passion, hysteria, and paralysis. For her—for feminists generally—irony

> is a way of communicating across barriers, a way of extending dialogue where there has been no firm basis. It is a way of forming remote ties of interaction, of building communities of sorts, where natural "commonality" may be in question. In irony, persons seek out and recognize each other on the basis of little more than a shared pretense. . . . [It] might be a way of generating participation and commitment out of ambivalence. . . . It seems to have much in common with politics itself: a combination of distance and engagement. . . .[22]

In this splendid passage, John Evan Seery has almost taken that small (though immensely critical) step from *comparing* irony to politics to fully *realizing* that to live in irony *is* to live in politics—in "shared pretense," in realities as ungrounded and specious as all make-believe.

Irony is believed to be impotent politically only where politics is defined in Hobbesian terms of power and domination, of real masters and real slaves, and therefore of battles rather than transactions. It is as potently impotent as Gandhi's *satyagraha*—that form of active resignation which manages without expectation of real change. Today it does its work by explicating the invisible grid of modernity in a series of postmodernist experiments that are as pointless as the play of children, as gratuitous as the all-is-well expressions of the terminally ill who accept their fate. Having no ulterior motive, ironic discourse produces no definitive texts, and thus yields to readers who hold their breath and wonder—wonder if a conventional solution (say, the enfranchising of the fetus) is a problem (say, the disenfranchising of the mother) that begs to be reformulated in an endless game played between a welter of texts.

Given space and time by the indeterminacy of irony, such readers are free to attribute it to discourse that appears to tell things unironically the way they are—whether it's Max Weber's account of bureaucratic rationality or a journalist's report on the dexterity with which George Bush's son distanced himself from the most spectacular economic scandal in American history.

Readers (and writers) ironize the world when they believe exits to be closed and death to be impending. At such times, they may conclude that no other trope offers redemption, that recyling remains their sole option. Although initially, as Marx had noted, they may see history to repeat itself as farce, they may finally regard it as irony. When reality has become so encompassing that no other trope makes it bearable, survivors of the vicissitudes of history may be sustained by reading *every* text as ironic. Unshaded matter-of-fact statements will turn out to be understood as deliberately overwrought, and hence as ironic.

Whether or not a text—one's very career—is ironic will depend on the situation of its readers—its audiences, spectators, listeners. If readers read it as ironical, it's *their* action that, for the moment, will have made it so. The text does no more than represent representations, interpret interpretations, reinscribe inscriptions. It leaves a stimulating if troublesome vacuum insofar as it makes no statement of intentions, issues no marching orders. It is this vibrant vacuum that invites readers to make comments, interpretations, and further representations—that is, to make notes at the margins which may yet move to the center. It enlists those who risk articulating their inarticulate misgivings about monolithic discourse.

The effectiveness of the irony of postmodern projects depends on the readiness of a community to share that sense of fatalism that is based on the assumption that it's too late to redirect events. At that point they will look for no moral basis for resolving contradictions. They will appreciate an end as irreducibly ambiguous as *The Deerhunter*'s concluding banquet: After having come to know the horrors of America's most psychedelic war, its military and nonmilitary participants thoughtfully sing "God Bless America!" They are the pilots returning from combat who tell newsmakers that everything is going just fine.

When judgments are wanted, it is hard not to feel cheated by such inconclusive conclusions. To commemorate the rightness or wrongness of crises, one wants more than Maya Ying Lin's Vietnam Veterans Memorial. For the ironist, to label phenomena unpatriotic, dirty, irrational, or psychopathic is but to restate the problem: It is to terminate discourse that the ironist keeps alive by treating problems not as real but as subjects for ongoing elaborations, further fictions, more comprehensive stories.

If the community recoils from treating its experience as ironical, it simply hasn't managed to incorporate the text in its life. Reading a text (say, *The Protocols of the Elders of Zion* or a speech by Saddam Hussein) as ironical makes severe demands on a community which is convinced that some voices are so unambiguously evil that they should not be interpreted as ironical. Understandably, irony is barely tolerable, for its voice invariably amplifies the very forces threatening the community—monopolies of power and language that generate consolidation and termination.

Open-ended discourse is easily dismissed by a society whose media serve to assemble entertainments sustained by endings, solutions, answers, and conclusions—all settlements that are assumed to be as unambiguous as liberal pluralist capitalist democracy. In such a society, every switching of channels depicts but more of the same settled background. The rejection of the comprehensive irony of postmodernism is understandable when the content and pace of the media leave no time for reflection, for designing independent strategies for coping with Otherness. A seamless sequence in which commercials are part of the show cuts no more deeply into alleged reality than a disinfected "Cosby Show," "Sesame Street," or "Mac-Neil/Lehrer NewsHour." Irony will be perceived as pathological playfulness at the assembly line unless it becomes a profitable and ontologically frozen Warhol print on the wall of a corporate dining room or a Kubrick movie reified in a scholarly journal. Those captivated by the promise of freedom in a post–technological pastoral field of dreams are understandably irritated by projects no more conclusive than the nonutopian discourse of irony. They recoil from irony's indifference to the claim that ground remains for overcoming present troubles. They think of the ironist as a virus that fails to sanction the politics of instrumentalism, that, like a god, will not darken the heavens during a holocaust.

To become aware of the resentment of others—of one's own resentment—is to become ambivalent toward his strategy for encompassing modernity's trajectory. Who but a spiritualized Caesar, as Nietzsche put it, has enough nerve to enact his life—to enact his death—in the absence of all possibility of salvation, of any circuit breaker that might arrest technology's readiness to satisfy the cultural desire to nudge history toward its end? Who will accept irony's strategy for postponing the obliteration of consciousness in the global movement toward coherence, resolution, homogeneity, consolidation? And who can finally accept irony's participation in eliminating the arena in which it can still manage to operate?

When the world becomes indistinguishable from ironic narratives, irony has reached its end, for irony and the mass media are one. There is no point to define an event as a disaster, as anything special. Judgments are as irrelevant as they were to Claude Lanzmann's *Shoah* or Truman Capote's *In Cold Blood*. When reality is so effectively mediated there is no Heaven or Nature to which to refer. Why inquests, autopsies, inquiries? What findings would matter? Running ahead of his time and his readers, Jean Baudrillard has maintained that it is no longer sensible to review the actions of villains or the events of the Holocaust. The meaning of concepts such as "cause" and "responsibility"—George Bush spoke of America's "unique responsibility" in his second inaugural address—are but media effects:

> Exchangeability of victim and executioner, destruction and dissolving of feel-
> ings of responsibility—those are the virtues of our marvelous communication
> system. . . . Who can speak of amnesty when all are guilty? And as far as autopsy
> is concerned, no one today still believes in the anatomical truth content of facts:
> we labor with models.[23]

Even if facts did assert themselves, they would not convince. The cata-clysms of the century exist no more than its "victims." The significance of events is but a media product. Baudrillard finally asks: Doesn't Foursson's claim that there were no gas chambers express the movement of the entire culture?

V. Irony as Unavoidable and Intolerable

The postmodern ironist's diagnosis of modernity—at times my own—is so sublime that it is barely acceptable: Radical feminism tends to return to the Subject, deconstructionism to Theory, philosophic discourse to Philosophy, critical jurisprudence to Law, my circular discourse to an unmovable bottom line. Fervent polemics about the need for postmodernist practices do not themselves embody their message. Reproducing the deadly logic of moder-nity, they arrive at conclusions. I, too, repress my awareness that our desire to finish, our death wish, will be granted if we fail to live in ironic contra-diction, that we will destroy ourselves to save ourselves.

To be unreflectively at home I furtively retreat from Nietzsche's gay science, from that lightness of being which empowers us to buoyantly fictionalize reality at will. A sad necessity contradicts the belief that virtue is but a human convention. At the edge I betray my public posture. I *fail* to give up hope and cling to convictions that validate unmediated private passions. Though I should know better, I find myself mourning the dead and saving for the future. I find myself holding that ironic discourse will save me from succumbing to alleged necessities, that the permutations of narratives and life are indeterminate, that contingency is universal. But I still act otherwise. I keep promises, pay life insurance premiums, correct my son's spelling errors. Leaking faucets need fixing, ambiguities beg to be reduced. At home, real problems demand real solutions.

Still, I keep corrupting private commitments by irony and public ones by favoring what Richard Rorty calls solidarity. In my quite ordinary utopia the commitment to irony and to solidarity are continuously enacted and reenacted in a process that integrates them; however polarized they appear, they are treated as intertwined on various public stages—even when they are stubbornly perceived as private possessions or private quarters. In this utopia the muddled politics that integrate irony and solidarity, indifference and passion, keep no one from deciding that at some specific time and place shoulder-shrugging irony is intolerable because cruelty and pain are so real that they demand action here and now. There is room for the ethnographer's or novelist's or filmmaker's detailed narratives to extend the range of comprehension of the miseries of outcasts, strangers, and others, including the Otherness within ourselves.

While professing that in contemporary public life irony is the only alternative to obsessive purity, I am a fellow traveler of assorted realists and foundationalists who rightly fear the terror induced by efforts to sustain the illusion of unbroken equanimity. I keep contradicting my stoic detachment and recurrently reveal my incapacity for living in the present moment. I solidify my life by turning verbs into nouns, fertile fields into fortifications— into findings, causes, conclusions, terminals. Recurrently I find myself unable to keep up with those high-spirited Sioux warriors who, knowing that every day is precisely what it is, go into battle rejoicing that "it's a good day to die."

Yet, forever hedging, I also know that at this very moment it's a good time for me to end. Beginning or ending—it makes no difference, for neither time is special.

NOTES

1. Ian Frazer, *Great Plains* (New York: Farrar, Straus & Giroux, 1989), pp. 166-167.
2. Charles Krauthammer, "Our System's Rivals are Routed," *Honolulu Star-Bulletin and Advertiser* (March 26, 1989), p. B-2.
3. Howard Nemerov, "On an Occasion of National Mourning," *War Stories* (Chicago: University of Chicago Press, 1980).
4. See Christopher Arterton, *Teledemocracy: Can Technology Protect Democracy?* (Newbury Park, CA: Sage, 1987).
5. It gained global recognition in the summer of 1989 thanks to Francis Fukuyama's essay entitled "The End of History?" *The National Interest* (Summer 1989), pp. 3-18, after its scholarly elaboration by Barry Cooper in 1984.
6. Frances FitzGerald makes this point, but her account also makes it easy to see Jim Bakker as victim of the residual constraints of a society that is not yet ready to honor its creed of consumption and materialism. Defying the strictures of puritanism, Bakker had created a postmodernist world of surfaces so sumptuous and extensive that they left no space for reality, sin, penance, and redemption. He created a theologically indeterminate TV community as well as a media-wise, deregulated, tax-exempt Reaganite imperium, a shamelessly overblown amusement park—Heritage USA—a monument to kitsch, a parody of popular art and popular culture. An inadvertent ironist, Bakker subverted rules and regulations, genders and genres. When the judicial system and his evangelical colleagues turned on him, he had no ground to stand on. See Frances FitzGerald, "Jim and Tammy," *The New Yorker* (April 23, 1990), pp. 45-87.
7. In *Hegemony and Socialist Strategy*, trans. Winston Moore and Paul Cammack (London: Verso, 1985), Ernest Laclau and Chantal Mouffe have challenged the buoyant apolitical determinism of postmodernist irony. They maintain that the realities created by the symbols and images of society are always overdetermined, that articulation necessarily subverts the larger field within which it takes place. For them the distance between the reality and appearance is ineradicable.
8. *The New Yorker* (April 23, 1990), pp. 51-66.
9. Stephen Tyler, "Post-Modern Ethnography: From Document of the Occult to Occult Document," in *Writing Culture: The Poetics and Politics of Ethnography*, ed. J. Clifford and G. Marcus, (Berkeley: University of California Press, 1986), pp. 130-131, 134.
10. Hans Magnus Enzensberger, "In Praise of Illiteracy," in *Performance and Reality*, ed. Ben Sonnenberg (New Brunswick, NJ: Rutgers University Press, 1989), p. 369.

11. Alexis de Tocqueville, *Democracy in America* (New York: Harper, 1966), pp. 666-667.

12. John Updike, "The Sweatless Creations of Andy Warhol: Fast Art," *The New Republic* (March 27, 1989), p. 26.

13. Andy Warhol, *The Philosophy of Andy Warhol: From A to B and Back Again* (New York: Harcourt Brace Jovanovich, 1975), p. 5, 26.

14. Carl Rogers, *On Becoming a Person* (Boston: Houghton Mifflin, 1961), p. 268.

15. "And perhaps there will come a great day on which a nation distinguished for wars and victories and for the highest development of military discipline and thinking, and accustomed to making the heaviest sacrifices on behalf of these things, will cry of its own free will: *'we shall shatter the sword'*— and demolish its entire military machine down to its last foundations. *To disarm while being the best armed,* and out of an *elevation* of sensibility— that is the means to *real* peace. . . ." F. Nietzsche, *Human, All too Human,* trans. R.J. Hollingdale (Cambridge: Cambridge University Press, 1986), p. 380.

16. *Götzen-Dämmerung,* in Karl Schlechta, ed., *Nietzsches Werke* (Munich: Carl Hansweser, 1954), Vol 2, p. 1019.

17. See Søren Kierkegaard, *The Concept of Irony, with Constant Reference to Socrates* (Bloomington: Indiana University Press, 1968).

18. See Robert Hughes, "The Decline of the City of Mahagonny," *The New Republic* (June 25, 1990), pp. 27-38.

19. Daniel Boorstin, *The Image* (London: Weidefeld and Nicholson, 1961), p. 240.

20. Quoted by Leslie Savan, "Titular Head," *The Voice* (February 21, 1989), p. 56.

21. *The New Yorker,* Vol 65 (March 13, 1989), pp. 51-58.

22. John Evan Seery, *Political Returns: Irony in Politics and Theory from Plato to the Antinuclear Movement* (Boulder, CO: Westview Press, 1990), pp. 195-96.

23. Jean Baudrillard, "Zu Spaet!" in *Die Heidegger Kontroverse,* ed. Jung Altwegg (Frankfurt: Atheneum, 1988), p. 168.

Part III

THE ONGOING DISCOURSE OF IRONY:
AN EXCHANGE

9

Don't Be Cruel:
Reflections on Rortyian Liberalism

Jean Bethke Elshtain

There is only the fight to recover what has been lost
And found and lost again and again; and now, under
conditions
That seem unpropitious. But perhaps neither gain nor
loss
For us, there is only the trying. The rest is not our
business.

Home is where one starts from. As we grow older
The world becomes stranger, the pattern more complicated

Of dead and living.

—T.S. Eliot, "East Coker," 1914

We are living in remarkable times. Even as nations and peoples formerly under the domination of the Soviet Empire proclaim their political ideals in language that inspired and secured our own political founding; even as Russia herself flails toward democracy, our own democracy is faltering, not flourishing. People confront one another as aggrieved groups rather than free citizens. And our political philosophers all too often merrily whistle a pick-me-up sort of tune as animosities old and new grow and the storm clouds gather.

One current enthusiasm is an up-to-date version of American pragmatism that reassures us things are pretty much moving along as they were meant to. I refer to the pervasive presence and influence of the philosopher Richard Rorty. Rorty is an intelligent and canny thinker and, at times, a powerful writer. But he undercuts whatever *gravitas* might inhere in his own position with moves in a direction that signals the unbearable lightness of liberalism, or at least one dominant modern version of it. If we are considering the future in light of the unraveling of Marxism, Rortyian liberalism is a good place to start.

By George, I think I get it. Then I seem to lose it. That is characteristic of my Rorty experience. I find his arguments slippery, hard to engage. But I don't think engagement is what Rorty is about. I think he means to embrace us, each and everyone, or at least all we who feel comfortable being part of "we liberal ironists," "we liberal reformers," "we pragmatists," "we anti-essentialists," we who "don't do things this way," we . . . we . . . we. In his *Contingency, Irony, and Solidarity*, Rorty uses the we-word nine times in one short paragraph.[1] This is a veritable love fest. As the Beatles sang long ago and far away, "I don't want to spoil the party, so I'll go." What follows may be read as the complaints of a party pooper. (Although, let me just add, I'm happy to be invited to attend.)

I will begin with a primer of assorted discontents that evolve into deeper engagements, a fleshed-out counterpoint to Rorty's positions where Freud, cruelty and self-creation, and redescription, among others, are concerned. I use as my point of departure *Contingency, Irony, and Solidarity* as well as Rorty's recently published philosophical papers.[2]

Reading Rorty, I find myself mumbling "He remains too much the analytic philosopher." That is a vacant complaint as mumbled, so what is at stake in this lament? It has to do with the nature of argument and the menu of options Rorty presents as alternatives. Rorty has a tendency to argue along these lines: Either you are part of "we liberal ironists," or you are an essentialist or foundationalist. He effectively debunks the pretensions of foundationalism, but he fails in his attempt to chart an alternative because that alternative is cast as a thin version of self-creation, wholly contingent, wholly constructed, utterly historicist, nominalist "through and through," or "all the way down, " as Rorty might put it.

Further, Rorty insists that we either seek or require "proof" the old-fashioned way, by *refusing* to earn it, relying instead on analytic philosophical or metaphysical reassurances and closures, or we join the ranks of his army of the contingent "we." Surely the universe of argument is far richer than this formula allows. Surely one can reject the correspondence theory of truth or strong convictions concerning the "intrinsic nature of reality," without opting for the view that truth is solely a property "of linguistic entities," the latter being a position he uses to lump together all sorts of folks he likes of the idealist, revolutionary and romantic sort. Rorty links his commitment to contingency to a rough-and-ready progressivist teleology (even though he cannot permit himself teleological arguments, he relies tacitly on Whiggish history) when he claims, as but one example: "Europe gradually lost the habit of using certain words and gradually acquired the habit of using others."[3] Aside from the peculiarity of granting agency to a continent, what is at work here appears to be a conviction that although there is nothing intrinsic or essential about anything that has happened, or that led to the construction of "we liberal ironists," we are still in pretty good shape if we endorse a loose liberal utopia in which things pretty much continue to move along the way they have been moving because, it must be said, the contingencies seem to be on "our side." At least that is the only way I can interpret a statement such as: "A liberal society is one which is content to call 'true' whatever the upshot of such encounters turns out to be."[4] The encounters in question here are basic bad guys versus good guys stuff in which, over time, the good guys appear to be winning, more or less.

The good guys combine commitment with contingency. The bad guys are all commitment—rigid and unyielding. The good guys reject any notion of intrinsic or essentialist anything and insist that so long as everybody has a "chance at self creation," life is pretty good. The good guy—actually, this character of the ideal sort gets to be a "she" throughout Rorty's discussion— accepts that "all is metaphor" and neither God nor nature designed anything to some preordained purpose, or at least any human anything. I thought of Rorty's "all is metaphor" during a recent van ride in a driving rain down Route 91 headed from Amherst, Massachusetts, to Bradley Airport in Windsor Locks, Connecticut. My pony-tailed, perpetually grinning van driver decided to strike up a postmetaphysical (I think) conversation. "For me, life is one big metaphor," he said. And then he spelled out his general philosophy of life. It was a brief story. My only concern was whether or not the rain-slicked pavement, the low visibility, and the presence of other vehicles was to be construed metaphorically as well. I thought this might be the case because he insisted on turning to me—I was seated opposite in the passenger seat up front—as he celebrated the basic unreality of existence.

Now: what connected my reading of Rorty to this metaphorical ride to the airport? (By the way, I was rather relieved to be back in Nashville, Tennessee, where cabbies are unlikely to describe life as one big metaphor as they drive you home.) I think it is the insistence that life is either to be taken straight up, as grounded and certain, or it is altogether contingent, up for grabs. As I said earlier, surely there are other options. That will be the burden of the case I intend to make.

I am also struck by the fact that Rortyian antiphilosophy is not terribly helpful to the political theorist who rejects Platonism and Kantianism (as do I) but wants, at the same time, to avoid the error of underlaboring, of offering far too thin an account of the body politic. When, for example, I read Rorty's characterization of the ideal liberal society, to which he believes we are heading, I learn that it is one in which the "intellectuals would still be ironists, although the nonintellectuals would not."[5] What spares this from being a bit of what in the old days would have been called a piece of class snobbery is Rorty's conviction that the latter—the vast majority, one must presume—would "be commonsensically nominalist and historicist. That is, they, too, would see themselves as contingent through and through, without feeling any particular doubts about the contingencies they happened to be." So they are in on the heady project of self-creation, although not so aware of its ironic dimension, as the true cognoscenti, "we intellectuals." Somehow I don't think historicist nominalism is going to fly with Joe Six-Pack. And I don't mean fly as an argument—I mean as "story" about reality, about his, or their (the nonintellectuals), reality, despite the fact that this thoroughgoing contingency is the thing Rorty calls "moral progress," one small step for men, one big leap for humankind in the direction of "greater human solidarity."

On Rorty's account, we become more solid the thinner we get because we recognize as contingent all the things that constitute who we are. This means jettisoning as core to our identity that which traditionally constituted it (tribe, religion, race, custom), recognizing them as inessential. All that matters is a brotherhood and sisterhood of pain and humiliation. This smuggles universalism back in, of course, but that isn't the most important point. The most important point is that even in our would-be liberal utopia, people don't and, I would argue, cannot think of themselves as "thoroughly" contingent because when they think of themselves they see concrete fears, pains, hopes, and joys embodied in concrete others—say a grandchild—and it is impossible for them to construe that grandchild, or to tell the story of the coming into being of that grandchild, in the way Rorty says we must.

Minimally, all those nonintellectuals out there would be unable to practice the incessant self-scrutiny required in order to purge "any particular doubts about the contingencies they happened to be." Leaving aside recent evidence on just how deep and wide are the religious commitments of Americans, including belief in God and personal immortality, a noncontingent fragment that appears to infect over 85 percent of the American people, the nonintellectuals I presume, Rorty's evidence for the capacity of nonironists to be wholly historicist and nominalist is pretty thin; indeed such evidence isn't proffered.[6] Rorty holds up the claim, eschewing coming to grips with the evidence. That is a further reason for the difficulties I have when I try to engage his arguments: They are cast at such a level of generality and diffuseness it is hard to know what one is endorsing, if one goes along, or what it might mean to oppose what is being said. At this point, Rorty owes us some stories—some postmodern, liberal-ironical, antifoundational, historicist, nominalist stories. "We" party poopers remain ironical about his ironical liberalism. We need exemplars. We need narratives that do not require the bogeyman of foundationalism and essentialism to frighten us into an under–specified alternative.

Sharing his view that in a liberal-democratic society overly precise and highly programmatic demands and policies are neither required nor desired, we nevertheless ponder: What is his alternative? And when we do that the images the come to mind are: a world in which nothing is ever distinct or ever stands out in stark relief and in which I am not called upon to make tough decisions of the sort that might require that I reject one version of multiculturalism in favor of a more authentic version of diversity—a choice Rorty would be loath to make because he would want to associate all the things that come down the pike with a vaguely progressivist air or flair as vaguely progressivist, hence worthy of endorsement or at least not worth opposing. I imagine the liberal ironist at a roller-skating rink—watch me whiz by, catch me if you can, I know I'm going in circles but at least I'm moving in the right direction. What does it mean to "acknowledge contingency?" How can I avoid using any "inherited language game?" What can it mean to use a "new language" in a world in which language is always already before me, in me, through me? What counts as a record of failure or success in the Rortyian world of self-creation? Is there an example of a group of persons, a movement, an ethico-politics that has successfully transcended transcendence of the bad universalist sort in order to achieve an authentic universalism of the contingent sort?

A genuinely ironic history and account should puncture our illusions. The Rortyian ironist, remember, is *first* a historicist and nominalist. The ironic part is the bonus, the door prize, in the ideal liberal utopia. The possibility of such a utopia is aided and abetted by a decline of religious faith (I have already called this into question as an empirical matter); the rise of literary criticism that, although it widens the gap between intellectuals and nonintellectuals, all in all seems a good thing: the consensus, or growth toward a consensus that everybody should have a chance at "self-creation"; and the hope that "with luck"—Lady Luck is a pretty important figure in Rorty's world—modern liberal society can keep telling optimistic tales about itself and how things are getting better. He, for one, sees "no insuperable obstacles in this story's coming true."[7] This is the basis of hope.

By contrast to this rather blithe account, would not the genuine ironist, one with a well-developed tragic sensibility, insist that "we" come to recognize the illusions—the political illusions—imbedded in the progressivist story as Rorty retells it? His ironist—once again a "she"—fulfills three conditions. Each of these conditions is presented as an intramural debate—a matter of "final vocabulary," of "present vocabulary," and the repudiation of some "real" vocabulary, real in the sense of being closer "to reality" or closer to some outside "power" (usually called God, though Rorty might also have Nature in mind). Ironists are folks who do battle over vocabularies and who recognize that "anything can be made to look good or bad by being redescribed." Given this recognition, they renounce any attempt "to formulate criteria of choice between final vocabularies. . . ."[8] This puts the Rortyian ironist in a "metastable" position.

Surely Rorty's "meta" is a bit too stable, hence not nearly ironic enough. Rorty's ironist is insular and self-enclosed, fighting a fight of words, words, words. Far easier to stabilize this world in the name of destabilization than to confront the thicker reality of lived life, the densities and intractabilities of a world I did not create and do not control. Rorty also encases his ironic self in a cocoon of private self-creation; yet he clearly means to endorse and to serve liberal democratic society as "we liberal ironists" construct the ironic identity as a form of loose community. There is a lot of seepage of private to public and public to private within Rorty's argument. That being the case, it is fair play to take him to task on whether his ironism stabilizes or destabilizes and makes problematic that which the nonironist would cast in the mold of dogmatic certitude. Return with me, then, to the those not-so-golden days of yesteryear Rorty describes thus:

> The French Revolution had shown that the whole vocabulary of social relations, the whole spectrum of social institutions, could be displaced almost overnight. This precedent made utopian politics the rule rather than the exception among intellectuals. Utopian politics set aside questions about both the will of God and the nature of man and dreams of creating a hitherto unknown form of society.[9]

Presumably Rorty would say this is "we anti-essentialist's" description of the French Revolution, descriptions being inventions that serve certain purposes. His description aims to show how contingent, even arbitrary, our political characterizations are, and this, in turn, serves to deepen the ironic stance. But that isn't the cause his description of the French Revolution serves: Rather, his bland depiction wipes the blood off the pages. Utopian politics becomes the stuff of intellectual politics. The French Revolution takes on a quasi-foundational status as the mother of all political redescriptions. The modern liberal utopian ironist moves away from the guillotine, to be sure, under the "don't be cruel" rule, but the French Revolution continues to edify, to lie at the heart of the project of political hope.

Rorty describes events in a way that misses the terrible tragedy, hence the deep irony, of the Revolution. In the name of the Rights of Man, or under that banner, tens of thousands were imprisoned and at least seventeen thousand guillotined between 1792 and 1794 alone. One avid executioner bragged that the revolution would "turn France into a cemetery rather than fail in her regeneration."[10] This statement is horrifically funny: the sort of thing that makes the blood run cold. The genuine ironist would describe in a way that foregrounds the Terror and the horror, that holds it up for all would-be Utopians to see. Rorty does the opposite. Why, I wonder? Surely we need continually to be reminded of the mounds of bodies on which nationalistic and revolutionary politics rests. Surely the liberal, above all, must proffer such reminders. Contrast the thinness of Rorty's characterization of the French Revolution in terms of vocabulary change with Camus's story of the Republic of the Guillotine.

> Saint-Just exclaims: "Either the virtues or the Terror." Freedom must be guaranteed, and the draft constitution presented to the Convention, already mentions the death penalty. Absolute virtue is impossible, and the republic of forgiveness leads, with implacable logic, to the republic of the guillotine.... But at the heart of this logical delirium, at the logical conclusion of this morality of virtue, the scaffold represents freedom. ... Marat, making his final calculations, claimed two hundred and seventy three thousand heads. But he compromised the therapeutic aspect of the operation by screaming during the massacre: "Brand them with hot irons, cut off their thumbs, tear out their tongues." [11]

The strong ironist would be certain that her description of Revolutionary virtue included a (be)headed count. For her task would be one of making as clear as possible, in as dramatic a way as possible short of some blunt laying down of the law, that virtue all too easily translates into vice; that the tragic and the ironic keep very close company; that self-deception is most visible when illusions are greatest; that any and all claims to purity must be punctured. Rorty does none of these in his few words on the French Revolution. This omission of any mention of the bloodiness of one of history's most grandiose movements of redescription permits, in turn and in tandem with Rorty's overall rhetoric and narrative strategy, far too smooth sailing over tranquilized waters to the present moment as one in which there are no "insuperable obstacles" to the liberal progressivist story.

Writes Richard Reinitz in his volume *Irony and Consciousness*: "Belief in the inevitable growth of human knowledge and progress, and in America as an exemplar of that progress, is one of those pretensions. [The pretensions he here discusses are those depicted by Reinhold Niebuhr as characteristic of American society.] Like all modern liberal cultures, America's culture has for the most part rejected the doctrine of original sin in favor of the irony-inducing pretense to 'objectivity,' the belief that we can keep selfish interests from affecting our understanding."[12]

Don't get me wrong: Rorty would never endorse the cruelty of the Terror. But by holding it at arm's length, by not allowing it into the picture, he more easily preserves intact his own endorsements and future projections and promises. Thus his claim that anything can be made to look good or bad by being redescribed *is* genuinely troubling—ethically and politically. Take the following story, one Camus offered in a speech at Columbia University in 1946 as a way to characterize "a crisis of world-dimensions, a crisis in human consciousness:"

> In Greece, after an action by the underground forces, a German officer is preparing to shoot three brothers he has taken as hostages. The old mother of the three begs for mercy and he consents to spare one of her sons, but on the condition that she herself designate which one. When she is unable to decide, the soldiers get ready to fire. At last she chooses the eldest, because he has a family dependent on him, but by the same token she condemns the two other sons, as the German officer intends.[13]

How might this story be redescribed in order to make it "look good?" Rorty, remember, insists on this possibility. I will put the point in stronger terms: He *requires* this possibility in order to sustain his larger argument about the utter contingency and arbitrariness of our characterizations. So it is something that "just happened" that Europe acquired a habit of using other words, words that promote "don't be cruel." Camus describes a moment of genuine terror. He means to evoke our horror and revulsion. He means to do this to alert us to how dangerous the world is and how necessary it is to sustain an ethical-political stance that limits the damage.

Were I to suggest that Camus's story is but one way of describing something that could be as easily described in an alternative way designed to make it look good, I would make myself loathsome; I would become a ravager. Rorty surely agrees with this because he, too, hopes to lower the body count; thus I think it is fair to ask of him whether Camus's story puts pressure on his rather carefree advocacy of the infinite possibilities of redescription. This is a point I will return to in my discussion of just what sorts of stories—political stories—"we liberal ironists" might tell. Camus is an ironist and many call him liberal, but he locates us in the heart of darkness, a place we must visit from time to time, not as one textual experiences among many possible textual experiences but as a historic reality and ever-present possibility that cannot be contained by being transported behind a private *cordon sanitaire*. If, as Rorty claims, solidarity is created "by increasing our sensitivity to the particular details of the pain and humiliation of other, unfamiliar sorts of people,"[14] it is puzzling indeed that he steps back from the opportunity to deepen the pool of sensitivity by telling the story of all those unfamiliar sorts of people—peasants in the Vendeé as well as aristocratic families and intellectuals (of the wrong sort) in Paris—who lost their heads to revolutionary virtue.

Rorty's Freud is as puzzling in this regard as his French Revolution. Freud is a pivotal thinker for Rorty, serving as one of the masters of redescription and decentering of the self central to the rise and future hope of "we liberal ironists." But I have a rather hard time recognizing his Freud. Freud becomes either too mechanistic (in Rorty's discussion in volume 2 of his philosophical papers) or too much the flower child, an odd combination of scientism and expressivism. Briefly, the story Rorty tells about Freud depicts his project as a knowing demolition of many received understandings—fair enough—and offering, as a consequence, simply "one more vocabulary," his own chosen metaphoric. Pressing just "one more description" is an extraordinary taming of a project whose father characterized himself as Hannibal, Moses, a conquistador. Conquistadors usually aim a bit higher than "one more description." They seek to impress themselves on a territory and a people—to conquer. Freud saw his project in similarly dramatic terms, and, as well, he claimed the imprimatur of science and truth. His demolition of his opponents is scarcely the work of a man tossing out "one more vocabulary" for our consideration!

As well, Freud's awareness not simply of life's contingencies but its tragedies; his insistence that psychoanalysis is not primarily a cure-all but the basis for a very "grave philosophy" disappears in Rorty's story. Instead, Freud is assimilated to a too-simple version of socialization theory, not unlike that favored by functionalists and structuralists. Here as elsewhere, in exposing the too-grandiose presumptions of traditional metaphysics and strong Aristotelian teleology, Rorty falls into an overreliance on the categories of analytic philosophy. That is, the absence of an "intrinsic" human nature or of moral obligations that are preprogrammed leads Rorty into a world that is at one and the same time too open and plastic ("any and every dream") or too constricted ("blind impress"). These too-restricted alternatives are strikingly in evidence when he takes up Freud. For Freud's aims went much beyond showing how we are determined and might be free for self-creation nonetheless. *Contra* Rorty, Freud did not give up "Plato's attempt to bring together the public and the private, the parts of the state and the parts of the soul, the search for social justice and the search for individual perfection."[15] Freud's discussions of ego and superego; of war and the self; of the trajectory of individual development—all turn on the connections Rorty claims Freud severed.

A long exposé or unpacking is not possible. I will serve up just a couple of points to put pressure on Rorty's redescription of Freud's project, beginning with "blind impress," which I take to be Rorty's way of insisting that instinct as a form of preprogramming may not be "unworthy of programming our lives or our poems," although this is not terribly clear.[16] "Private obsessions" is another way Rorty talks about what he calls "blind impresses" unique "to an individual or common to members of some historically conditioned community."[17] One way or the other, Rorty is depicting conditioning—conditioning that he doesn't sort out into the biological and the historical although "blind impress" suggests both.

Either way this rather misses the Freudian boat. Freud could never agree that "socialization . . . goes all the way down—that there is nothing 'beneath' socialization or prior to history which is definatory of the human."[18] To be sure, this is a slippery Rortyian formulation. Perhaps Rorty here means to incorporate bio-evolutionary dimensions within the historical. But it needs to be stressed that, for Freud, the human being is a complex physiological entity, driven in ways not at all historically contingent. We are critters of a particular kind. There is a biology, a morphology, a neurophysiology definatory of "the human" and prior to our historic construction in a particular family, time, and place.

For an individual to be forged out of the human, certain things are required, first and foremost human love for we are "exquisitely social." Freud's understanding of the very possibility for human freedom turns on there being something to us humans that is not thoroughly and exhaustively defined and captured by history. There would be nothing to be discontented were we as totally historicized as Rorty suggests. Where Freud is powerful— in offering a developmental account, teleologically driven, of what is required in order that a distinctive individual might emerge from the human—Rorty falters. Rorty does insist that one cannot, from the day of a child's birth, rear a child to be tentative and "dubious" about his or her society and culture. But that is pretty much it. Freud goes much further. He does lay down the law (again, the Moses analogy Freud used to understand himself is not unimportant in this regard) and sketches out a clear and mordant theory of development. Conscience—necessary to the don't-be-cruel rule—is not, Freud insists, simply "there," is not given. But it can and must emerge if aggression—the greatest problem in civilization—is to be tamed, curbed, and muted if not eliminated.

Rorty offers us no developmental account. We cannot, therefore, understand where noncruelty comes from. Freud is insistent on this score. He reverses conventional accounts of the rise of moral ideals. For persons capable of a moral point of view (that is, capable of occupying the position of the other: capable of empathy and identification with those different from themselves) to emerge what is required is: (1) Specific powerful others (usually called parents) who are libidinally cathected, the objects of both love and hate. This demands constancy in early object-identification. (2) In order for reality testing, essential to mature development and the emergence of genuine individuality to occur, those others cannot be absent or remote, nor will "objective" structures and institutions do the job; they must be real human beings to whom the child is erotically attached. This and this alone lays the groundwork for the child to become a social being.

The superego has a specific history; it bears a double burden of aggression, a combination of the child's own aggressivity and the child's introjection of parental authority. In order that this aggressivity be bound, the child must engage in a series of complex experiments of thought and action within an environment of loving discipline. Ethical and erotic are necessarily intertwined in moral life. This intertwining escapes the confines of particular families and feeds into, even as it is fueled by, the wider culture.[19] The development of the individual is, of course, contingent in many ways: No one selects his or her parents, place or culture of birth, and so on, but it is not arbitrary. Development has a teleological thrust; it bears within it the seeds of possibility. That possibility is best understood as an attempt to work out what it means to be free and to be responsible in light of predeterminations of an embodied sort and determinations of a cultural sort.

Freud never shirked from specifying the sorts of environments and worlds that gave rise, or had a fighting chance of giving rise, to individuals and those that did not. As well, there would be no point at all in therapy if an ideal of the structural unity of the self were not held up. This is tied, in turn, to the possibility of truth. Hysterics and neurotics suffer from reminiscences, from the telling of inappropriate, false, or obsessive stories. The truth *does* set one free, but it cannot be any old construction—it must "take"; it must be a construction that leads to a recollection that invites a "yes," a liberating "yes," from the analysand.

Now none of this makes any sense at all if it is severed from a strong developmental account that enables us to sift and winnow some ways of rearing children from others; that enables us to say this is rotten and awful; this is better; this is better yet. Writes Jonathan Lear: "From all we know of cruelty, it is not lovingly instilled. It is cruelty that breeds cruelty: and thus the possibility of a harmonious cruel soul, relatively free from inner conflict and sufficiently differentiated from the cruel environment, begins to look like science fiction." Lear goes on in a footnote to write unabashedly, as did Freud, of the formation of the soul as being "dependent on a certain type of responsiveness. Sanity is a constitutive condition of a fully formed soul. Clinical experience suggests that the closest example of a happy torturer is a torturer who is happier than he normally is when he is torturing. Such people are not stably happy or well-integrated humans. On the whole, it is a tough life to be a torturer."[20]

The upshot of all this is that Freud does *not* deuniversalize the moral sense, as Rorty claims; he reuniversalizes it. Rorty claims that Freud made the moral sense as "idiosyncratic as the poet's inventions."[21] Freud would not recognize this description of his project. It is precisely bad and destructive idiosyncrasy that he aims to reveal and to alter in order that the too-idiosyncratic obsessive, as one example, may take his or her place in the human community, more or less following those rules that make social life possible and dangerous aggressivity against self or others less likely. It is important to bear in mind that Freud is displacing Kantian-Christian teaching about universal moral claims and dispositions, but not in order to eradicate such claims altogether. If Rorty were right about Freud, private life would become impossible—a world of self-creating idiosyncratics continually searching for new descriptions—and public life uninteresting, severed as it is from all that private creativity. But Freud insists that there is truth to be found; that a metapsychological account relocates our understanding of the self by offering a strong story of development, including the emergence of conscience in a way that puts pressure on older projects; that central to this project is love—the work of Eros—which he links specifically to Plato's *Symposium*.

On one account, it is cruel to chide a woman wearing a fur coat: It hurts her feelings. On the other hand, more than the fox's feelings have been hurt in creating that sign of vanity and conspicuous consumption. A careless putdown is cruel, but systematic torture is far more cruel and reprehensible. But leave this aside. I want instead to home in on just where the don't-be-cruel rule comes from. I have already suggested that Freud offers, and would require, a developmental account of restraint from cruelty. In order not to be cruel we must learn that cruelty hurts and harms, and we learn this because the ethico-politics of eroticized moral learning have worked out: We can identify with the other. Freud always bows in the direction of those universal moral norms and rules he challenges, especially Christianity and the Sermon on the Mount, by saying such rules are impossible to live out fully but they may, nonetheless, serve a vital purpose in stemming the tide of aggression.

Our century has been very cruel, probably the most cruel on a public-political scale. Rorty doesn't really offer an account of public cruelty of the fascist-Stalinist sort either, though he clearly stands in opposition to it. But how robust is his stance? With the don't-be-cruel rule in mind, he poses alternatives that, I fear, make us dumber than we have any right to be at this late stage. It "just happened" that liberal societies condemn torture because liberals want to be reasonable and they want this because the contingencies fell out this way. But it didn't just happen. Liberal society and democratic possibility are the heirs of a very strong account—a Hebrew-Christian story—of why cruelty is sinful and must be stopped, beginning with the Roman games and the exposing of children. These were the first cruelties Christianity forbade. You don't torture people because that is a violation and it is a violation because we are all children of God.

If one jettisons the metaphysical underpinning of the don't-be-cruel rule, one must offer an alternative. That alternative is usually cast these days in the form of "universal human rights." Amnesty International doesn't talk about reasonableness; it talks about violation of fundamental human dignity taken as an ontological given, not a historic contingency. It might be an interesting exercise for Rorty to rewrite the declaration of human rights so that it retains its power to condemn, separate, and define yet abandons the basis on which it now does so. Celebrating the decline of religious faith, which served initially to underscore natural law and natural right, Rorty wants to maintain and sustain the injunctions imbedded in such earlier formulations. Here I will take up just one instance where I think Rorty misses the boat on cruelty.

Specifically, I have in mind the stories of rescuers—those who put their own lives at risk to stop the torture and destruction of fellow human beings. Having said "fellow human beings" I have already distanced myself from Rorty's account, for he insists that rescuers who saved Jewish neighbors (his examples, very underspecified, are Danes and Italians) did so not because

Jews were "fellow human beings" but by using "more parochial terms," for example that a particular Jew was a "fellow Milanese, or a fellow Jutlander, or a fellow member of the same union or profession, or a fellow bocce player, or a fellow parent of small children."[22] I have read many accounts of rescue and I have never once encountered "fellow bocce player" as a reason proffered by a life-risker for why he came to put his life and that of his family at risk. Ironical reasonableness didn't have a lot to do with life-risking. Indeed, rescuers during the Nazi years talk the sort of talk Rorty aims to supplant. Here are brief examples drawn from five accounts of anti-Nazi activism and rescue:

1. Students from the White Rose society, an anti-Nazi student group from Munich, who were caught, tried, and executed, left behind Five Leaflets designed to animate anti-Nazi sentiment.

> Therefore every individual, conscious of his responsibility as a member of Christian and Western civilization, must defend himself as best he can at this late hour, he must work against the scourges of mankind, against fascism and any similar system of totalitarianism. . . . For, according to God's will, man is intended to pursue his natural goal, his earthly happiness, in self-reliance and self-chosen activity, freely and independently within the community of life and work of the nation. . . . It is not possible through solitary withdrawal, in the manner of embittered hermits, to prepare the ground for the overturn of this "government" or bring about the revolution at the earliest possible moment.[23]

The White Rose students cite Aristotle, St. Augustine, Kant. To be sure, many who endorsed this final vocabulary remained quiescent during the Nazi era; others, to their shame, offered support. But that isn't what's at stake here; what's at stake is the basis for resistance.

2. Rescue in Italy. The Italians spared 85 percent of their Jewish population. The definitive work on this story offers the following by way of insight:

> In many cases after the war, nonJewish Italians who had saved Jews, when asked about their motivations, were annoyed and even angered by the very question: "How can you ask me such a question?" one man inquired. "Do you mean to say that you do not understand why a devout Catholic like myself had to behave as I did in order to save human beings whose lives

were in danger?" Other rescuers insisted, simply, "I did my duty."[24]

3. Samuel and Pearl Oliner interviewed authenticated rescuers identified by Yad Vashem, Israel's memorial to victims of the Holocaust. These rescuers came from Poland, Germany, France, Holland, Italy, Denmark, Belgium, and Norway. Probing the circumstances and the reasons for rescue, they learned that rescuers were "ordinary" people—farmers and teachers, entrepreneurs and factory workers, rich and poor, Protestants and Catholics, distinguished by "their connections with others in relationships of commitment and care." The point the Oliners make runs opposite to Rorty's about immediate identification serving as the basis for rescue—"fellow Jutlander" and the like. Rather, rescuers moved from strong grounding in family, community, church—all were rooted in this way—to "broad universal principles that relate to justice and care in matters of public concern." They rescued because they could generalize beyond their immediate attachments rather than merely enact them.[25] Religious affiliation—overwhelming for both rescuers and nonrescuers—did not per se propel individuals into danger, but the way religious obligation was interpreted by rescuers and nonrescuers did mark a sharp distinction between the two groups.

4. Nechama Tec, a rescued Polish Jew, also relies on Yad Vashem identification of bona fide rescuers. Tec is fascinated and horrified that some Polish peasants "were executed for their selfless help, while others were busy rounding up Jews and delivering them to the authorities." Within Poland, to help Jews was to risk one's life. This extended to one's family. Among rescuers there were many religious anti-Semites, but there was something in their religious upbringing that led them to the conclusion that "cruel, glaringly murderous behavior towards the Jews was a sin." What religion offered was no certain guarantee of rescue but the possibility of such in light of religious values and teachings. Religion was, then, a necessary but not complete explanation for rescue, according to Tec, and it is unclear that anything other than a fundamental, first language of sin and justice could have propelled "ordinary" people (those Rorty would have us construe as thoroughly historic, nominalist, and contingent through and through) into the danger zone.[26]

5. Finally, the best known of rescue books—Philip Hallie's account of the village of Le Chambon, a Protestant commune that, to the man,

woman, and child, committed itself to rescue. The entire village was put at risk of massacre. Public duty took precedence. The Chambonnais opened their homes to those unlike themselves—Jewish refugees—at great risk to themselves. They spoke of an ethic of responsibility; of not wanting to increase the harm in the world; of following the example of Jesus. None talked of an immediate identification with those they risked their lives to save—these were strangers, aliens in our midst, but Christian responsibility is cast universally and meant to be applied concretely so we did what we had to do. Led by their pastor, André Trocmé, the villagers prayed and acted. By attacking evil, they cherished "the preciousness of human life. Our obligation to diminish the evil in the world must begin at home; we must not do evil, must not ourselves do harm."[27] Trocmé's sermons offered no blueprint but they did animate a spirit of resistance that required, in order that it be enacted, precisely the identification Rorty denatures. The Chambonnais did not rescue "neighbors." They rescued strangers. And their determination not to be cruel rested for them on imperatives that were obligatory, not contingent; necessary, not incidental. They could not have acted otherwise, they said.

Now I am acutely aware, as I wind down, of how easy it is to be taken for a moral scold, if not a scourge. (I hope I haven't been that heavy-handed.) These are the days of lightness and froth as well as political correctness, an odd combination of "anything goes" and micromanagement of every word I say and thought I think. Ah well, tribulations of the spirit come and go. And my final point goes like this: What would a Rortyian redescription of rescue that omitted the first vocabularies and noncontingent (to their eyes) actions of the rescuers look like? Have we "progressed" beyond the need for any such "justification"? It seems not if I may judge from what I was told by the Mothers of the Disappeared in Argentina who speak of universal human rights, of obligations and immunities, of human beings who must not by definition be violated, a strong ontoethical political claim. What would a liberal ironist account of ethical heroism be? I understand what a tragic-ironic account is; one can turn to Camus, among others, for that. But an account that insists on its own incessant displacement is trickier by far.

I am struck by the fact that Vàclav Havel, former dissident, current president, always playwright, published his collection of essays under the title: *Living in Truth*. Havel is insistent that there is an absolute horizon of being; that the world is possible only because we are grounded; that there is such a thing as a "metaphysical offense," an assault on the mystery of the absolute. Here he has in mind the violation of forests, rivers, streams, living creatures. This is the don't-be-cruel rule, but with teeth. As a performer of political thought—my way to describe him—Havel is working with a very rich script that requires the language of totalitarianism, truth, lies, violation, being, nature, the "very notion of identity itself." Truth and lies are contextual but not *merely* contextual. There are false and true vocabularies, and one can distinguish between and judge them and dissent or assent to them. There may not be a human nature but there is a *human condition*, described by Hannah Arendt thus: "the conditions of human existence—life itself, natality and mortality, worldliness, plurality, and the earth—can never'explain' what we are or answer the question of who we are for the simple reason that they never condition us absolutely."[28] It is recognition of this condition as the horizon of thought and action that makes possible freedom and responsibility. This recognition escapes the Rortyian net, comprised as it is of either preordained natures, identities, being, and reality or a thoroughgoing contingency with no "left-over," no "surplus," nothing that is not arbitrary in the first and last instance. Havel's and Arendt's positions elude Rorty's alternatives.

The final words shall be Havel's. I conclude in this way because I want to suggest that without the possibility of creating a Havelian sort of "I," a modern identity at once committed yet aware of the irony and limits to all commitments; prepared to suffer but wary of all calls to sacrifice, we would live in a moral universe impoverished beyond our poor powers of imagination. This Havelian "I" is a thicker being by far than "we liberal ironists."

> The problem of human identity remains at the center of my thinking about human affairs . . . as you must have noticed from my letters, the importance of the notion of human responsibility has grown in my meditations. It has begun to appear with increasing clarity, as that fundamental point from which all identity grows and by which it stands or falls; it is the foundation, the root, the center of gravity, the constructional principle or axis of identity, something like the "idea" that determines its degree and type. It is the mortar binding it together, and when the mortar dries out, identity too begins irreversibly to crumble and fall apart. (That is why I wrote you that the secret of man is the secret of his responsibility.)[29]

My mission, Havel insists, is to "speak the truth about the world I live in, to bear witness to its terrors and miseries, in other words, to warn rather than hand out prescriptions for change."[30] My hunch is that Rorty wouldn't characterize his mission all that differently, although he would probably want to drop "mission" as too religious sounding. "Truth" would also have to go

in order that it be absolutely clear that truth is a characteristic assigned to
linguistic properties rather a strong contrast to lie and a claim that truth and
lies are linked to definable realities, as Havel intends. "The world" might
also be a bit tricky as it has too solid and universalistic a ring to it as Havel
deploys it. "Bear witness" derives from Christian witness, so it should
probably be jettisoned. This leaves warning. But would "to warn" retain its
force were all else redescribed or excised? I don't think so.

NOTES

1. Richard Rorty, *Contingency, Irony, and Solidarity*. (Cambridge: Cambridge University Press, 1989), pp. 79-80.
2. Richard Rorty, *Objectivity, Relativism, and Truth*, Vol. 1, and *Essays on
Heidegger and Others*, Vol. 2 of *Philosophical Papers* (Cambridge: Cambridge University Press, 1991).
3. Rorty, *Contingency, Irony, and Solidarity*, p. 6.
4. Ibid., p. 52.
5. Ibid., p. 87.
6. Rorty recognizes that most "nonintellectuals are still committed either to
some form of religious faith or to some forth of Enlightenment rationalism"
but he quickly forgets this recognition as a limiting condition to his own
argument in the body of his text, perhaps because he construes as contingent
commitments what for those thus committed are anything but. *Contingency,
Irony, and Solidarity*, p. xv.
7. Ibid., p. 86.
8. Ibid., p. 73.
9. Ibid., p. 3.
10. Eugene Weber, "A new order of loss and profit," *Times Literary Supplement*
(January 15-21, 1988), pp. 51-52. See also Richard John Neuhaus's biting,
"Joshing Mr. Rorty," *First Things*, No. 8 (December, 1990), pp. 14-24.
11. Albert Camus, *The Rebel* (New York: Vintage Books, 1956), pp. 124-26.
12. Richard Reinitz, *Irony and Consciousness*, (Lewisburg, PA: Bucknell
University Press, 1980), p. 65.
13. Camus, "The Human Crisis," *Twice a Year* (Vol. 1, 1946-47), lecture
delivered in America, Spring, 1946, p. 21.
14. Rorty, *Contingency, Irony, and Solidarity*, p. xvi.
15. Ibid., pp. 303-34.
16. Ibid., p. 35.
17. Ibid., pp. 37—38.
18. Ibid., p. xiii.

19. On this see Freud's complex discussions of the interpenetration of state aggressivity—war—and the moral enactments of individuals in "Thoughts for the Times on War and Death," *Standard Edition*, Vol. 14, pp. 273-330; and "Why War?" *Standard Edition*, Vol. 22, pp. 196-215.

20. Jonathan Lear, *Love and Its Place in Nature. A Philosophical Interpretation of Freudian Psychoanalysis* (New York: Farrar, Straus and Giroux, 1990), p. 189.

21. Rorty, *Contingency, Irony, and Solidarity*, p. 30.

22. Ibid., p. 190.

23. Inge Scholl, ed., *The White Rose: Munich 1942-1943* (Middletown, CT: Wesleyan University Press, 1983), pp. 74, 82.

24. Susan Zuccotti, *The Italians and the Holocaust* (New York: Basic Books, 1987), pp. 281-282.

25. Samuel P. Oliner and Pearl M. Oliner, *The Altruistic Personality: Rescuers of Jews in Nazi Europe* (New York: The Free Press, 1988), pp. 259-260.

26. Nechama Tec, *When Light Pierced the Darkness: Christian Rescue of Jews in Nazi-Occupied Poland* (New York: Oxford University Press, 1986), pp. 117, 104.

27. Philip Hallie, *Lest Innocent Blood Be Shed* (New York: Harper Colophon, 1979), p. 85.

28. Hannah Arendt, *The Human Condition* (Chicago: University of Chicago Press, 1958), p. 11.

29. Vàclav Havel, *Letters to Olga* (New York: Henry Holt, 1989), p. 145.

30. Vàclav Havel, *Disturbing the Peace* (New York: Knopf, 1990), p. 8.

10

Robustness:
A Reply to Jean Bethke Elshtain

Richard Rorty

Professor Elshtain employs, in her remarks on my book, a notion that presupposes just the view about the relation of religion and philosophy to moral choice which I reject. This is the notion of a "robust stance," as in Elshtain's question "How robust is his [Rorty's] stance?"

Elshtain agrees with Camus that, when faced with examples like that of the German officer who asks a mother to choose which of her sons shall be shot, it is necessary "to sustain an ethical-political stance that limits the damage." If this meant simply "we should be repelled, and raise our children to be repelled, by what the officer did," then Elshtain and I would have no quarrel. But Elshtain means more than that. In response to my claim that you can describe anything in a way that makes it look good, she suggests that this officer is a counterexample — that such a man is beyond the power of words to excuse. (She even suggests that to *try* to make such man's behavior look good is to make oneself "loathsome," "to become a ravager.")

It is not, alas, a counterexample. Suppose that the German officer in question had been, before the war and while a student, a member of one of those little circles of Nietzsche fans—circles that specialized in vaguely sadomasochistic, homoerotic male bonding—which were dotted about the German universities in the 1930s. He and his friends prided themselves on their ability to rise above slave morality. They strove to outdo each other in scorn for the weak, in *Entschlossenheit* and a concomitant contempt for everything stemming from Platonism and Christianity. Home on leave, the officer tells his friends the story of how he broke a Greek mother's heart. He tells it as an episode in the saga of German will gradually cleansing Europe, enforcing its distinction between the pure and noble races and the ignoble and despicable ones. His friends, hearing his story, are envious of the robustness of his moral stance; they secretly wonder if they themselves might not, at the last moment, have succumbed to weakness and sentimentality, might not have heard their own mother's sobs when the Greek mother was faced with her choice. They swear to themselves that, when they return to their posts, they will imitate the good example their friend has set.

Saying, as I do, that you can make anything look good (not, obviously, to Elshtain or me—but certainly to yourself and a few select fellow spirits) is just to seize upon the grain of truth in Socrates' claim that nobody knowingly does evil. Everybody (usually just before doing evil, but if not, then shortly afterward) tries to whip up a story according to which he or she did the right thing, and usually succeeds. Ever since Socrates noticed this, philosophers and theologians have asked: What could stop us from telling such stories? What large story can we tell that, once internalized, will make these little self-exculpatory stories harder to tell? More specifically they have asked: What allies can we call upon when we undertake the moral education of our children?

The Platonic answer to this latter question is repeated in Jonathan Lear's version (quoted by Elshtain) of Freud. This answer says that doing evil tends to make you unhappy by making your soul unharmonious. On this view, a Freudian metapsychological account—an account that is good for all people in all ages and climes—shows not only that parents and societies have to instill a conscience in children in order to curb in-built aggression, but that the conscience instilled by Christian parents will give these children more harmonious souls than that instilled by Aztec, or ancient Chinese, or Nazi parents. In other words, instilling the sort of sympathy for strangers that (some) Christians are better than most people will give your child a better chance for peace of mind than raising him or her to be fiercely proud of a certain community and to despise people who are not "like us." I am not sure that Freud really thought that, but if he did I do not see that he had much evidence for his view. I suspect that the souls of the Aztec priests painstakingly gouging out their prisoners' hearts and, for that matter, those of the Catholic bureaucrats whose *mission civilizatrice* made the Congo so profitable to King Leopold, and of the Unitarian captains of the slave ships, were as harmonious as most. I suspect that all it takes to let you feel at peace with yourself is the thought that those whom you were raised to respect would approve of what you are doing. I see no reason to doubt that many torturers sleep very well indeed, secure in the approval of their ghastly peers.

Before leaving Freud let me hasten to agree with him and Elshtain that we have a biology, a morphology, and a neurophysiology "definatory of 'the human.' " The trouble is that such a physiological definition isn't much use to us. History suggests that human neurophysiology is as compatible with different (often antithetical) consciences as the structure of a random access memory is with different programs. So I see no reason to think that contemporary neurophysiology supplies a more robust ally than the Platonic tripartite soul.

When neither metapsychology nor neurophysiology will do the trick, we usually turn to metaphysics. This is what Elshtain does when she tells us that Amnesty International "talks about violation of fundamental human dignity taken as an ontological given, not a historic contingency." I take it that Elshtain thinks ontological givens more *robust* than historical givens. But does this mean that there really is an ally out there doing something causal—stiffening and backing up your better nature— or does it just mean that we are so built as to need metaphysical or religious beliefs to keep our moral courage up?

If Elshtain means the former, then she owes us an account of the nature of this causal influence, and in particular an account of why it sometimes fails to operate. She owes us something like a full-fledged theodicy. She needs to tell us more about the nature of robustness, and to develop a considerably thicker cosmology, and a psychology more interwoven with that cosmology, than anything Freud ever dreamed of offering. If she means the latter, she is offering a psychological generalization about what will and won't strengthen people's resolves. My objection to the generalization is simply that not all moral heroes and heroines—only most of them—have felt the need she suggests. A few of them have acted in the name of something unreal—a possible utopian future for human beings—rather than in the name of something already existent. I am suggesting that we raise our children to imitate these few rather than the many whom Elshtain describes.

The question of how to raise the children is Elshtain's chosen ground for argument, and it seems to me a good one. We both, I take it, want to raise them to admire the good things about the French Revolution and the Christian religion (fewer tyrants, redistribution of wealth, less torture, etc.) while not being led to imitate the bad things (the Terror, the Inquisition, etc.). My suggestion is that this might best be done by decosmologizing such notions as "human rights" and "Christian charity."

I can suggest what I mean by "decosmologizing" by saying that maximal cosmologization of the good side of Christianity occurred when we tried to get children to believe that they would fry in hell forever if they fell short of ideal generosity, tolerance, and sensitivity to the feeling of others. This strategy did not work well, because the children tended to imitate divine vengefulness rather than divine tolerance. So, in recent centuries, we have softened things down in various ways. We have been trying to make the divine sound less like Daddy at his angriest and more like Mommy at her most relaxed. This softening process has resulted in less emphasis on power and more on love. It has meant less metaphysics and more edification, fewer attempts to overawe and more coaxing.

The price we paid for this gradual decosmologization, for playing down the claim that the very structure of the universe (or of the human soul) is our ally, has been (just as Nietzsche was always complaining) a loss in robustness. The gains included a decrease in fanaticism—in willingness to go out and save Christian civilization by killing lots of non-Christians, or borderline Christians. Unquestionably, however, this shift has meant that it has become harder and harder to answer the obstreperous child who asks "Why should I be good, if nothing bad is going to happen to me if I am not?"

I suggest that when such questions are posed, either by our children or by our innermost selves, we just smile bravely and say "Gee, you just don't get the idea, do you? Let me tell you some more stories about how nice things would be if everybody were generous, tolerant, and sensitive. In particular, let me tell you about the pain endured by people who seem quite strange to us, the humiliation and agony they suffer when we treat them as badly as we are often tempted to treat them." I take Elshtain as preferring a more robust answer—along the lines of "Actually, a lot of terrible, though admittedly rather abstract and hard-to-visualize, things will happen to you if you are bad, if you succumb to those temptations." Such a robust answer can be filled in by one or another description of the forces allied with the parents' moral pedagogy. My answer, by contrast, does not rely on claims about powerful allied forces. This is because I see no way to tell an even halfway convincing story about a noncontingent relation between love and power. So I see cosmology, metapsychology, and neurophysiology as irrelevant to ethics.

Is my stance insufficiently robust to do the job of moral education? Must we continue to tell a large story about God, or the universe, or the human condition, or the human soul, in order to inhibit the little self-exculpatory stories? I don't know, but I think we should give a different strategy a try. Certainly, as Elshtain shows in her stories about the rescuers, lots of good and brave people have relied upon such larger stories. Equally certainly, however, a lot of horrible and dangerous people have also relied upon them. Counting up how many people of each sort there have been—trying to figure out whether, on balance, the claim to have powerful allies has done more harm than good—will get us no farther than totting up the good and bad after-effects of the French Revolution, or of the institutionalization of Christianity.

Sometimes nothing will help except a hazardous experiment. Elshtain sees more hazards than promise in the experiment I propose, and she may be right. But we shall never know until we give a totally decosmologized ethics more of a chance than it has had so far. It is not the smallest advantage of such an ethics that it helps a child realize that, had Lady Luck given him or her the wrong parents in the wrong country at the wrong time, he or she might have been that German officer. Making such ironies vivid is, it seems to me, important for the inculcation of tolerance and sensitivity.

CONTRIBUTORS

JANE BENNETT is assistant professor of politics at Goucher College. She is the author of *Unthinking Faith and Enlightenment* (New York University Press) and is currently working on a book on Thoreau.

SARA B. BLAIR is assistant professor of English and director of the Modern Studies Program at the University of Virginia. She is currently completing a book on irony and authority in the writings of Henry James.

JANE K. BROWN is chair of the department of Germanics and professor of Germanics and comparative literature at the University of Washington. She is also president of the Goethe Society of North America. Her books include *Goethe's Faust: The German Tragedy* (Cornell University Press); *Goethe's Cyclical Narratives* (University of North Carolina Press); and an English edition of *Wilhelm Meisters Wanderjahre* (Suhrkamp).

WILLIAM E. CONNOLLY is professor of political science at the Johns Hopkins University. He is the editor of *CONTESTATIONS: Cornell Studies in Political Theory*. His recent books include *Politics and Ambiguity* (University of Wisconsin Press); *Political Theory and Modernity* (Blackwell); and *Identity/Difference: Democratic Negotiations of Political Paradox* (Cornell University Press).

DANIEL W. CONWAY is assistant professor of philosophy and co-director of the Center for Ethics and Value Inquiry at The Pennsylvania State University. He is currently completing a book on Nietzsche's politics.

JEAN BETHKE ELSHTAIN is Centennial Professor of political science and professor of philosophy at Vanderbilt University. Her books include *Public Man/Private Woman* (Princeton University Press); *Meditations on Modern Political Thought* (Praeger); *Women and War* (Basic Books); and *Power Trips and Other Journeys* (University of Wisconsin Press).

HENRY S. KARIEL is professor of political science at the University of Hawaii, Honolulu. His works include *The Desperate Politics of Postmodernism* (University of Massachusetts Press); *The Decline of American Pluralism* (Stanford University Press); *In Search of Authority* (Free Press of Glencoe); and *The Promise of Politics* (Prentice-Hall).

RICHARD RORTY is University Professor of the Humanities at the University of Virginia. In 1991 he published *Essays on Heidegger and Others* (Cambridge University Press) and *Philosophical Papers: Objectivity, Relativism and Truth* (Cambridge University Press).

JOHN E. SEERY is assistant professor in the department of politics at Pomona College. He is the author of *Political Returns: Irony in Politics and Theory from Plato to the Antinuclear Movement* (Westview).

JOHN TRAUGOTT is professor of English at the University of California at Berkeley. His works include *Discussions of Jonathan Swift* (Heath); *Laurence Sterne: A Collection of Critical Essays* (Prentice-Hall); and *Tristam Shandy's World: Sterne's Philosophical Rhetoric* (University of California Press).